Instructor's Manual with Test Bank

for

Babbie's

The Practice of Social Research
Tenth Edition

Margaret Platt Jendrek
Miami University

THOMSON

WADSWORTH

Australia • Canada • Mexico • Singapore • Spain • United Kingdom • United States

Printed in the United States of America
1 2 3 4 5 6 7 06 05 04 03

Printer: Victor Graphics

ISBN: 0-534-62034-5

For more information about our products,
contact us at:
**Thomson Learning Academic Resource Center
1-800-423-0563**

**For permission to use material from this text,
contact us by:**
Phone: 1-800-730-2214
Fax: 1-800-731-2215
Web: http://www.thomsonrights.com

Asia
Thomson Learning
5 Shenton Way #01-01
UIC Building
Singapore 068808

Australia
Nelson Thomson Learning
102 Dodds Street
South Street
South Melbourne, Victoria 3205
Australia

Canada
Nelson Thomson Learning
1120 Birchmount Road
Toronto, Ontario M1K 5G4
Canada

Europe/Middle East/South Africa
Thomson Learning
High Holborn House
50/51 Bedford Row
London WC1R 4LR
United Kingdom

Latin America
Thomson Learning
Seneca, 53
Colonia Polanco
11560 Mexico D.F.
Mexico

Spain
Paraninfo Thomson Learning
Calle/Magallanes, 25
28015 Madrid, Spain

CONTENTS

Preface
Special Resources
Resource Integration Guide

PREFACE

This Instructor's Manual with Test Bank has been developed for use with the Tenth Edition of Earl Babbie's text, *The Practice Of Social Research* and the Tenth Edition of the student study guide, *Practicing Social Research*, by Theodore Wagenaar and Earl Babbie. This manual is designed to help you teach research methods more effectively. It contains chapter outlines, behavioral objectives, in-class lecture materials and projects, and exam questions. The manual also contains solutions and guidelines to selected exercises in the Study Guide. Each chapter of the Instructor's Manual is designed as follows:

CHAPTER OUTLINE: The outline of the text chapter provides a quick overview of both the content and the organization of the chapter.

BEHAVIORAL OBJECTIVES: Approximately ten objectives are listed for each chapter. Although not exhaustive, the objectives do state the most important topics covered in each chapter. You may wish to use this list during your class presentations to help students focus on the major topics. A similar listing is presented in the Study Guide.

TEACHING SUGGESTIONS AND RESOURCES: This section provides some *in-class* lecture materials, ideas, and projects. Please read these sections ahead of time. Some suggestions will require additional preparation on your part (i.e., copying transparencies or ordering data sets, pamphlets, films, etc.). These suggestions have been successful either in getting students involved in doing research or in highlighting important concepts. The films listed in this manual were reviewed in film guides as being appropriate for college audiences.

POSSIBLE ANSWERS TO STUDY GUIDE QUESTIONS: When appropriate this section gives you answers or guidelines for reviewing the exercises presented in the Study Guide. This section should be read before giving the assignment, as suggestions are sometimes made for guiding students through the project. Please note that for some exercises there is no one "correct" answer. Rather, the answer given is simply intended to help you establish guidelines for reviewing your students' answers.

INFOTRAC EXERCISES: Four months of FREE anywhere, anytime access to InfoTrac College Edition, the online library, is automatically packaged with this book. The new and improved InfoTrac College Edition puts cutting edge research and the latest headlines at your students' fingertips, giving them access to an entire online library for the cost of one book! This fully searchable database offers more than 20 years' worth of full-text articles (more than 10 million) from almost 4000 diverse sources, such as academic journals, newsletters, and up-to-the-minute periodicals including "Time," "Newsweek," "Science," "Forbes," and "USA Today." To access InfoTrac College Edition go to **http://www.infotrac-college.com/wadsworth** on the World Wide Web and enter the password that came with your copy of *The Practice of Social Research*. (If your textbook did not come packaged with a password, contact your local ITP/Wadsworth representative for information about how to access InfoTrac College Edition.). Where appropriate, this manual lists keywords for the students to examine using INFOTRAC. The keywords were checked to be sure that there were articles of interest to social scientists that used those concepts. You might want to assign a particular article to the students from the keywords listed in this manual or you may ask students to select articles that are of interest to them.

INTERNET EXERCISES: Where appropriate, this manual suggests student assignments using the Internet. Please note that sites disappear, undergo name changes, etc. Consequently, check the site before making the assignment.

MULTIPLE-CHOICE QUESTIONS: Approximately fifteen to thirty items are presented for each chapter. Some items test facts and some test the application of the facts. The items vary in their level of difficulty. The correct answer is starred and text page references are included.

TRUE-FALSE QUESTIONS: Approximately ten to fifteen items are presented for each chapter. These items also differ in their level of difficulty and their testing of fact or application. The correct answer is given and text page references are included.

ESSAY QUESTIONS: Two to four essay questions are presented in each chapter. These may be used for exams or to stimulate class discussions.

As always, I want to thank Carol Kist for her incredible help in formatting this manual. If you have any comments or suggestions on this manual, I would be delighted to hear from you.

Margaret Platt Jendrek

Miami University

Oxford, Ohio

SPECIAL RESOURCES

Resources of special interest to instructors of research methods include:

A. Instructors who adopt the Study Guide, *Practicing Social Research*, may write on school
    letterhead to:
Sales Service Department
Wadsworth Publishing Company
Ten Davis Drive
Belmont, California 94002

You will be sent a complimentary copy of the General Social Survey (GSS) data set used in
some of the Study Guide exercises. The GSS have occurred almost annually since 1972 and
typically involve samples of about 1500 Americans 18 years old or older. Samples are full
probability samples, and the samples reflect multistage area probability samples to
the block level. The data file you will be using contains random samples of 500 cases for each of
the years of 1975, 1980, 1985, 1990, 1994 (there was no survey in 1995), and 2000, resulting in a
total sample of 3000. The data set contains many more variables than are used in the exercises.
This feature allows you maximum flexibility in developing additional exercises or extending
those in the Study Guide.

B. The American Sociological Association (ASA)
Teaching Resources Center
1722 N Street, N.W.
Washington, D.C. 20036
Phone: 202-833-3410 ext. 318 or 323
E-mail: APAP@ASANET.ORG

Many materials are available through the ASA Teaching Resources Center. Of particular interest
in a methods course are:

Qualitative Research Methods: Syllabi and Instructional Materials (Third Edition)
Edited by James David Ballard. Twenty-seven syllabi and six teaching assignments and
exercises represent the collective teaching experiences of many of the finest qualitative
methodology educators working today. This collection exhibits a variety of qualitative research
approaches, from the traditional Chicago school, to approaches based on feminist methodologies,
to the most ambitious post-modern variety of qualitative scholarship. Both Undergraduate and
Graduate research courses are included in this set. 220 pp., revised 2001. Stock #339.Q01.

Research Methods Courses: Syllabi, Assignments and Projects (Fifth Edition)
Edited by Kevin P. Mulvey. Ten syllabi for courses in undergraduate methods, field methods,
and graduate methods. Topics covered include linear structural equation models,
ethnomethodology, questionnaire design, and sampling. Final section offers thoughts on issues
related to teaching research methods courses. 157pp., revised 2000. (10% discount to members
of the Undergraduate Education Section). Stock #340.R00.
Research Methods in Cyberspace: Internet Exercises for Social Science Research Courses.

By Norah D. Peters-Davis and Susan G. Lehmann. The new book was developed for use in undergraduate research methods courses. It provides students with hands on research experience, and makes effective use of available technology. Five chapters with numerous internet exercises include: Evaluating the Internet, Sampling, Quantitative Methods, Qualitative Methods, and Demography. 98 pp., 2002. Stock#228.R02.

Simulation and Gaming and the Teaching of Sociology (Eighth Edition)
Compiled by Richard L. Dukes. A comprehensive annotated bibliography of books and articles on simulations and games used for teaching sociology. Includes suggestions for how to use these unique teaching devices in the classroom. 21 pp., revised 2001. Stock #207.S01.

Software and Sociology: An Annotated Bibliography of Programs, Journals, and Articles (2nd Edition). By Dan Cover. This resource provides updates and reviews of the latest of computer hardware and software developments, with a focus on how these innovations open new opportunities for computer assisted instruction, social research and teaching. Chapters cover software development, authoring software, reviews, lists of recent articles of interest, an annotated bibliography, a list of relevant journals, and a section on data resources. 108 pp, revised in 1998, Stock #222.S98.

Syllabi and Instructional Materials for Social Statistics.
Edited by Cynthia Line. Contains three essays on teaching undergraduate statistics. Contains nine undergraduate syllabi, 3 handouts and tips for students, 8 in class group work, and many assignments for early in the semester, and at the end of the semester. This set also have sections that are solely devoted to t-tests, correlations and regressions, chi-square, and ANOVA. Plus, sample quizzes and tests are provided. 210 pp., 2000. Stock #349.S00.

Online Brochures: These are available at: http://www.asanet.org/pubs/pubs.html
Careers in Sociology
• What can you do with a degree in sociology?

Do You Want to Enhance Your Workforce? Employ the Sociological Advantage
• The professional sociologist can contribute many skills to organizations and businesses.

Majoring in Sociology: A Guide for Students
• Sociology is a valuable liberal arts major for students planning careers in a wide variety of fields.

The Sociology Major: As Preparation for Careers in Business and Organizations
• A degree in sociology is an excellent springboard for entering many professions.

C. *Teaching Sociology* contains many articles and notes on teaching research methods. See the special issue on teaching research methods and statistics—April 1987. Call the ASA office to subscribe.

D. World Wide Web Sites: This is not an exhaustive list of sites but a sample of what is "out there" that might interest research methods students and instructors. Please note that both the text and the Study Guide list many more web sites. Also note that listings change and so you may have to update an address.

ICPSR at the University of Michigan. They have many data sets.
Homepage: http//www.icpsr.umich.edu
Use: http//www.icpsr.umich.edu/nacjd to access the National Archive of Criminal Justice Data
Use: http//www.icpsr.umich.edu/gss to access the General Social Survey

U.S. Bureau of the Census
Homepage: http://ftp.census.gov/
Contains tables and graphs detailing census data.

Department of Labor, Bureau of Labor statistics
Homepage: http://stats.bls.gov
Contains statistical reports, bibliographies, and descriptions of surveys.

Gallup Poll
Homepage: http://www.gallup.com
Contains poll results and current events information.

National Coalition for the Homeless
Homepage: http://nch.ari.net
Contains facts, figures, and legislation about the homeless.

U.S. Postal Service
Homepage: http://www.usps.gov/
Great for survey research as it includes zip codes by street address.

E.   The Annenberg/CPB series entitled "Against All Odds" is a 26-part, half-hour each video series that is very useful in teaching research methods and statistics. The brochure on the series states that, "With an emphasis on "doing" statistics rather than on passive learning, this series goes on location to help uncover statistical solutions to the puzzles of everyday life. You learn how data collection and manipulation--paired with intelligent judgment and common sense--lead to greater understanding of the world." Where appropriate, the half-hour program is references in this manual. The complete series is listed below.

Annenberg/CPB
401 9th Street, NW
Washington, DC 20004
phone: (202) 879-9654
fax: (202) 879-9696
E-mail: info@learner.org

Program Descriptions: 26 half-hour video programs

1: What is Statistics?
Discover how this complex discipline has evolved.

2: Picturing Distributions

3: Describing Distributions
Examine the difference between mean and median and learn of quartiles, box-plots, interquartile range, and standard deviation.

4: Normal Distributions
Shows the progression from histogram to a single normal curve for standard measurement.

5: Normal Calculations
Emission standards and cholesterol studies give examples of normal calculations at work.

6: Time Series
Statistics identify patterns over time, answering questions about stability and change, as seen in the stock market.

7: Models for Growth
Topics include linear growth, least squares, exponential growth, and straightening an exponential growth curve by logic.

8: Describing Relationships
Scatterplots, smoothing scatterplots of response versus explanatory variables by median trace, and least squares regression lines are covered.

9: Correlation
How to derive and interpret the correlation coefficient using the relationship between a baseball player's salary and his home run statistics.

10: Multidimensional Data Analysis
This program recaps the data analysis by showing computing technology at Bell Communications Research.

11: The Question of Causation
The relationship between smoking and lung cancer is examined, and a study of admissions data illustrates Simpson's paradox.

12: Experimental Design
Distinguish between observational studies and experiments, and learn the basic principles of design, including comparison, randomization, and replication.

13: Blocking and Sampling

Understand random sampling and the difference between single-factor and multi-factor experiments.

14: Samples and Surveys

Stratified random sampling is explained. A 1936 Gallup election poll yields information about undercoverage.

15: What Is Probability?

Distinguishes between deterministic phenomena and random phenomena.

16: Random Variables

Topics covered include independence, the multiplication rule for independent events, and discrete and continuous random variables.

17: Binomial Distributions

Calculate the mean and standard deviation of binomial distributions, and see a representative example of binomial distribution.

18: The Sample Mean and Control Charts

Roulette and business demonstrate the use of the central limit theorem, control chart monitoring of random variation, creation of x-bar charts, and definitions of control limits.

19: Confidence Intervals

Explains the confidence interval using population surveys to show how margin of error and confidence levels are interpreted.

20: Significance Tests

A hiring discrimination case illustrates the basic reasoning behind tests of significance.

21: Inference for One Mean

Study inference about the mean of a single distribution, with an emphasis on paired samples and the t confidence interval and test.

22: Comparing Two Means

Learn to recognize a two-sample problem and to distinguish it from one- and paired-sample situations.

23: Inference for Proportions

See confidence intervals and tests for comparing proportions applied in government estimates on unemployment.

24: Inference for Two-Way Tables

The chi-square test and the relationship between two categorical variables are covered.

25: Inference for Relationships
Understand inference for simple linear regression, emphasizing slope, and prediction.

F.   The following assignment is the semester's research project that I give students on the first day of class. Modified from an assignment that Theodore Wagenaar uses in his class, I find the project an extremely useful vehicle for enabling students to "put it all together" in an area that interests them.

A Research Proposal Assignment: Putting It All Together
For this assignment you must develop a bivariate (or multivariate) hypothesis that interests you and carry it through the research process described in class and in the text. DO NOT select hypotheses used in class or in the readings. Although you will not actually collect* the data, the proposal should be of sufficient detail and clarity that you (or someone else) could do the research following the proposal description.

The following issues should be addressed in your paper. These steps can be used as an outline for the proposal or the items can be integrated. In addition,

1.   State the general problem area. What topic are you investigating and why? Note previous studies in the area.
2.   What are the two (or more) concepts that you are trying to link? Conceptualize your two main concepts. (Be sure that at least one concept is abstract. That is, relating gender to last year in school completed will not get many points).
3.   Working with your conceptualization, operationalize your concepts. I need to be clear on how you will measure each concept.
4.   State the specific hypothesis(es) that you wish to examine.
5.   Identify the independent variable and the dependent variable in the hypothesis. How did you determine which variable was independent and which was dependent?
6.   At what level is each variable measured?
7.   Discuss the reliability and validity of your measurements. What techniques will you use to assess the reliability and validity of each variable?
8.   What type of research design will you use to collect and analyze your data? Why did you select that design? What are the advantages and disadvantages of the selected design?
9.   Do you plan to sample? If yes, what kind of sampling design will you use and why? Explain your sampling procedure. If you do not plan to sample, why not?
10. What type of data collection technique will you use and why? Note the advantages and disadvantages of the selected technique.
11. What kind of data analysis do you plan to use? Will you do descriptive and/or inferential analysis and why?
12. Set up mock tables to indicate support for your hypothesis. Since you do not need to actually collect data, you will need to make up data for these tables.
13. What variables, if any, will you control for and why?
14. What, if any, ethical considerations enter into your project? How do you plan to handle these issues?

15. Discuss any special problems or issues that you might experience in doing your research. How will you deal with these issues?

* My students do not collect the data for their project. You may, however, have them collect data and thus modify the assignment. Variations on the assignment include: requiring students to complete your school's human subjects forms. These forms should be reviewed by your colleagues with feedback to the student. You will also need to decide whether to request drafts of the proposal as students work through it. I find that the papers I receive at the end of the semester are far more thoughtful when drafts are required. You will also need to decide on the paper's length. I typically require no more than 10 pages.

Instructors: Welcome to your Resource Integration Guide!
This guide correlates every text chapter with the many instructor and student resources that accompany Babbie's *The Practice of Social Research*, 10th Edition

Chapter 1: Human Inquiry and Science

Instructor Resources	Readers and Guides*	Media Resources	Online Resources
Instructor's Manual with Test Bank See Chapter 1 for teaching resources and 20–25 Multiple-Choice, 10–15 True/False, and 2–5 Essay questions Also available electronically through **ExamView®** **Multimedia Manager for Sociology** Choose from figures, tables, and CNN® video clips to create customized Microsoft® PowerPoint® lecture presentations	*Guided Activities for The Practice of Social Research,* **Tenth Edition** See Chapter 1 ***Readings in Social Research Methods,* Second Edition** See Chapter 1, "Why Do You Need to Understand Research Methods?" for readings such as "From the Sociological Imagination" (Mills) ***Experiencing Social Research: An Introduction Using MicroCase®*** See Exercise 1, "Scientific Inquiry into Social Reality: An Introduction" ***SPSS Companion for Research Methods,* Third Edition** See SPSS exercises for Chapter 1, "Human Inquiry and Science"	**Research Writer CD-ROM** Guides students through the stages of writing a research report. They can email their reports, export to Word, and have their reports automatically formatted. Video clips of Earl Babbie highlight important points in the text. *The Research Writer* section, "Introduction," relates to this chapter **SPSS 11.0 CD-ROM** Student version allows students to use real-world software to do data analysis. Use with *SPSS Companion* exercises noted on the left **GSS Data Disk** Use these data sets to complete exercises 1.5 and 1.6 in the *Guided Activities* and the Chapter 1 exercises in the *SPSS Companion*	**InfoTrac® College Edition** *Keywords:* deductive reasoning, idiographic, inductive reasoning, nomothetic, postmodernism research, qualitative, quantitative **Web Site Highlights** http://sociology.wadsworth.com *For this chapter:* • Tutorial Quizzes • Internet Links and Exercises • InfoTrac® College Edition Exercises • Flashcards • Chapter Tutorials • Extended Projects • Social Research in Cyberspace • Primers for using SPSS, NVivo, and other data analysis software **WebTUTOR Advantage** See Chapter 1 for chapter-specific quizzing, discussion threads, interactive games and exercises, and other study tools

Chapter 2: Paradigms, Theory, and Social Research

Instructor Resources	Readers and Guides*	Media Resources	Online Resources
Instructor's Manual with Test Bank See Chapter 2 for teaching resources and 20–25 Multiple-Choice, 10–15 True/False, and 2–5 Essay questions Also available electronically through **ExamView®** **Multimedia Manager for Sociology** Choose from figures, tables, and CNN® video clips to create customized Microsoft® PowerPoint® lecture presentations	*Guided Activities for The Practice of Social Research,* **Tenth Edition** See Chapter 2 ***Readings in Social Research Methods,* Second Edition** See Chapter 2, "Combining Theory with Methods" for such readings as "School Tracking and Student Violence" (Yogan) ***Experiencing Social Research: An Introduction Using MicroCase®*** See Exercise 2, "Connecting Theory and Research" ***SPSS Companion for Research Methods,* Third Edition** See SPSS exercises for Chapter 2, "Paradigms, Theory, and Social Research"	**Research Writer CD-ROM** Guides students through the stages of writing a research report. They can email their reports, export to Word, and have their reports automatically formatted. Video clips of Earl Babbie highlight important points in the text. *The Research Writer* sections on "Review of the Literature" and "Bibliography" relate to this chapter **SPSS 11.0 CD-ROM** Student version allows students to use real-world software to do data analysis. Use with *SPSS Companion* exercises noted at left **GSS Data Disk** Use these data sets to complete exercise 2.5 in the *Guided Activities* and the Chapter 2 exercises in the *SPSS Companion*	**InfoTrac® College Edition** *Keywords:* conflict theory, ethnomethodology, feminism, logical positivism, macro-theory, micro-theory, social sciences functionalism, sociological theory **Web Site Highlights** http://sociology.wadsworth.com *For this chapter:* • Tutorial Quizzes • Internet Links and Exercises • InfoTrac® Exercises • Flashcards • Chapter Tutorials • Extended Projects • Social Research in Cyberspace • Primers for using SPSS, NVivo, and other data analysis software **WebTUTOR Advantage** See Chapter 2 for chapter-specific quizzing, discussion threads, interactive games and exercises, and other study tools

Chapter 3: The Ethics and Politics of Social Research

Instructor Resources	Readers and Guides*	Media Resources	Online Resources
Instructor's Manual with Test Bank See Chapter 3 for teaching resources and 20–25 Multiple-Choice, 10–15 True/False, and 2–5 Essay questions Also available electronically through **ExamView®**. **Multimedia Manager for Sociology** Choose from figures, tables, and CNN® video clips to create customized Microsoft® PowerPoint® lecture presentations	***Guided Activities for The Practice of Social Research,* Tenth Edition** See Chapter 3 ***Readings in Social Research Methods,* Second Edition** See Chapter 3, "The Ethics of Research" for readings such as "Problems of Ethics in Research" (Milgram) ***SPSS Companion for Research Methods,* Third Edition** See SPSS exercises for Chapter 3, "The Ethics and Politics of Social Research"	**Research Writer CD-ROM** Guides students through the stages of writing a research report. Students can email their reports, export to Word, and have their reports automatically formatted. Video clips of Earl Babbie highlight important points in the text **SPSS 11.0 CD-ROM** Student version allows students to use real-world software to do data analysis. Use with the SPSS *Companion* exercises noted on the left **GSS Data Disk** Use these data sets to complete the Chapter 3 exercises in the *SPSS Companion*	**InfoTrac® College Edition** *Keywords:* anonymity, code of ethics, confidentiality, informed consent, institutional review board, research ethics **Web site Highlights** http://sociology.wadsworth.com *For this chapter:* • Tutorial Quizzes • Internet Links and Exercises • InfoTrac® College Edition Exercises • Flashcards • Chapter Tutorials • Extended Projects • Social Research in Cyberspace • Primers for using SPSS, NVivo, and other data analysis software WebTUTOR Advantage See Chapter 3 for chapter-specific quizzing, discussion threads, interactive games and exercises, and other study tools

Chapter 4: Research Design

Instructor Resources	Readers and Guides*	Media Resources	Online Resources
Instructor's Manual with Test Bank See Chapter 4 for teaching resources and 20–25 Multiple-Choice, 10–15 True/False, and 2–5 Essay questions Also available electronically through **ExamView®**. **Multimedia Manager for Sociology** Choose from figures, tables, and CNN® video clips to create customized Microsoft® PowerPoint® lecture presentations.	***Guided Activities for The Practice of Social Research,* Tenth Edition** See Chapter 4 ***Readings in Social Research Methods,* Second Edition** See Chapter 4, "Research Design" for such readings as "Public Assistance Receipt Among Immigrants and Natives" (VanHook/Glick/Bean) ***Experiencing Social Research: An Introduction Using MicroCase®*** See Exercises 3 and 4, "Establishing Cause and Effect Relationships" and "Designing Research" ***SPSS Companion for Research Methods,* Third Edition** See SPSS exercises for Chapter 4, "The Idea of Causation in Social Research" and "Research Design"	**Research Writer CD-ROM: with Chapter Tutorials** Guides students through the stages of writing a research report. Students can email their reports, export to Word, and have their reports automatically formatted. Video clips of Earl Babbie highlight important points in the text. *The Research Writer* sections "Introduction" and "Study Design" relate to this chapter **SPSS 11.0 CD-ROM** Student version allows students to use real-world software to do data analysis. Use with the *SPSS Companion* exercises noted on the left **GSS Data Disk** Use these data sets to complete exercises 4.5 and 4.6 in the *Guided Activities* and the Chapter 4 exercises in the *SPSS Companion*	**InfoTrac® College Edition** *Keywords:* cross-sectional study, ecological fallacy, longitudinal study, panel study, reductionism, trend study, unit of analysis, spuriousness, necessary cause, sufficient cause **Web site Highlights** http://sociology.wadsworth.com *For this chapter:* • Tutorial Quizzes • Internet Links and Exercises • InfoTrac® College Edition Exercises • Flashcards • Chapter Tutorials • Extended Projects • Social Research in Cyberspace • Primers for using SPSS, NVivo, and other data analysis software WebTUTOR Advantage See Chapter 4 for chapter-specific quizzing, discussion threads, interactive games and exercises, and other study tools

Chapter 5: Conceptualization, Operationalization, and Measurement

Instructor Resources	Readers and Guides*	Media Resources	Online Resources

Instructor's Manual with Test Bank
See Chapter 5 for teaching resources and 20–25 Multiple-Choice, 10–15 True/False, and 2–5 Essay questions

Also available electronically through **ExamView®**

 Multimedia Manager for Sociology
Choose from figures, tables, and CNN® video clips to create customized Microsoft® PowerPoint® lecture presentations

Guided Activities for The Practice of Social Research, Tenth Edition
See Chapter 5

Readings in Social Research Methods, Second Edition
See Chapter 5, "Conceptualization, Operationalization, and Measurement" for readings such as "Conceptualization of Terrorism" (Gibbs)

 Experiencing Social Research: An Introduction Using MicroCase®
See Exercises 5 and 6, "Connecting Conceptualization and Measurement" and "Measuring Social Reality"

SPSS Companion for Research Methods, Third Edition
See SPSS exercises for Chapter 5, "Conceptualization, Operationalization, and Measurement"

 Research Writer CD-ROM
Guides students through the stages of writing a research report. Students can email their reports, export to Word, and have their reports automatically formatted. Video clips of Earl Babbie highlight important points in the text. *The Research Writer* section, "Measurement of Variables," relates to this chapter

SPSS 11.0 CD-ROM
Student version allows students to use real-world software to do data analysis. Use with the *SPSS Companion* exercises noted on the left

 GSS Data Disk
Use these data sets to complete exercises 5.6 and 5.7 in the *Guided Activities* and the Chapter 5 exercises in the *SPSS Companion*

 **InfoTrac® College Edition**
Keywords: anomie, attributes and variables, cohort study, conceptualization, construct validity, operationalization, panel study, trend study, validity and reliability

Web site Highlights
http://sociology.wadsworth.com
For this chapter:
• Tutorial Quizzes
• Internet Links and Exercises
• InfoTrac® College Edition Exercises
• Flashcards
• Chapter Tutorials
• Extended Projects
• Social Research in Cyberspace
• Primers for using SPSS, NVivo, and other data analysis software

WebTUTOR Advantage
See Chapter 5 for chapter-specific quizzing, discussion threads, interactive games and exercises, and other study tools

Chapter 6: Indexes, Scales, and Typologies

Instructor Resources	Readers and Guides*	Media Resources	Online Resources

Instructor's Manual with Test Bank
See Chapter 6 for teaching resources and 20–25 Multiple-Choice, 10–15 True/False, and 2–5 Essay questions

Also available electronically through **ExamView®**

Multimedia Manager for Sociology
Choose from figures, tables, and CNN® video clips to create customized Microsoft® PowerPoint® lecture presentations

Guided Activities for The Practice of Social Research, Tenth Edition
See Chapter 6

Readings in Social Research Methods, Second Edition
See Chapter 6, "Indexes and Scales" for readings such as "The Reverse Social Distance Scale" (Lee/Sapp/Ray)

 Experiencing Social Research: An Introduction Using MicroCase®
See Exercise 7, "Constructing and Evaluating Scales and Indexes"

SPSS Companion for Research Methods, Third Edition
See exercises for Chapter 6, "Indexes, Scales, and Typologies"

Research Writer CD-ROM
Guides students through the stages of writing a research report. Students can email their reports, export to Word, and have their reports automatically formatted. Video clips of Earl Babbie highlight important points in the text. *The Research Writer* section, "Measurement of Variables," relates to this chapter.

 SPSS 11.0 CD-ROM
Student version allows students to use real-world software to do data analysis. Use with the *SPSS Companion* exercises noted on the left

GSS Data Disk
Use these data sets to complete exercise 6.5 in the *Guided Activities* and the Chapter 6 exercises in the *SPSS Companion*

InfoTrac® College Edition
Keywords: composite and measure, intelligence tests and validity, Likert, sociological and index, sociological and scale, Thurstone

Web site Highlights
http://sociology.wadsworth.com
For this chapter:
• Tutorial Quizzes
• Internet Links and Exercises
• InfoTrac® College Edition Exercises
• Flashcards
• Chapter Tutorials
• Extended Projects
• Social Research in Cyberspace
• Primers for using SPSS, NVivo, and other data analysis software

 WebTUTOR Advantage
See Chapter 6 for chapter-specific quizzing, discussion threads, interactive games and exercises, and other study tools

Chapter 7: The Logic of Sampling

Instructor Resources	Readers and Guides*	Media Resources	Online Resources
Instructor''s Manual with Test Bank See Chapter 7 for teaching resources and 20–25 Multiple-Choice, 10–15 True/False, and 2–5 Essay questions Also available electronically through **ExamView®** **Multimedia Manager for Sociology** Choose from figures, tables, and CNN® video clips to create customized Microsoft® PowerPoint® lecture presentations	*Guided Activities for The Practice of Social Research,* **Tenth Edition** See Chapter 7 *Readings in Social Research Methods,* **Second Edition** See Chapter 7, "Sampling Made Logical" for readings such as "Sex in America"(Michael/Gagnon/Laumann/Kolata) *Experiencing Social Research: An Introduction Using MicroCase®* See Exercise 8, "Probability Sampling" *SPSS Companion for Research Methods,* **Third Edition** See SPSS exercises for Chapter 7, "The Logic of Sampling"	**Research Writer CD-ROM: with Chapter Tutorials** Guides students through the stages of writing a research report. Students can email their reports, export to Word, and have their reports automatically formatted. Video clips of Earl Babbie highlight important points in the text. *The Research Writer* section, "Study Design," relates to this chapter **SPSS 11.0 CD-ROM** Student version allows students to use real-world software to do data analysis. Use with the *SPSS Companion* exercises noted on the left **GSS Data Disk** Use these data sets to complete the Chapter 7 exercises in the *SPSS Companion*	**InfoTrac® College Edition** *Keywords:* cluster sample, confidence interval, confidence level, nonprobability sample, probability sample, quota sample, sampling bias, sampling distribution, sampling error, sampling frame, stratified sample **Web site Highlights** http://sociology.wadsworth.com *For this chapter:* • Tutorial Quizzes • Internet Links and Exercises • InfoTrac® College Edition Exercises • Flashcards • Chapter Tutorials • Extended Projects • Social Research in Cyberspace • Primers for using SPSS, NVivo, and other data analysis software **WebTUTOR™ Advantage** See Chapter 7 for chapter-specific quizzing, discussion threads, interactive games and exercises, and other study tools

Chapter 8: Experiments

Instructor Resources	Readers and Guides*	Media Resources	Online Resources
Instructor's Manual with Test Bank See Chapter 8 for teaching resources and 20–25 Multiple-Choice, 10–15 True/False, and 2–5 Essay questions Also available electronically through **ExamView®** **Multimedia Manager for Sociology (icon)** Choose from figures, tables, and CNN® video clips to create customized Microsoft® PowerPoint® lecture presentations	*Guided Activities for The Practice of Social Research,* **Tenth Edition** See Chapter 8 *Readings in Social Research Methods,* **Second Edition** See Chapter 8, "Experimental and Survey Research" for readings such as "Intraoperative Progress Reports Decrease Family Members' Anxiety" (Leske) *Experiencing Social Research: An Introduction Using MicroCase®* See Exercise 9, "Doing Experiments" *SPSS Companion for Research Methods,* **Third Edition** See SPSS exercises for Chapter 8, "Experiments"	**Research Writer CD-ROM** Guides students through the stages of writing a research report. Students can email their reports, export to Word, and have their reports automatically formatted. Video clips of Earl Babbie highlight important points in the text. *The Research Writer* section, "Study Design," relates to this chapter **SPSS 11.0 CD-ROM** Student version allows students to use real-world software to do data analysis. Use with the *SPSS Companion* exercises noted on the left **GSS Data Disk** Use these data sets to complete exercise 8.4 in the *Guided Activities* and the Chapter 8 exercises in the *SPSS Companion*	**InfoTrac® College Edition** *Keywords:* double-blind experiment, experiment and control group, experiment and matching, experiment and placebo, experiment and stimulus, natural experiment **Web site Highlights** http://sociology.wadsworth.com *For this chapter:* • Tutorial Quizzes • Internet Links and Exercises • InfoTrac® College Edition Exercises • Flashcards • Chapter Tutorials • Extended Projects • Social Research in Cyberspace • Primers for using SPSS, NVivo, and other data analysis software **WebTUTOR™ Advantage** See Chapter 8 for chapter-specific quizzing, discussion threads, interactive games and exercises, and other study tools

Chapter 9: Survey Research

Instructor Resources	Readers and Guides*	Media Resources	Online Resources
Instructor's Manual with Test Bank See Chapter 9 for teaching resources and 20–25 Multiple-Choice, 10–15 True/False, and 2–5 Essay questions Also available electronically through **ExamView®** **Multimedia Manager for Sociology** Choose from figures, tables, and CNN® video clips to create customized Microsoft® PowerPoint® lecture presentations	*Guided Activities for The Practice of Social Research,* **Tenth Edition** See Chapter 9 *Readings in Social Research Methods,* **Second Edition** See Chapter 8, "Experimental and Survey Research" for readings such as "The Internet and Opinion Measurement: Surveying Marginalized Populations" (Koch/California State University/Emrey) *Experiencing Social Research: An Introduction Using MicroCase®* See Exercise 10, "Conducting Surveys" *SPSS Companion for Research Methods,* **Third Edition** See SPSS exercises for Chapter 9, "Survey Research"	**Research Writer CD-ROM** Guides students through the stages of writing a research report. Students can email their reports, export to Word, and have their reports automatically formatted. Video clips of Earl Babbie highlight important points in the text. *The Research Writer* section, "Study Design," relates to this chapter **SPSS 11.0 CD-ROM** Student version allows students to use real-world software to do data analysis. Use with the *SPSS Companion* exercises noted on the left **GSS Data Disk** Use these data sets to complete exercise 9.6 in the *Guided Activities* and the Chapter 9 exercises in the *SPSS Companion*	**InfoTrac® College Edition** *Keywords:* CATI, mail survey, opinion poll, questionnaire, respondent, self-administered, telephone poll, telephone survey **Web site Highlights** http://sociology.wadsworth.com *For this chapter:* •Tutorial Quizzes •Internet Links and Exercises •InfoTrac® College Edition Exercises •Flashcards •Chapter Tutorials •Extended Projects •Social Research in Cyberspace •Primers for using SPSS, NVivo, and other data analysis software **WebTUTOR Advantage** See Chapter 9 for chapter-specific quizzing, discussion threads, interactive games and exercises, and other study tools

Chapter 10: Qualitative Field Research

Instructor Resources	Readers and Guides*	Media Resources	Online Resources
Instructor's Manual with Test Bank See Chapter 10 for teaching resources and 20–25 Multiple-Choice, 10–15 True/False, and 2–5 Essay questions Also available electronically through **ExamView®** **Multimedia Manager for Sociology** Choose from figures, tables, and CNN® video clips, to create customized Microsoft® PowerPoint® lecture presentations	*Guided Activities for The Practice of Social Research,* **Tenth Edition** See Chapter 10 *Readings in Social Research Methods,* **Second Edition** See Chapter 9, "Field Research and Unobtrusive Measures" for readings such as "Tally's Corner: A Study of Negro Streetcorner Men" (Liebow) *Experiencing Social Research: An Introduction Using MicroCase®* See Exercise 11, "Connecting Field Observation and Quantitative Measurement" *SPSS Companion for Research Methods,* **Third Edition** See SPSS exercises for Chapter 10, "Qualitative Field Research"	**Research Writer CD-ROM** Guides students through the stages of writing a research report. Students can email their reports, export to Word, and have their reports automatically formatted. Video clips of Earl Babbie highlight important points in the text. *The Research Writer* section, "Study Design," relates to this chapter **SPSS 11.0 CD-ROM** Student version allows students to use real-world software to do data analysis. Use with the *SPSS Companion* exercises noted on the left **GSS Data Disk** Use these data sets to complete the Chapter 10 exercises in the *SPSS Companion*	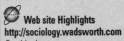 **InfoTrac® College Edition** *Keywords:* ethnomethodology, field research, grounded theory, in-depth interview, naturalism, participant observation, participatory action research **Web site Highlights** http://sociology.wadsworth.com *For this chapter:* •Tutorial Quizzes •Internet Links and Exercises •InfoTrac® College Edition Exercises •Flashcards •Chapter Tutorials •Extended Projects •Social Research in Cyberspace •Primers for using SPSS, NVivo, and other data analysis software **WebTUTOR Advantage** See Chapter 10 for chapter-specific quizzing, discussion threads, interactive games and exercises, and other study tools

Chapter 11: Unobtrusive Research

Instructor Resources	Readers and Guides*	Media Resources	Online Resources
Instructor's Manual with Test Bank See Chapter 11 for teaching resources and 20–25 Multiple-Choice, 10–15 True/False, and 2–5 Essay questions Also available electronically through **ExamView®** **Multimedia Manager for Sociology** Choose from figures, tables, and CNN® video clips to create customized Microsoft® PowerPoint® lecture presentations	**Guided Activities for The Practice of Social Research, Tenth Edition** See Chapter 11 **Readings in Social Research Methods, Second Edition** See Chapter 9, "Field Research and Unobtrusive Measures" for readings such as "The Evolution of Al-Anon: A Content Analysis of Stories in Two Editions of its 'Big Book'" (Martin) **Experiencing Social Research: An Introduction Using MicroCase®** See Exercise 12, "Doing Unobtrusive Research" **SPSS Companion for Research Methods, Third Edition** See SPSS exercises for Chapter 11, "Unobtrusive Measures"	**Research Writer CD-ROM** Guides students through the stages of writing a research report. Students can email their reports, export to Word, and have their reports automatically formatted. Video clips of Earl Babbie highlight important points in the text. *The Research Writer* section, "Study Design," relates to this chapter **SPSS 11.0 CD-ROM** Student version allows students to use real-world software to do data analysis. Use with the *SPSS Companion* exercises noted on the left **GSS Data Disk** Use these data sets to complete the Chapter 11 exercises in the *SPSS Companion*	**InfoTrac® College Edition** *Keywords:* content analysis, Emile Durkheim, historical/comparative, Karl Marx, latent content, manifest content, Max Weber, unobtrusive **Web site Highlights** http://sociology.wadsworth.com *For this chapter:* • Tutorial Quizzes • Internet Links and Exercises • InfoTrac® College Edition Exercises • Flashcards • Chapter Tutorials • Extended Projects • Social Research in Cyberspace • Primers for using SPSS, NVivo, and other data analysis software **WebTUTOR Advantage** See Chapter 11 for chapter-specific quizzing, discussion threads, interactive games and exercises, and other study tools

Chapter 12: Evaluation Research

Instructor Resources	Readers and Guides*	Media Resources	Online Resources
Instructor's Manual with Test Bank See Chapter 12 for teaching resources and 20–25 Multiple-Choice, 10–15 True/False, and 2–5 Essay questions Also available electronically through **ExamView®** **Multimedia Manager for Sociology** Choose from figures, tables, and CNN® video clips to create customized Microsoft® PowerPoint® lecture presentations	**Guided Activities for The Practice of Social Research, Tenth Edition** See Chapter 12 **Readings in Social Research Methods, Second Edition** See Chapter 10, "Existing Data and Evaluation Research" for readings such as "Women's Opposition to Race-Targeted Interventions" (Stack) **Experiencing Social Research: An Introduction Using MicroCase®** See Exercise 13, "Evaluating Social Interventions" **SPSS Companion for Research Methods, Third Edition** See SPSS exercises for Chapter 12, "Evaluation Research"	**Research Writer CD-ROM** Guides students through the stages of writing a research report. Students can email their reports, export to Word, and have their reports automatically formatted. Video clips of Earl Babbie highlight important points in the text. *The Research Writer* section, "Study Design," relates to this chapter **SPSS 11.0 CD-ROM** Student version allows students to use real-world software to do data analysis. Use with the *SPSS Companion* exercises noted on the left **GSS Data Disk** Use these data sets to complete the Chapter 12 exercises in the *SPSS Companion*	**InfoTrac® College Edition** *Keywords:* capital-punishment evaluation, computer social simulation, evaluation research, program assessment, program evaluation, quasi-experiment, social indicators research **Web site Highlights** http://sociology.wadsworth.com *For this chapter:* • Tutorial Quizzes • Internet Links and Exercises • InfoTrac® College Edition Exercises • Flashcards • Chapter Tutorials • Extended Projects • Social Research in Cyberspace • Primers for using SPSS, NVivo, and other data analysis software **WebTUTOR Advantage** See Chapter 12 for chapter-specific quizzing, discussion threads, interactive games and exercises, and other study tools

Chapter 13: Qualitative Data Analysis

Instructor Resources	Readers and Guides*	Media Resources	Online Resources
Instructor's Manual with Test Bank See Chapter 13 for teaching resources and 20–25 Multiple-Choice, 10–15 True/False, and 2–5 Essay questions Also available electronically through **ExamView®** **Multimedia Manager for Sociology** Choose from figures, tables, and CNN® video clips to create customized Microsoft® PowerPoint® lecture presentations	***Guided Activities for The Practice of Social Research, Tenth Edition*** See Chapter 13 ***SPSS Companion for Research Methods,* Third Edition** See SPSS exercises for Chapter 13, "Qualitative Data Analysis"	**Research Writer CD-ROM** Guides students through the stages of writing a research report. Students can email their reports, export to Word, and have their reports automatically formatted. Video clips of Earl Babbie highlight important points in the text. *The Research Writer* section, "Data Analysis," relates to this chapter **SPSS 11.0 CD-ROM** Student version allows students to use real-world software to do data analysis. Use with the *SPSS Companion* exercises noted on the left **GSS Data Disk** Use these data sets to complete the Chapter 13 exercises in the *SPSS Companion*	**InfoTrac® College Edition** *Keywords:* concept mapping, conversation analysis, grounded theory, qualitative data analysis, semiotics **Web site Highlights** http://sociology.wadsworth.com *For this chapter:* • Tutorial Quizzes • Internet Links and Exercises • InfoTrac® College Edition Exercises • Flashcards • Chapter Tutorials • Extended Projects • Social Research in Cyberspace • Primers for using SPSS, NVivo, and other data analysis software **WebTUTOR Advantage** See Chapter 13 for chapter-specific quizzing, discussion threads, interactive games and exercises, and other study tools

Chapter 14: Quantitative Data Analysis

Instructor Resources	Readers and Guides*	Media Resources	Online Resources
Instructor's Manual with Test Bank See Chapter 14 for teaching resources and 20–25 Multiple-Choice, 10–15 True/False, and 2–5 Essay questions Also available electronically through **ExamView®** **Multimedia Manager for Sociology** Choose from figures, tables, and CNN® video clips to create customized Microsoft® PowerPoint® lecture presentations	***Guided Activities for The Practice of Social Research, Tenth Edition*** See Chapter 14 ***Experiencing Social Research: An Introduction Using MicroCase®*** See Exercise 14, "Continuities in Quantifying Data" ***SPSS Companion for Research Methods,* Third Edition** See SPSS exercises for Chapter 14, "Quantifying Data" and "Elementary Quantitative Analysis"	**Research Writer CD-ROM** Guides students through the stages of writing a research report. Students can email their reports, export to Word, and have their reports automatically formatted. Video clips of Earl Babbie highlight important points in the text. *The Research Writer* section, "Data Analysis," relates to this chapter **SPSS 11.0 CD-ROM** Student version allows students to use real-world software to do data analysis. Use with the *SPSS Companion* exercises noted on the left **GSS Data Disk** Use these data sets to complete exercises 14.5 and 14.6 in the *Guided Activities* and the Chapter 14 exercises in the *SPSS Companion*	**InfoTrac® College Edition** *Keywords:* bivariate analysis, central tendency, continuous variable, discrete variable, multivariate analysis technique, univariate analysis **Web site Highlights (icon)** http://sociology.wadsworth.com *For this chapter:* • Tutorial Quizzes • Internet Links and Exercises • InfoTrac® College Edition Exercises • Flashcards • Chapter Tutorials • Extended Projects • Social Research in Cyberspace • Primers for using SPSS, NVivo, and other data analysis software **WebTUTOR Advantage** See Chapter 14 for chapter-specific quizzing, discussion threads, interactive games and exercises, and other study tools

Chapter 15: The Elaboration Model

Instructor Resources	Readers and Guides*	Media Resources	Online Resources
Instructor's Manual with Test Bank See Chapter 15 for teaching resources and 20–25 Multiple-Choice, 10–15 True/False, and 2–5 Essay questions Also available electronically through **ExamView®** **Multimedia Manager for Sociology** Choose from figures, tables, and CNN® video clips to create customized Microsoft® PowerPoint® lecture presentations	***Guided Activities for The Practice of Social Research, Tenth Edition*** See Chapter 15 ***SPSS Companion for Research Methods, Third Edition*** See SPSS exercises for Chapter 15, "The Elaboration Model"	**Research Writer CD-ROM** Guides students through the stages of writing a research report. Students can email their reports, export to Word, and have their reports automatically formatted. Video clips of Earl Babbie highlight important points in the text. *The Research Writer* section, "Data Analysis," relates to this chapter **SPSS 11.0 CD-ROM** Student version allows students to use real-world software to do data analysis. Use with the *SPSS Companion* exercises noted on the left **GSS Data Disk** Use these data sets to complete exercises 15.3 and 15.4 in the *Guided Activities* and the Chapter 15 exercises in the *SPSS Companion*	**InfoTrac® College Edition** *Keyword:* Paul F. Lazarsfeld **Web site Highlights** http://sociology.wadsworth.com *For this chapter:* • Tutorial Quizzes • Internet Links and Exercises • InfoTrac® College Edition Exercises • Flashcards • Chapter Tutorials • Extended Projects • Social Research in Cyberspace • Primers for using SPSS, NVivo, and other data analysis software **WebTUTOR Advantage** See Chapter 15 for chapter-specific quizzing, discussion threads, interactive games and exercises, and other study tools

Chapter 16: Social Statistics

Instructor Resources	Readers and Guides*	Media Resources	Online Resources
Instructor's Manual with Test Bank See Chapter 16 for teaching resources and 20–25 Multiple-Choice, 10–15 True/False, and 2–5 Essay questions Also available electronically through **ExamView®** **Multimedia Manager for Sociology** Choose from figures, tables, and CNN® video clips to create customized Microsoft® PowerPoint® lecture presentations	***Guided Activities for The Practice of Social Research, Tenth Edition*** See Chapter 16 ***Readings in Social Research Methods, Second Edition*** See Chapter 11, "An Introduction to Statistics" for such readings as "Elementary Applied Statistics: For Students in Behavioral Science" (Freeman) ***SPSS Companion for Research Methods, Third Edition*** See SPSS exercises for Chapter 16, "Social Statistics"	**Research Writer CD-ROM** Guides students through the stages of writing a research report. Students can email their reports, export to Word, and have their reports automatically formatted. Video clips of Earl Babbie highlight important points in the text. *The Research Writer* section, "Data Analysis," relates to this chapter **SPSS 11.0 CD-ROM** Student version allows students to use real-world software to do data analysis. Use with the *SPSS Companion* exercises noted on the left **GSS Data Disk** Use these data sets to complete the Chapter 16 exercises in the *SPSS Companion*	**InfoTrac® College Edition** *Keywords:* descriptive statistics, inferential statistics, regression analysis, path analysis, statistically significant, nonsampling error, null hypothesis **Web site Highlights (icon)** http://sociology.wadsworth.com *For this chapter:* • Tutorial Quizzes • Internet Links and Exercises • InfoTrac® College Edition Exercises • Flashcards • Chapter Tutorials • Extended Projects • Social Research in Cyberspace • Primers for using SPSS, NVivo, and other data analysis software **WebTUTOR Advantage** See Chapter 16 for chapter-specific quizzing, discussion threads, interactive games and exercises, and other study tools

Chapter 17: Reading and Writing Social Research

Instructor Resources	Readers and Guides*	Media Resources	Online Resources
Instructor's Manual with Test Bank See Chapter 17 for teaching resources and 20–25 Multiple-Choice, 10–15 True/False, and 2–5 Essay questions Also available electronically through **ExamView®** **Multimedia Manager for Sociology** Choose from figures, tables, and CNN® video clips to create customized Microsoft® PowerPoint® lecture presentations	**Guided Activities for The Practice of Social Research, Tenth Edition** See Chapter 17 **Readings in Social Research Methods, Second Edition** See Chapter 12, "Reading and Writing for the Social Sciences" for such readings as "AIDS and the Media" (Wysocki/Harrison) **SPSS Companion for Research Methods, Third Edition** See SPSS exercises for Chapter 17, "The Ethics and Politics of Social Research" and "The Uses of Social Research"	**Research Writer CD-ROM** Guides students through the stages of writing a research report. Students can email their reports, export to Word, and have their reports automatically formatted. Video clips of Earl Babbie highlight important points in the text. *The Research Writer* sections on "Abstract," "Introduction," "Review of the Literature," "Study Design," "Measurement of Variables," "Data Analysis," and "Conclusion and Bibliography" relate to this chapter **SPSS 11.0 CD-ROM** Student version allows students to use real-world software to do data analysis. Use with the *SPSS Companion* exercises noted on the left **GSS Data Disk** Use these data sets to complete the Chapter 17 exercises in the *SPSS Companion*	**InfoTrac® College Edition** *Keyword:* plagiarism **Web site Highlights** http://sociology.wadsworth.com *For this chapter:* • Tutorial Quizzes • Internet Links and Exercises • InfoTrac® College Edition Exercises • Flashcards • Chapter Tutorials • Extended Projects • Social Research in Cyberspace • Primers for using SPSS, NVivo, and other data analysis software **WebTUTOR Advantage** See Chapter 17 for chapter-specific quizzing, discussion threads, interactive games and exercises, and other study tools

*Wagenaar & Babbie, *Guided Activities for The Practice of Social Research*, Tenth Edition
*Wysocki, *Readings in Social Research Methods*, Second Edition
*Ayers, *Experiencing Social Research: An Introduction Using MicroCase®*
*Turner, *SPSS Companion for Research Methods*, Third Edition

CHAPTER 1: HUMAN INQUIRY AND SCIENCE

OUTLINE

I. Introduction

II. Looking For Reality
    A. Ordinary human inquiry
    B. Tradition
    C. Authority
    D. Errors in inquiry and some solutions
        1. Inaccurate observations
        2. Overgeneralization
        3. Selective observation
        4. Illogical reasoning
    E. What's really real?
        1. The premodern view
        2. The modern view
        3. The postmodern view

III. The Foundations of Social Science
    A. Theory, not philosophy or belief
    B. Social regularities
        1. The charge of triviality
        2. What about exceptions?
        3. People could interfere
    C. Aggregates, not individuals
    D. A variable language

IV. Some Dialectics of Social Research
    A. Idiographic and nomothetic explanation
    B. Inductive and deductive theory
    C. Qualitative and quantitative data
    D. Pure and applied research

V. The Ethics of Social Research
    A. Voluntary participation
    B. No harm to subjects

BEHAVIORAL OBJECTIVES

Upon completion of this chapter, the student should be able to:

1. Define and illustrate agreement reality.

2. Define and illustrate experiential reality.

3. Identify the two criteria for scientists to accept the reality of something they have not personally experienced.

4. Differentiate epistemology from methodology.

5. Define and illustrate causal reasoning and probabilistic reasoning.

6. Differentiate the scientific approach from the ordinary human inquiry approach to causal and probabilistic reasoning.

7. Differentiate prediction from understanding.

8. Describe the roles of tradition and authority as sources of secondhand knowledge.

9. Define and illustrate each of the following errors in inquiry: inaccurate observation, overgeneralization, selective observation, and illogical reasoning.

10. Show how a scientific approach attempts to provide safeguards against each one of these errors.

11. Compare premodern, modern and postmodern views of reality.

12. Describe what is meant by science being logico-empirical.

13. Describe the three major aspects of the overall scientific enterprise.

14. Define theory and indicate how it differs from philosophy or belief.

15. Give three examples of social regularities.

16. Respond to the three objections commonly raised regarding social regularities.

17. Define aggregate and present a rationale for why social scientists examine aggregates.

18. Give four examples of variables and their respective attributes.

19. Differentiate independent and dependent variables by definition and example, and show how they contribute to understanding causality.

20. Define and compare idiographic and nomothetic explanations.

21. Define and compare induction and deduction as ways of developing theories.

22. Define and give examples of quantitative data and qualitative data.

23. Define and compare pure and applied research.

24. Identify two basic ethical rules in doing social research.

TEACHING SUGGESTIONS AND RESOURCES

1. The following "True-False" questions can be used to illustrate two points. First, it illustrates that the social sciences do not simply document trivial "common sense" ideas. Second, it illustrates how we know the things we know.

   Ask students to answer whether the following statements are true or false. In addition, ask them to write down how they knew whether the statements were true or false.

   After students complete the "quiz" pick one of the items for discussion. Ask who answered "true" and who said "false." Ask those who said "true" how they **knew** that the statement was true and those who said "false" how they **knew** it was false. It will become clear to the students that how we/they "knew the answer" was from reading, something they heard, or their experience. All statements are false.

   A. Teen pregnancies account for most unwed births today.
      False
      http://www.cdc.gov/nchs/data/hus/tables/2002/02hus009.pdf
      Ask students to access this site from the CDC (Center for Disease Control) and NCHS (National Center for Health Statistics). The table on nonmarital childbearing clearly illustrates that in 1970 about 50% of the births were to women under 20 years of age and 18.1% to women 25 or older. However, by 2000 the figures changed. About 28% of the births were to women under 20 years of age and 34.6% to women 25 years of age or older. The data demonstrates that in recent years teenage pregnancies DO NOT account for most of the unwed births.

   B. The typical family structure in the United States is comprised of a married couple with their children.
      False

http://www.census.gov/prod/2001pubs/p20-537.pdf
This Census Bureau site presents the June 2001 report on America's Families and Living Arrangements. Figure 1 of the report shows that married couples with children constituted 24.1% of households in 2000 (it had been 40.3% in 1970). The modal category was married couples without children (28.7%).

C. In comparison to other age groups, the elderly are more likely to be in poverty.
False
http://www.census.gov/hhes/poverty/poverty01/pov01hi.html
The data presented at this site are from the "Current Population Survey (CPS), 2002 Annual Demographic Supplement (ADS), the source of official poverty estimates. The CPS ADS is a sample survey of approximately 78,000 households nationwide. These data reflect conditions in calendar year 2001." This site states that "At 16.3 percent, the poverty rate for children remained higher than that of other aged groups..."

2. To help students think about the process of doing research and how we as a society are constantly bombarded with research findings, bring in (or have students bring in) research reported in the media. I have found that studies reported in *Glamour Magazine, Esquire,* or *Cosmopolitan* seem to capture their attention as do articles from newspapers. One report that I heard while listening to *NPR* is "Would *one thousand young American women rather increase the size of their income, political power, or breasts.*" 1994 (February) *Esquire*. The survey results raise questions about question construction, sampling, generalizability, etc.

3. FILMS

Inventing Reality
60 min. PBS Video
MILL-108-CR94
ISBN 0-7936-0674-8
In Western society, science and magic are seen as opposing views of reality. Is there in fact a balance to strike? Travel to the Huichol Indian villages of Central Mexico to witness a Mexican doctor and a tribal shaman battling an epidemic of a rare strain of deadly measles. Then visit a cancer treatment center in Canada.

Perception
28 min. Color. 1979. Penn State Univ.
Shows how we perceive situations differently.

The Cave
10 min. Color. Bosustow Productions.
To lead into a discussion of the question "How do we know?" show this film. Based on Book VI of Plato's *The Republic*, the film depicts four men viewing the reflections on the wall as truth. One escapes to see reality. This film was reviewed in the ASA's "Using Films in Sociology

Courses: Guidelines and Reviews." See the Preface for the ASA Teaching Resource Center address.

The Eye of the Beholder
25 min. 1954. Indiana Univ.
To illustrate the errors we make in observation, show this film. It develops the idea that no two people see the same thing or situation in the same way.

See chapter 3 for a listing of films that involve the ethics of social research.

POSSIBLE ANSWERS TO STUDY GUIDE EXERCISES

Exercise 1.6: SPSS Computer Printout

INCOME3   INCOME IN THIRDS   * SEX RESPONDENTS

INCOME3 INCOME IN THIRDS			RESPONDENT'S SEX	SEX SEX	Total
			1 MALE	2 FEMALE	
INCOME IN THIRDS	1 LOW	Count	278	493	771
		% within SEX	26.8%	39.6%	33.8%
	2 MODERATE	Count	380	386	766
		% within SEX	36.7%	31.0%	33.6%
	3 HIGH	Count	378	366	744
		% within SEX	36.5%	29.4%	32.6%
Total		Count	1036	1245	2281
		% within SEX	100.0%	100.0%	100.0%

These data indicate that females are more likely than males to be in the lower third of income (39.6% of females as compared to 26.8% of males). Furthermore, males are more likely than females to earn both moderate and high incomes. Consequently, the data indicate that men earn more than women.

INFOTRAC EXERCISES

1. The future of the behavioral and social sciences. Philip M. Smith, Barbara Boyle Torrey. *Science*, Feb 2, 1996 v271 n5249 p611(2).What do the authors feel are the five main ways of meeting the needs of social research in the future?

2. Research misconduct. (Fraud in research.) Marcel C. LaFollette. *Society*, March-April 1994 v31 n3 p6(5). How does the author feel a social scientist should address the issue of scientific fraud?

3. Use the keyword option to look up quantitative research/data and qualitative research/data. How many "hits" did you get using each term? Read and summarize one social science article that focuses on qualitative research and one social science article that focuses on quantitative research.

4. Use the keyword option to locate articles on pure research and articles on applied research. Select one article that focuses on pure research within the social sciences and one that focuses on applied research within the social sciences. Provide a brief summary of each article.

INTERNET EXERCISES

If you used the "common sense quiz" noted in the Teaching Suggestions and Resources section, ask students to verify the information using the websites. If you did not use the "common sense quiz," ask students to examine whether these common sense beliefs are true or false using the previously noted websites.

MULTIPLE-CHOICE QUESTIONS

1. Methodology could best be described as
    a. the science of knowing
    b. the science of finding out
    c. the discovery of reality through agreement
    d. the discovery of reality through personal experience
    e. the logical aspect of science
        ANS: C
        PG: 6

2. Our attempts to learn about the world we live in come from
    a. direct experience
    b. tradition
    c. direct, personal inquiry
    d. authority
    e. all of the above
        ANS: E
        PG: 7

3. Pregnant at age 15, Tammy decided to have the baby. Her parents were upset with her decision and threatened to "cut her off" if she did not complete high school. A difficult pregnancy and embarrassment resulted in her dropping out of school. After the baby was born her parents said that they would raise the baby but that she would have to leave the house. At age 16 Tammy was on her own and without any money or job market skills. She began to work as a prostitute. This explanation of Tammy's prostitution is:
    a. Idiographic
    b. Nomothetic
    c. Probabilistic
    d. Quantitative
    e. Based on agreements
        ANS: A
        PG: 21

4. Today, social scientific theory addresses
    a. what should be
    b. what is and why
    c. matters of value
    d. only a and b are correct
    e. only b and c are correct
        ANS: B
        PGS: 12-13

5. Which of the following would a sociologist be LEAST likely to study?
    a. why crime rates are increasing in rural areas
    b. the incidence of child abuse in middle-income families
    c. why Mr. Smith quit his job
    d. the incidence of employment among the mentally retarded
    e. why unemployment rates are higher for black teens than white teens
        ANS: C
        PGS: 15-16

6. The expectation that increased education leads to a reduction in prejudice illustrates
    a. a relationship between variables
    b. the notion of causation
    c. the associations that might logically be expected to exist between particular attributes of different variables
    d. a hypothesis
    e. all of the above
        ANS: E
        PG: 20

7. Using data collected between 1957 and 1978, from 15 samples of adults, Professor Rodgers (1982 *Social Forces*) found that (1) the average level of happiness reported by people under 65 years of age declined from 1957 to 1970. For this same group, the average level of happiness increased slightly from 1970 to 1978. (2) The average level of happiness reported by people age 65 and older increased from 1957 to 1978. A(the) variable(s) in this study is(are)
   a. aged 65 and older
   b. less than age 65
   c. age
   d. age 65
   e. all of the above are variables
   ANS: C
   PGS: 16-17

8. Assume that Professor Rodgers from question #7 had studied only three people aged 65 or older. Suppose he had concluded that people under 65 years of age also experienced increasing levels of happiness from 1957 to 1970. He would have committed
   a. the error of overgeneralization
   b. the error of inaccurate observation
   c. the error of illogical reasoning
   d. the error of selective observation
   e. no error
   ANS: A
   PG: 8

9. The statement "Knowledge for knowledge's sake" describes:
   a. Pure research
   b. Applied research
   c. Inductive logic
   d. Deductive logic
   e. Probabilistic thinking
   ANS: A
   PG: 28

10. A study reported in *American Sociological Review* (1994) was entitled "Race Differences in Sexual Activity Among Adolescent Women." The independent variable was probably
   a. Race
   b. Sexual activity
   c. Adolescence
   d. Women
   e. There is probably no independent variable
   ANS: A
   PG: 20

11. One of your friends scored in the 90s on her last ten exams. Although she has been studying for this exam and feels prepared, she told you, "I know I'm going to flunk this exam. I've been doing too well on exams." Your friend is committing the error of
    a. illogical reasoning
    b. theory
    c. inaccurate observation
    d. selective observation
    e. overgeneralization
    ANS: A
    PG: 9

12. Some people claim that social scientists merely document the obvious. How might a social scientist respond to this claim?
    a. What appears obvious may be incorrect.
    b. What appears obvious may not have been, before the findings of the social scientist were reported.
    c. People may know something is so, without knowing why it is so—social science aims at both tasks.
    d. All of the above are responses.
    e. Only a and b are correct.
    ANS: D
    PGS: 13-14

13. The statement "wealthy countries should give aid to poorer countries" is a(an)
    a. hypothesis
    b. theory
    c. error in selective observation
    d. value judgment
    e. error in premature closure of inquiry
    ANS: D
    PG: 12

14. After examining court records, Jenny concludes that Mom's are more likely to obtain custody of their children than are Dad's. This type of statement is:
    a. Nomothetic.
    b. Idiographic
    c. Probabilistic
    d. Nomothetic and probabilistic
    e. Idiographic and probabilistic
    ANS: D
    PGS: 22-23

15. Which of the following is NOT an aim of social science?
    a. judging social values
    b. predicting social phenomena
    c. understanding social regularities
    d. explaining social regularities
    e. all of the above are aims of social science
    ANS: A
    PG: 12

16. Sally begins to think about the classes she's enrolled in at her university. She notices that she speaks a lot in three of her class and very little in two of her classes. She also notices that the classes in which she speaks have female instructors and that she rarely speaks in the two classes with male instructors. She begins to list all her college courses, the gender of the professor and whether or not she spoke in the class. She notices that she tends to speak in classes where the instructor is female and rarely speaks when the instructor is male. Sally is using
    a. Inductive reasoning
    b. Qualitative analysis
    c. Deductive reasoning
    d. Ordinary human inquiry
    e. Nomothetic reasoning
    ANS: A
    PG: 25

17. Safeguards against error in social research include
    a. making observations more deliberate
    b. replications under slightly varying circumstances
    c. the use of simple and complex measurement devices
    d. totally independent replications by other researchers
    e. all of the above
    ANS: E
    PGS: 8-9

18. In comparison to nonscientific inquiry, scientific inquiry
    a. takes special precaution to avoid error
    b. is a semiconscious activity
    c. is an activity where we are less concerned about making mistakes
    d. guards against all errors
    e. none of the above
    ANS: A
    PG: 9

19. An independent variable is a
     a. theoretical concept
     b. variable influencing other variables
     c. variable influenced by other variables
     d. set of attributes
     e. either b or c depending upon the variable
         ANS: B
         PG: 20

20. Which of the following is a list of variables?
     a. female, Jewish, educational level
     b. plumber, professor, dentist
     c. occupation, political party preference, birthrate
     d. 21, violent, social class
     e. dishonest, conservative, farmer
         ANS: C
         PGS: 16-17

21. Samantha agreed to participate in a study about use of health care facilities. After completing a questionnaire on her use of various medical facilities she declined to participate in an interview session. The researchers insisted that since she had agreed to participate she had to participate in the interview session. Which of the following ethical considerations were the researchers most clearly violating
     a. No harm to subjects
     b. Voluntary participation
     c. The unfairness of revealing damaging information
     d. Samantha's right to a nomothetic explanation
     e. None of the above
         ANS: B
         PG: 28

22. Which of the following views of reality does the statement "Beauty is in the eyes of the beholder" best reflect?
     a. The postmodern view
     b. The premodern view
     c. The modern view
     d. The ultramodern view
     e. All of the above
         ANS: C
         PG: 10

23. Which of the following is TRUE of quantification
    a. It often makes our observations more explicit
    b. It can make it easier to aggregate data
    c. It can make it easier to summarize data
    d. It opens up the possibility of statistical analysis
    e. All of the above are TRUE
       ANS: E
       PG: 26

24. The two pillars of science are:
    a. Qualitative and quantitative data
    b. Logic and observation
    c. Idiographic and nomothetic explanation
    d. Variable and attributes
    e. Tradition and authority
       ANS: B
       PG: 12

25. Nomothetic explanations
    a. Enable us to fully understand the causes of a particular instance
    b. Give us an exhaustive understanding of a particular instance
    c. Seek to explain a class or situations or events
    d. Are not useful in everyday life
    e. A and b are correct
       ANS: C
       PG: 22

TRUE-FALSE QUESTIONS

1. If an exception is found to a sociological pattern, the pattern is invalid.
   ANS: F
   PG: 14

2. Theory that is logically inconsistent is acceptable as long as it is empirically accurate.
   ANS: F
   PG: 12

3. Science offers total protection against the errors that nonscientists commit in casual, day-to-day inquiry.
   ANS: F
   PG: 29

4.   We study people for the purpose of seeing how variables are related to one another.
     ANS: T
     PG: 21

5.   The variable *plumber* has the attribute of occupation.
     ANS: F
     PGS: 16-17

6.   The misuse of authority refers to experts who discuss their area of expertise in public.
     ANS: F
     PGS: 7-8

7.   Social scientific theory aims at the determination of logical and persistent patterns of regularities in social life.
     ANS: T
     PG: 16

8.   We can predict without understanding.
     ANS: T
     PG: 7

9.   The premodern view assumes that we see things as they really are.
     ANS: T
     PG: 10

10. Every observation is quantitative at the outset.
     ANS: F
     PG: 26

11. Theories describe the relationship we might logically expect between variables.
     ANS: T
     PG: 20

12. Idiographic explanation provide partial explanations of a particular instance.
     ANS: F
     PG: 22

13. Deductive reasoning refers to movement from a set of specific observations to the discovery of a pattern.
     ANS: F
     PG: 25

14. Nomothetic explanations are more easily achieved through quantification.
    ANS: T
    PG: 28

ESSAYS

1. Describe how scientific inquiry differs from nonscientific inquiry.

2. Discuss how scientific inquiry tries to avoid the common pitfalls that produce error in nonscientific inquiry.

3. Name five sociological variables and their attributes.

4. Explain what is meant by the statement "Tradition and authority are the two-edged swords in the search for knowledge about the world."

CHAPTER 2: PARADIGMS, THEORY, AND SOCIAL RESEARCH

OUTLINE

I. Some Social Science Paradigms
   A. Macrotheory and microtheory
   B. Early positivism
   C. Social Darwinism
   D. Conflict paradigm
   E. Symbolic interactionism
   F. Ethnomethodology
   G. Structural functionalism
   H. Feminist paradigms
   I. Rational objectivity reconsidered

II. Elements of Social Theory

III. Two Logical Systems
   A. The traditional model of science
      1. Theory
      2. Operationalization
      3. Observation
   B. Deductive and inductive reasoning: A case illustration

IV. Deductive Theory Construction
   A. Getting started
   B. Constructing your theory
   C. An example of deductive theory

V. Inductive Theory Construction

VI. The Links Between Theory and Research

BEHAVIORAL OBJECTIVES

Upon completion of this chapter, the student should be able to:

1. List the three functions of theory for research.

2. Define paradigm.

3. Differentiate macrotheory from microtheory.

4.   Provide synopses for each of the following paradigms: early positivism, social Darwinism, conflict, symbolic interactionism, ethnomethodology, structural-functionalism, and feminist.

5.   Differentiate theory from paradigm.

6.   Define and show how each of the following terms is used in theory construction: observation, fact, law, theory, concepts, variables, axioms (or postulates), propositions, and hypotheses.

7.   Show the role of theory, operationalization, and observation in the traditional model of science.

8.   Define hypothesis testing.

9.   Differentiate inductive logic from deductive reasoning by definition and example.

10. Outline the steps in deductive theory construction.

11. Summarize the links between theory and research.

TEACHING SUGGESTIONS AND RESOURCES

1.   A method for demonstrating the steps in the traditional model of science comes from the ASA's "Eighty-one Techniques For Teaching Sociological Concepts." The technique was written by Reed Geertsen. See the preface for ASA Teaching Resources address.

The demonstration requires two clear glasses. Fill one glass with water and the other with rubbing alcohol. You will also need several ice cubes. The students should be unaware as to what the materials are.

Write on the blackboard, PROBLEM or TOPIC OF INTEREST. Tell the students you want to know what will happen when the CUBES are placed in the LIQUID. Ask them for their suggestions and write these on the board. When the students are done, label these HYPOTHESES. Explain to them that their suggestions are hypotheses. Ask the students how to TEST these hypotheses. As you go through the list you will find the issue of MEASUREMENT coming up. For example, a typical hypothesis is that the temperature of the liquids will change. Ask them how they will test that. This will lead into a discussion of a before and after thermometer measurement of temperature. After going through the hypotheses list with the issues of testing and measurement in mind, select one to test. An easy one to test in class is the hypothesis that the cubes will float. Define *float* and *sink*. Place the cubes in the liquids. Ask what happened and write FINDINGS on the board. Ask what CONCLUSIONS they draw from these findings. Typically, they will respond that the liquids are different or that the cubes are different. Write ADDITIONAL RESEARCH on the board and ask them what they would call their suggestions - HYPOTHESES. Point out that they are back into the research process. You might switch the cubes and go through the process again.

After going through the stages with this demonstration, go through them with a sociological example.

2.   A wonderful demonstration for teaching students about the blind spots of our perceptions/paradigms is developed by Reed Geertsen 1993. "Simulating the Blind Spot of Everyday Experience." *Teaching Sociology* 21:392-396. All you need is chalk and a board. The demonstration is done in several rounds during which you tell the students which word is part of the pattern and which word is not. You ask students to guess the pattern. So, the first round might include a pattern of words that begin with a vowel (e.g., around, extra, interesting, Ann but not guess, child. or Tom). The second round might have a pattern of words that include double letters (e.g., teen, letters, Sally but not Fred, tired, or theory). The third round might include a pattern of 3 letter words (e.g., Tom, try, or cry but not Sally, theory, or Marx). You can develop any patterns in this part as long as the focus is on the word (though you do not tell the students to focus on the word). Finally, start writing words on the board in the last round and again tell the students which words are in the pattern and which are not. However, this time the pattern is determined by where you stand when you write the word. If you're on the left of the word, for example, it's in the pattern and if you stand to the right of the word it's not. Students will have a tough time switching from focusing on the words to focusing on your position. Gradually exaggerate your stance. The demonstration clearly illustrates that once our attention is focused we have difficulty seeing other patterns.

3.   FILMS

Application of the Scientific Method
27 min. B/W. 1966. Univ. of Utah.
Applies the scientific method to four different experiments: (1) Bernard's discovery of the cause of diabetes, (2) Priestley's discovery of the need for oxygen in healthy air, (3) Leverrier's discovery of the planet Neptune, and (4) Freud's theory of the cause of dreams.

Methodology: The Psychologist and the Experiment
30 min. Color. 1975. Indiana Univ.
The scientific method is demonstrated in two different experiments. Steps illustrated are (1) generation of hypotheses; (2) manipulation of relevant environmental conditions; (3) random assignment of subjects; (4) experimental control; (5) observation of the effects of manipulation on the behavior under study; (6) interpretation of the findings; (7) replicability and generalizations.

Research Methods for the Social Sciences
33 min. 1995. Insight Media
An introduction to research methods for the social sciences. The video details 7 steps of the
scientific method and explains how to gather and interpret data.

Sociological Thinking and Research
30 min. 1991. Insight Media Phone: (212)721-6316
This program describes how to structure a research study by defining the problem to be studied,
reviewing the relevant literature, formulating a hypothesis, and selecting a research design.
William Kornblum explains his methods for studying the effects of planned renewal on the
Times Square neighborhood.

POSSIBLE ANSWERS TO STUDY GUIDE QUESTIONS

Exercise 2.5: SPSS Computer Results

HAPPY GENERAL HAPPINESS * **PRESTIG3** OCCUPATIONAL PRESTIGE IN THIRDS

			OCCUPATIONAL	PRESTIGE		
			1 LOW	2 MODERATE	3 HIGH	Total
GENERAL HAPPINESS	1 VERY HAPPY	Count	259	302	347	908
		% within PRESTIG3	27.9%	32.6%	36.1%	32.3%
	2 PRETTY HAPPY	Count	537	537	531	1605
		% within PRESTIG3	57.9%	57.9%	55.3%	57.0%
	3 NOT TOO HAPPY	Count	131	88	83	302
		% within PRESTIG3	14.1%	9.5%	8.6%	10.7%
	Total	Count	927	927	961	2815
		% within PRESTIG3	100.0%	100.0%	100.0%	100.0%

INFOTRAC EXERCISES

1. Feminist theory and sociology: underutilized contributions for mainstream theory. Janet Saltzman Chafetz. *Annual Review of Sociology*, 1997 v23 p. 97(24). What four criteria did the author use to select theories for this analysis?

2. Positivism in sociological practice: 1967-1990. C. David Gartrell, John W. Gartrell. *The Canadian Review* of Sociology and Anthropology, May 1996 v33 n2 p 143(16). What are the criteria by which the authors define positivism?

3. Symbolic interaction theories. (Theories of ethnicity.) Barbara Ballis Lal. *American Behavioral Scientist*, Jan 1995 v38 n3 P421(21). Who are some of the key founders of symbolic interactionism?

4. Using the key word option, ask student to select one of the theoretical perspectives with which they view the world and read a social science article that uses that perspective. Ask students to critique the article and its use of the perspective. Ask them how someone using one of the other paradigms would apply that paradigm to the topic under inquiry.

5. Ask students to select a theoretical perspective that they DO NOT use to view the world and to find an article that uses that perspective. Ask student to critique the article and whether the author(s) correctly applied the perspective to the topic of inquiry. Would another perspective be useful in studying the topic? If so, which paradigm and why? If no, why not?

INTERNET EXERCISES

1. Ask your students to use the SOSIG: Social Science Information Gateway site at: http://sosig.esrc.bris.ac.uk

Once accessed tell students to click on "Schools and Theories" under sociology. Ask students to select a category (e.g., critical theory or ethnomethodology) and to read and summarize an article from that category.

2. Ask students to visit the Marx/Engels Internet Archive site.
http://csf.colorado.edu/psn/marx
http://www.marxists.org/archive/marx/

Once accessed ask students to review the site and to select and summarize the information presented on a topic of their choice. For example, after accessing the site they could select "Marxist Writers" and summarize either what is available in that category or the writing of an individual author.

3. Ask students to go to the following site for a discussion of the scientific method. http://www.scientificmethod.com/index_nofla.html

Tell students to read the following three sections: 1) scientific methods vs scientific method, 2) the 11 stages and 3 supporting ingredients of the SM-14 formula, and 3) practical help with everyday problems and decisions. After reviewing these three sections ask students:
1) What are the stages in the scientific method?
2) Why is the scientific method used?
3) What does the scientific method enable researchers to conclude?

MULTIPLE-CHOICE QUESTIONS

1. While doing research on crime, Professor Middler noted that crime creates jobs in law enforcement and related careers. He also noticed that crime reinforces norms when criminals are caught and punished. Professor Middler has probably adopted a(n) _____ approach to the study of crime.
   a. conflict theory
   b. social Darwinism
   c. structural functionalism
   d. ethnomethodology
   e. symbolic interactionism
      ANS: C
      PG: 39

2. Which of the following is NOT a function of theory for research?
   a. theory helps to prevent our being taken in by flukes
   b. theory helps us to explain occurrences
   c. theory helps us to make sense out of observed patterns
   d. theory shapes and directs research efforts
   e. all of the above ARE functions of theory for research
      ANS: E
      PG: 33

3. The fundamental models or frames of reference we use to organize our observations and reasoning are:
   a. paradigms
   b. theories
   c. hypotheses
   d. laws
   e. concepts
      ANS: A
      PGS: 33-34

4. In a study of women the following notation was used: $Y = f(X)$ where Y represented fertility plans and X represented occupational plans. This states
    a. that fertility plans are a function of (or are affected by) occupational plans
    b. that occupational plans are a function of (or are affected by) fertility plans
    c. a hypothesis
    d. only a and c are correct
    e. only b and c are correct
        ANS: D
        PG: 46

5. Which of the following outlines the steps in the traditional deductive model?
    a. Theoretical expectation, testable hypothesis, operationalization of concepts, observations
    b. Operationalization of concepts, theoretical expectation, testable hypothesis, observations
    c. Operationalization of concepts, testable hypotheses, observations, theoretical expectation
    d. Observations, theoretical expectation, operationalization of concepts, testable hypothesis
    e. Theoretical expectation, operationalization of concepts, testable hypothesis, observations
        ANS: E
        PG: 46

6. Which of the following is NOT TRUE of paradigms?
    a. paradigms shape the kinds of observations we are likely to make
    b. paradigms determine the kinds of facts we will discover
    c. paradigms shape the conclusions that we draw from facts
    d. paradigms determine whether we look at micro or macro concerns
    e. all of the above are TRUE about paradigms
        ANS: E
        PGS: 33-35

7. Which of the following illustrates the use of the inductive method?
    a. hypothesis, observations, accept or reject hypothesis
    b. observations, pattern finding, and generalizations
    c. theory, hypothesis, observations, generalizations
    d. theory, observations, and generalizations
    e. generalizations, theory, and observations
        ANS: B
        PGS: 51-52

8. Which of the following topics would a macrotheorist be more likely to study than a microtheorist?
    a. jury deliberations
    b. international relations among countries
    c. the grandparent-grandchild relationship
    d. student-faculty interactions
    e. dating behavior
        ANS: B
        PG: 35

9. Professor May wants to learn how grandparents define their role when they become the guardians of their grandchild. May asks grandparents questions like, "How did you come to have custody of your grandchild?" and "Do you feel more like a parent or a grandparent?" Which of the following paradigms is May probably using?
    a. conflict theory
    b. social Darwinism
    c. structural functionalism
    d. ethnomethodology
    e. symbolic interactionism
        ANS: E
        PGS: 37-38

10. The idea that knowledge is based on observation made through one of the five senses rather than on belief or logic alone is termed
    a. social Darwinism
    b. conflict theory
    c. positivism
    d. structural functionalism
    e. microtheory
        ANS: C
        PGS: 35-36

11. Grounded theory
    a. is an inductive method of theory construction
    b. is a deductive method of theory construction
    c. requires the researcher to begin constructing theory by first observing aspects of social life
    d. only a and c are true
    e. only b and c are true
        ANS: D
        PG: 55

12.   A sociologist with a symbolic interactionist orientation would be MOST likely to do
      research on which of the following question(s)?
      a. Is conflict inevitable in the sibling relationship?
      b. What function does marriage serve for society?
      c. What is the effect of economic conditions on the crime rate?
      d. Which unstated norms govern the interactions between family members?
      e. All of the above are equally likely to be asked by a symbolic interactionist.
          ANS: D
          PGS: 37-38

13.   Walking with an open umbrella on a beautiful day or using hands to eat mashed potatoes
      are techniques used by _____ to understand the social world.
      a. social Darwinists
      b. conflict theorists
      c. structural functionalists
      d. symbolic interactionists
      e. ethnomethodologists
          ANS: E
          PG: 38

14.   Which of the following statements is(are) TRUE?
      a. Laws are universal generalizations.
      b. Laws are created by scientists.
      c. Laws explain the phenomena under study.
      d. Laws are concerned with accidental patterns.
      e. All of the above are true.
          ANS: A
          PG: 43

15.   Which of the following is FALSE about Paradigms?
      a. they are a system of interrelated statements designed to explain some aspect of social
          life
      b. they are neither true or false
      c. they provide ways for looking at life
      d. they are grounded in sets of assumptions about the nature of reality
      e. All of the above are TRUE
          ANS: A
          PGS: 35, 43

16. Axioms are
    a. hypotheses
    b. fundamental assertions on which the theory is grounded
    c. assumed to be true
    d. concepts
    e. only b and c are correct
       ANS: E
       PG: 44

17. The *Minamata disease,* a disease which produced severe nervous disorders and birth defects, was traced to the fact that the Chisso Chemical Company dumped mercury into a bay where Japanese villagers fished. The villagers of Minamata, the village in which the company was located, refused to become involved in lawsuits with the chemical company for many years. However, the residents of Niigata, a fishing village forty miles up the river from the factory, filed lawsuits against the chemical company. Which of the following explanations flows from the conflict paradigm in attempting to explain the differences in lawsuits between the two villages?
    a. the Minamata victims were less likely to be tied socially, economically, and physically to the company than were the Niigata victims.
    b. the Japanese culture frowns on lawsuits
    c. the chemical company controlled more of the village resources in Minamata than in Niigata
    d. people in Niigata are not as nice as people in Minamata
    e. none of the above
       ANS: C
       PGS: 36-37

TRUE-FALSE QUESTIONS

1. Social scientists generally believe that the succession from one paradigm to another represents progress from a false view to a true one.
   ANS: F
   PG: 35

2. In deduction we start from observed data and develop a generalization that explains the relationship between the observed concepts.
   ANS: F
   PGS: 46-47

3. Symbolic interactionists tend to focus on macrotheoretical issues
   ANS: F
   PG: 37

4.   In practice, scientific inquiry typically alternates between deduction and induction.
     ANS: T
     PG: 52

5.   Variables are empirical whereas concepts are abstract.
     ANS: T
     PG: 44

6.   Logical integrity and empirical verification are essential to scientific inquiry and discovery.
     ANS: T
     PG: 57

7.   Laws are used to explain events.
     ANS: F
     PG: 43

8.   Theories, in contrast to paradigms, are general frameworks or viewpoints.
     ANS: F
     PG: 43

9.   Theories must always shape and direct research efforts.
     ANS: F
     PG: 33

10. While our subjectivity is individual, our search for objectivity is social.
     ANS: T
     PG: 42

11. Constructed knowledge is a major concept in positivism.
     ANS: F
     PG: 40

ESSAYS

1.   Contrast the inductive model of theory construction with the deductive model. Give examples of research that use each of these models.

2.   How are theory and research linked? Give examples.

3.   Briefly explain and give an example of a topic that a researcher might study for each of the following: conflict paradigm, symbolic interactionism, role theory, ethnomethodology, structural functionalism, feminist paradigm, and the exchange paradigm.

CHAPTER 3: THE ETHICS AND POLITICS OF SOCIAL RESEARCH

OUTLINE

I. Introduction

II. Ethical Issues in Social Research
   A. Voluntary participation
   B. No harm to participants
   C. Anonymity and confidentiality
   D. Deception
   E. Analysis and reporting
   F. Institutional Review Boards
   G. Professional codes of ethics

III. Two Ethical Controversies
   A. Trouble in the tearoom-Laud Humphreys
   B. Observing human obedience-Stanley Milgram

IV. The Politics of Social Research
   A. Objectivity and ideology
      1. Social research and race
      2. Project Camelot
   B. Politics with a little "p"
   C. Politics in perspective

BEHAVIORAL OBJECTIVES

Upon completion of this chapter, the student should be able to:

1. Discuss why ethical issues are frequently not apparent to the researcher.

2. Describe and illustrate the ethical issues involved in: voluntary participation, no harm to subjects, anonymity and confidentiality, the researcher's identity, and analysis and reporting.

3. Describe the role of the Institutional Review Boards (IRB).

4. Identify which of the ethical principles were violated in the Humphreys tearoom study.

5. Identify which of the ethical principles were violated in the Milgram shock study.

6.   Describe two ways in which ethical and political concerns differ.

7.   Summarize the link between objectivity and ideology.

8.   Compare the positions on the issue that social science can (or cannot) and should (or should not) be separated from politics.

9.   Illustrate how political issues exist in some of the research on race relations.

10. Identify the political issues in Project Camelot.

11. Identify the three main purposes of Babbie's discussion of politics.

TEACHING SUGGESTIONS AND RESOURCES

1.   The following technique generates a lively discussion on ethics and the participant-observer role. Use it here to discuss ethics and later you can refer to it when the class focuses on observation roles in data collection.

     During your in-class discussion of ethics, casually mention that a new member of your faculty is completing research on college student interaction patterns. State that your colleague assumed the role of the complete participant and lived in one of your college's dormitories. Student interest will immediately pick up! Students will begin to ask such questions as-what dorm? what's the person's major? did the person take tests? date? have a roommate? Be prepared for many questions. Some students will begin to express their distaste for the study-"My privacy has been invaded." Their comments and questions can be used to lead into a discussion of the ethical considerations researchers face.

     After discussion has "died down," and before class ends, debrief your students. Let them know that no such study is being done. I tell them that I had no desire to trick them, but only to get them to think about ethics. Tell them to take a look at their reactions to learning about such a study-these would be the reactions of people actually being observed.

2.   An interesting topic in ethics is that of informed consent. Discuss the notion of informed consent as it pertains to studies of prisoners, children, mental health patients, and so on. Can these people give informed consent, voluntary participation, and so forth?

3.   Invite a member of your school's IRB to talk to the class. Ask him or her to explain the guidelines used by the committee in assessing the ethical issues raised in proposals. Ask him or her to talk about ethical issues that created lengthy discussion among board members. Or, ask faculty who do research in different disciplines (e.g. anthropology, sociology,

psychology) to class and ask them questions about ethics within their disciplines. Try to find differences and similarities in the ethical treatment of subjects.

3. FILMS

Confidentiality
45 min. Color. 1983. Videocassette.
Docudrama vignettes portray an interview situation with a family in a clinical psychiatric setting. Seven vignettes detail ethical and legal issues involved in maintaining the confidentiality of clinical records.

Deadly Deception.
NOVA series
Investigates the Tuskegee study where black males believed that they were getting medical treatment for syphilis were actually getting no treatment at all.

Do Scientists Cheat?
58 min. Color. 1988. Penn State.
Examines the issue of scientific fraud, showing why scientists may be less than honest, analyzing how our scientific system deals with quality control, and questioning the adequacy of the scientific community's response when a researcher is involved in fraud.

The Human Experiment
60 min. 1989 Insight Media
Does the chance for finding a cure for disease justify putting subjects at risk?

POSSIBLE ANSWERS TO STUDY GUIDE QUESTIONS

Exercise 3.2
1. Voluntary participation might conflict with generalizability.
2. Anonymity might conflict with reliability since repeated measurements would be difficult to obtain. Confidentiality might conflict with validity and reliability since people might give different answers or false answers because you can link them to a particular answer.
3. No harm to subjects might conflict with measurement and specificity since the best measure from a methodological standpoint might not be ethically feasible.
4. Identifying yourself as a researcher might conflict with validity and reliability since people might give different answers.
5. Identifying the sponsor might conflict with validity and reliability since people might give different answers or not answer at all because of their feelings about the sponsor.

INFOTRAC

1. If not used from chapter 1, you might ask students to look at: Research misconduct. (Fraud in research.) Marcel C. LaFollette. *Society*, March-April 1994 v31 n3 p6(5). How does the author feel a social scientist should address the issue of scientific fraud?

2. Using the keyword option, ask students to select two social science articles that focus on the concept of informed consent. Ask them to briefly summarize how the concept of informed consent is used in the article and whether there are problems with the use of that guideline.

3. Using the keyword option, ask students to select one social science article that focuses on anonymity and one that focuses on confidentiality. Ask them to briefly summarize how each concept was used and to compare the issues that were raised by the use of each concept.

INTERNET EXERCISES

1. Ask students to go to the following site on ethics in biomedical and health care. Ask students to scroll and click on "RESEARCH ETHICS." This "hit" includes the Belmont Report which serves as the ethical basis for human subject guidelines used at many colleges and universities. Ask students to summarize that report and compare it to the guidelines used at your college or university. Or, you could ask students to summarize another article or report in that site that interests them.
http://www.ethics.ubc.ca/resources/biomed/topics.html

2. Ask students to go the Institute for Global Ethics website and summarize the site.
http://www.globalethics.org/
Within that site ask them to either click on "dilemma: right v right" or go to:
http://www.globalethics.org/dilemmas/default.tmpl
Check this site before making this assignment if you want to assign a particular dilemma. These dilemmas can be used as the basis for a class discussion.

3. Ask students to visit the U.S. Department of Health and Human Services website for the Office of the Protection of Human Subjects at:
http://ohrp.osophs.dhhs.gov/info.htm

Tell students to click on "Human Subjects Requirements (self instructional) Slide Show."
Ask them to summarize the "show." Ask them to discuss whether the "show" included information about human subjects that agrees with or disagrees with the information presented in the text.

MULTIPLE-CHOICE QUESTIONS

1. Ethics in social research
   a. is defined as general agreements shared by researchers as to what is proper and improper in the conduct of scientific inquiry
   b. may stem from religious, political, and pragmatic sources among others
   c. may vary from one social research community to another
   d. may vary from one point in time to another
   e. all of the above
      ANS: E
      PG: 63

2. The **primary ethical** research issue raised by the Milgram study was
   a. the willingness of people to harm others when "following orders" required it
   b. the administering of electrical shocks
   c. the effects of the methods on the experimental subjects
   d. the effects of the methods on the learner
   e. the examination of obedience as a topic for study
      ANS: C
      PG: 75

3. The **primary political** issue raised by the Milgram study was
   a. the willingness of people to harm others when "following orders" required it
   b. the administering of electrical shocks
   c. the effects of the methods on the experimental subjects
   d. the effects of the methods on the learner
   e. the examination of obedience as a topic for study
      ANS: E
      PG: 76

4. Professor Smith's research examines the dating behaviors of college students. Smith decides to track the dating behaviors of college students throughout their college careers. She decides to begin her research using her introductory class. She assures her students that all responses will be kept confidential. The students complete her survey during class. Her research most clearly impinges on
   a. Deception
   b. No harm to participants
   c. Voluntary participation
   d. The value placed on anonymity
   e. Value-free reports of the data
      ANS: C
      PG: 63

5. Which of the following statements is NOT found in the AAPOR Code of Professional Ethics and Practices?
    a. We shall maintain the right to approve the release of our findings, whether or not ascribed to us.
    b. We shall select research tools and methods of analysis because of their special capacity to yield a desired conclusion.
    c. We shall protect the anonymity of every respondent, unless the respondent waives such anonymity for specified uses.
    d. We shall not knowingly imply that interpretations should be accorded greater confidence than the data actually warrant.
    e. None of the above are correct.
        ANS: B
        PG: 73

6. The lack of intrusion of the researcher's own political position on research is called
    a. value-free research
    b. anonymity
    c. confidentiality
    d. the identity of the researcher
    e. deception
        ANS: A
        PG: 76

7. When names are removed from questionnaires and are replaced with identification numbers so that only the researcher can later link a response to a particular name, the researcher should tell the respondent that the information is
    a. anonymous
    b. confidential
    c. anonymous and confidential
    d. harmless
    e. none of the above
        ANS: B
        PGS:65-67

8. Ethical considerations are NOT invoked by
    a. the kinds of individuals serving as participants
    b. the setting in which the research is to take place
    c. the analysis of the data
    d. the reporting of the data
    e. all of the above may invoke ethical considerations
        ANS: E
        PGS: Entire chapter

9. Professor Winer sent a mail questionnaire to 2,000 subjects. Winer told subjects that their responses would be held in strict confidence. After the first mailing, 400 completed surveys were returned. For a second mailing, Winer should mail
   a. 2,000 questionnaires
   b. 1,000 questionnaires
   c. 400 questionnaires
   d. 1600 questionnaires
   e. 50 questionnaires
   ANS: D
   PG: 66

10. Which of the following does NOT harm subjects?
   a. having them face aspects of themselves that they do not normally consider
   b. asking them to reveal their unpopular attitudes
   c. asking them to identify their deviant behavior
   d. allowing them to identify themselves easily in the final report
   e. all of the above may harm respondents
   ANS: E
   PGS:64-65

11. Ethical obligations to one's colleagues in the scientific community
   a. require that technical shortcomings and failures of the study be revealed
   b. encourage researchers to ignore negative findings
   c. encourage researchers to describe their findings as the product of a carefully preplanned analytical strategy
   d. require researchers to report only the positive discoveries
   e. all of the above
   ANS: A
   PGS: 68-69

12. Jenny agreed to participate in a study of friendship patterns. During the study she was asked to name her three best friends. Jenny could not think of anyone to name. She felt awful because she suddenly realized that she had no friends. This research most clearly demonstrates the ethical problem of:
   a. Deception
   b. No harm to participants
   c. Voluntary participation
   d. The value placed on anonymity
   e. Value-free reports of the data
   ANS: B
   PG: 64

13.   Which of the following techniques of data collection is MOST likely to make a guarantee of anonymity difficult?
       a.   interviews
       b.   mailed questionnaires
       c.   secondary data analysis
       d.   unobtrusive measures
       e.   they are equally problematic
            ANS: A
            PG: 65

14.   Ethical issues are distinguished from political issues in research in that
       a.   ethics deals more with the substance of research
       b.   politics deals more with the methods of research
       c.   there are no formal codes of accepted political conduct whereas there are codes of ethical conduct
       d.   ethics deals more with the use of research
       e.   all of the above
            ANS: C
            PGS:75-76

TRUE-FALSE QUESTIONS

1.   Social scientists are totally objective in their research
      ANS: F
      PGS: 76,80

2.   The ethical issues are readily apparent in research projects.
      ANS: F
      PG: 62

3.   Once people are told that their participation in a research study is voluntary, there are no ethical problems.
      ANS: F
      PGS: 64-69

4.   It is often as important to report that two variables are unrelated as to report that they are related.
      ANS: T
      PG: 68

5. The norm of voluntary participation threatens the social research goal of generalizability.
ANS: T
PG: 64

6. Because social scientists rarely plan studies that could physically harm subjects, the issue of no harm to subjects is not a real problem.
ANS: F
PGS: 64-65

7. IRB's insure that the agency doing the research is protected against lawsuits by human subjects.
ANS: F
PGS: 69-72

8. Social scientists agree that objectivity is necessary for research.
ANS: F
PG: 76

9. Debriefing entails interviews with subjects to discover any problems generated by their research experience.
ANS: T
PG: 68

10. Informed consent combines the principles of voluntary participation and no harm to subjects.
ANS: T
PG: 64

11. It is easy to avoid harming subjects.
ANS: F
PG: 65

ESSAYS

1. Illustrate how ethics and politics affect social research.

2. Choose an ethical issue presented in this chapter, create a research situation where this issue could arise, and tell how you would handle it.

3. Are there any situations in which a researcher is justified in deceiving subjects? Explain your answer.

CHAPTER 4: RESEARCH DESIGN

OUTLINE

I. Three Purposes of Research
   A. Exploration
   B. Description
   C. Explanation

II. The Logic of Nomothetic Explanation
   A. Criteria for Nomothetic Causality
      1. Correlation
      2. Time Order
      3. Nonspurious
   B. False Criteria for Nomothetic Causality
      1. Complete causation
      2. Exceptional cases
      3. Majority of cases

III. Necessary and Sufficient Causes

IV. Units of Analysis
   A. Types
      1. Individuals
      2. Groups
      3. Organizations
      4. Social artifacts
   B. Faulty Reasoning About Units of Analysis: The ecological fallacy and reductionism

V. The Time Dimension
   A. Cross-sectional studies
   B. Longitudinal studies
      1. Trend
      2. Cohort
      3. Panel
      4. Comparing the three types of longitudinal studies
   C. Approximating longitudinal studies

VI. How to Design a Research Project
   A. Getting started
   B. Conceptualization
   C. Choice of research method
   D. Operationalization

    E. Population and sampling
    F. Observations
    G. Data processing
    H. Analysis
    I. Application
    J. Research design in review

VII.   The Research Proposal

BEHAVIORAL OBJECTIVES

Upon completion of this chapter, the student should be able to:

1.   Identify the two major tasks of research design.

2.   Define and illustrate the three basic purposes of research.

3.   List three reasons for performing exploratory studies.

4.   Contrast the idiographic and the nomothetic models of explanation by definition and example.

5.   List and illustrate the three prerequisites for establishing causality in nomothetic explanations.

6.   List and explain the three things that social scientists do not mean when they speak of causal relationships.

7.   Differentiate a necessary cause from a sufficient cause by definition and example.

8.   Define units of analysis and identify and illustrate each of the basic types.

9.   Define and illustrate the ecological fallacy.

10.   Define and illustrate reductionism.

11.   Compare cross-sectional and longitudinal studies in terms of the advantages and weaknesses of each.

12.   Differentiate among the three types of longitudinal studies by definition and example.

13.   Explain how longitudinal studies may be approximated using the cross-sectional design.

14.   Depict the research process in a diagram manner and describe the diagram.

15.   Identify the basic elements of a research proposal.

TEACHING SUGGESTIONS AND RESOURCES

1.   Divide students into small groups to discuss whether the following statements fit the criteria for a causal relationship.
      a.   Going to college causes people to become smarter.
      b.   Old age causes senility.

2.   To illustrate spurious relationships, use the following examples from Rosenberg, Morris. 1968. *The Logic of Survey Analysis*. New York: Basic Books.
      a.   In Sweden there is a relationship between the number of storks in an area and the number of births. Therefore, storks do bring babies. Control variable-region of country (urban/rural). There are more storks in rural areas, and rural areas have higher birthrates.
      b.   There is a positive association between the number of firefighters at a fire and the amount of damage. Therefore, firefighters cause damage. Control variable-the size of fire. Larger fires have more damage and more firefighters.

3.   The following overlays are extremely useful in demonstrating the time dimension in research designs. These overlays were suggested by Dr. Mildred Seltzer, a dearly missed colleague.

OVERLAY #1: This is the basic transparency.

<table>
<tr><td></td><td colspan="3" align="center">YEAR OF MEASUREMENT</td></tr>
<tr><td>YEAR OF
BIRTH
(COHORT)</td><td>1980</td><td>1990</td><td>2000</td></tr>
<tr><td>1960</td><td>A-20</td><td>B-30</td><td>C-40</td></tr>
<tr><td>1950</td><td>D-30</td><td>E-40</td><td>F-50</td></tr>
<tr><td>1940</td><td>G-40</td><td>H-50</td><td>I-60</td></tr>
</table>

Explain that the column variable represents the year that the measurements were taken. For example, this table could contain census data collected in 1980, 1990, and 2000. Tell students that the row variable represents the year that the respondents were born. So, for this table there are three cohorts, people born in 1940, 1950, and 1960. The cells are labeled A through I. The number within each cell represents the respondents' age at the time of measurement.

OVERLAY #2: Cross-sectional overlay.Outline cells A, D, and G in red. Or, outline the corresponding cells for the 1990 and 2000 censuses. This will illustrate that cross-sectional studies are conducted at one point in time. Point out that cross-sectional studies sometimes collect data on all cohorts. Leave overlay #2 down on overlay #1 and add overlay #3.

OVERLAY #3: Longitudinal overlay.
Outline cells A, B, and C or the corresponding cells for the 1950 or 1940 cohort in blue. Place this overlay on #1 and #2. Students will be able to see that longitudinal studies are done across time-measurements were taken in 1980, 1990, and 2000.

  a. To illustrate panel studies-explain that if the same people were surveyed in 1980, 1990, and 2000, it would constitute a panel study.

  b. To illustrate cohort studies-explain that for a cohort study you would trace one cohort through time: for example, cells D, E, and F. Point out that the same people need not be surveyed each year.

  c. To illustrate trend studies-explain that if you compared the measurements taken in the 1980 census with those obtained in 1990, you would be examining trends.

4. The following suggestion can be used alone or in conjunction with suggestion #3. Ask students why researchers might arrive at different conclusions using cross-sectional studies in comparison to longitudinal studies. For example, a classic issue to use is the relationship between age and intelligence. Cross-sectional studies indicate that IQ declines with age. Longitudinal studies claim that there is either no decline or less of a decline with age than cross-sectional studies indicate.

5. Divide students into small groups to design a cross-sectional study that would examine the relationship between income and education using:
   a. the individual as the unit of analysis
   b. the family as the unit of analysis
   c. the country as the unit of analysis

Then, have the students discuss whether these studies could lead to different conclusions about the relationship between income and education.

6. FILMS
Against All Odds: The Question of Causation, Part 11. See Preface for a more complete listing.
Against All Odds: Experimental Design, Part 12. See Preface for a more complete listing.

POSSIBLE ANSWERS TO STUDY GUIDE QUESTIONS

Exercise 4.5: SPSS Computer Printout

1. **ABORTION** IF WOMAN WANTS FOR ANY REASON * **YEAR** FOR RESPONDENT

			GSS	**YEAR**	FOR	RESPOND		Total
			1980	1985	1990	1994	2000	
ABORTION	YES	Count	182	183	159	171	147	842
IF WOMAN								
WANTS		% within YEAR	37.9%	38.0%	49.2%	51.7%	47.6%	43.8%
FOR ANY								
REASON								
	NO	Count	298	298	164	160	162	1082
		% within YEAR	62.1%	62.0%	50.8%	48.3%	52.4%	56.2%
Total		Count	480	481	323	331	309	1924
		% within YEAR	100.0%	100.0%	100.0%	100.0%	100.0%	100.0%

2. The percentage of respondents who said abortion was "okay" for any reason increased from 1980 to 1994 and then declined in 2000. However, 1994 was the only year in which more than half of the respondents said it was "okay." The 2000 percentage saying it was "okay" was below the 1990 percentage.

Exercise 4.6

1. **CAPPUN** FAVOR OR OPPOSE DEATH PENALTY FOR MURDER * **SEX**
   RESPONDENTS SEX

				RESPONDENTS	**SEX**	
				1 MALE	2 FEMALE	Total
CAPPUN FAVOR	1 FAVOR		Count	986	1036	2022
OR OPPOSE			% within SEX	78.8%	67.8%	72.8%
DEATH PENALTY	2 OPPOSE		Count	266	491	757
			% within SEX	21.2%	32.2%	27.2%
FOR MURDER			Count	1252	1527	2779
	Total	% within SEX		100.0%	100.0%	100.0%

2. Most respondents (72.8%) favor the death penalty for murder. However, males are more likely than females to favor its use (78.8% versus 67.8%).

3. Students will need to address: 1) *Time order*: it makes more sense to say that attitudes toward capital punishment are determined by sex than to say that sex determines attitude toward capital punishment, 2) *Correlation*: The data suggest that there is a correlation between sex and

attitude toward capital punishment; males are more likely than females to favor its use, and 3) *Non-spurious:* Is there some other variable that influences both one's sex and one's attitude toward capital punishment?

INFOTRAC EXERCISES

1. Ask students to read: What's cooking in the Ivory Tower: this year's social science research will surprise both conservatives and liberals. (Includes related article on annual meeting of American Political Science Association.) Nurith C. Aizenman, Rachel Pomerance. *Washington Monthly*, Sep 1997 v29 n9 p12(6). Which of the research projects discussed dealt with the "ecological inference problem," and what was the subject matter of the study?

2   Ask students to read: "Delinquency during the transition to early adulthood: family and parenting predictors from early adolescence." Karla Klein; Rex Forehand, Lisa Armistead, Patricia Long. Describe the longitudinal design of this study.

3. Using the keyword option, ask students to select a social science article that uses the cross-sectional design. Ask your students to briefly summarize the article and whether the cross-sectional design was the most appropriate design. If yes, why? If not, why not?

4. Using the keyword option ask students to examine one social science article that uses a panel design and one social science article that uses the cohort design. Ask students to briefly summarize each article and to indicate whether the selected design was the most appropriate. If yes, why? If not, why not and what design would they suggest?

INTERNET EXERCISES

1. To illustrate the differences between trend and cross-sectional data, have students access the following Gallup poll site   http://www.gallup.com/poll/
Ask students to click on "Social Issues and Policy" which is located on the left. Ask students to look at one or two of the public sites. For example, ask them to look at "Roe v. Wade Has Positive Public Image" or "Public Satisfaction at Lowest Point in Six Years." Ask students to pick one of the data points and describe what they learned about the selected topic. Then ask them to look at the longitudinal data and describe what they learned about the topic. Then ask students what they learned about cross sectional data as compared to longitudinal/trend data.

2. Ask students to go the Bureau of Labor Statistics site via:
http://stats.bls.gov/ and to click on "State and Local Unemployment Rates" which is located in the upper right corner under "Employment and Unemployment." Then ask them to click on "General Overview" and then "Most Requested Statistics." At this point, decide whether you want the students to examine the same data or whether you want them to select a state and city.

Data on labor force employment, unemployment, and the unemployment rate from 1992 to 2002 will be retrieved. Ask students what they learn from examining the October, 2002 unemployment rate as opposed to all the unemployment rate data points.

3. Ask students to read a brief note on cigarette smoking and causal relationships at: http://www.hlth.gov.bc.ca/guildford/pdf/086/00008740.pdf
Ask the students "how does the commentary link to Babbie's criteria for causality?"

MULTIPLE-CHOICE QUESTIONS

1. For a causal relationship to exist, there must be evidence
    a. of an empirical correlation between the variables
    b. that one variable precedes the other in time
    c. that a third variable did not cause the changes observed in the first two variables
    d. all of the above
    e. only a and b are correct
        ANS: D
        PGS: 90-92

2. Which of the following employs the nomothetic model of explanation?
    a. an examination of all the considerations that resulted in 85% of the senior class members being hired for the jobs of their choice
    b. an attempt to understand all the reasons concerning why five former presidents of the United States ran for office
    c. an isolation of the three most important reasons as to why men were selected to all the leadership positions at a former women's college that went coed
    d. a list of all the reasons given by first-year students for selecting the college they currently attend
    e. all of the above employ the nomothetic model of explanation
        ANS: C
        PG: 90

3. If a researcher wanted to know why there was a noticeable increase in the number of burglaries in the town of Southpaw during 1997, the researcher would design a(n)
    a. descriptive study
    b. explanatory study
    c. panel study
    d. study of characteristics
    e. exploratory study
        ANS: B
        PG: 89

4. Professor Dooley examined the literature on AIDS and could find nothing that examined children's attitudes toward parents and friends with AIDS. To examine this topic, Dooley should undertake a(n)
    a. Examination of reductionism
    b. A descriptive study
    c. An exploratory study
    d. An explanatory study
    e. A panel study
        ANS: C
        PGS: 87-89

5. If we can establish that variable X comes before variable Q in time, then we can say
    a. variable X is a cause of variable Q
    b. variable X is not a cause of variable Q
    c. variable Q is a cause of variable X
    d. variable Q is not a cause of variable X
    e. variable Q may cause variable X
        ANS: D
        PGS: 90-91

6. Which of the following hypotheses best fits the criteria of causality?
    a. males have higher suicide rates than females.
    b. As income increases, age tends to increase
    c. As education increases, income tends to increase
    d. As education increases, income tends to increase even after controlling for gender and race
    e. Gender tends to influence jury verdict
        ANS: D
        PGS: 90-92

7. The topic of surrogate mothers interested Professor Snyder. Snyder read the available materials on the topic and wanted to develop an age, education, and income profile of women who serve as surrogate mothers in the United States. To develop this profile, Snyder should undertake a(n)
    a. trend study
    b. descriptive study
    c. explanatory study
    d. panel study
    e. cohort study
        ANS: B
        PG: 89

8. A researcher examined newspaper editorials published in the newspapers of major cities in the United States that examined the topic of grade inflation. The unit of analysis was
    a. grade inflation
    b. the major cities
    c. the newspapers
    d. the newspaper editorials
    e. the United States
        ANS: D
        PGS: 95-96

9. Which of the following statements is(are) TRUE?
    a. Being arrested is a necessary cause for having a criminal trial.
    b. A child's birth is a sufficient cause for having a cigar.
    c. A child's birth is a necessary cause for having a cigar.
    d. Being arrested is a sufficient cause for having a criminal trial.
    e. All of the above are true.
        ANS: A
        PGS: 92-94

10. Which of the following statements is(are) FALSE regarding necessary and sufficient causes?
    a. A necessary cause represents a condition that, by and large, must be present for the effect to follow.
    b. A sufficient cause represents a condition that, if it is present, will pretty much guarantee the effect in question.
    c. In social science, we typically find a single necessary and sufficient cause to establish a causal relationship.
    d. Idiographic analyses typically yield sufficient causes for a particular result
    e. All of the above are true.
        ANS: C
        PG: 94

11. Which of the following is NOT a characteristic of a cross-sectional study?
    a. It is conducted at only one point in time.
    b. It can be exploratory, descriptive, or explanatory.
    c. It concentrates on the changes that take place among a specific sample over a period of time.
    d. It provides a means for studying a large population at the same point in time.
    e. All of the above are characteristics of the cross-sectional study.
        ANS: C
        PGS: 101-102

12. If a researcher were conducting a study of women's attitudes toward abortion, the unit of analysis would be
    a. the individual
    b. attitudes
    c. each abortion
    d. the women's attitudes
    e. the society
       ANS: A
       PG: 95

13. The 2000 Census is a ____study that when used with another decennial census could be considered a ____study.
    a. cross-sectional, trend
    b. cross-sectional, panel
    c. cross-sectional, cohort
    d. cross-sectional, cross-sectional
    e. trend, cohort
       ANS: A
       PGS: 101-103

14. Explanatory studies are designed to find answers to which of the following questions?
    a. What is the educational profile of people who change careers in midlife?
    b. Why are people changing careers in midlife?
    c. How many people change careers in midlife?
    d. Does the occupational prestige of a career tend to increase for midlife career changers?
    e. All of the above are questions are answered by explanatory research
       ANS: B
       PG: 89

15. Professor King examined all the reasons given by 100 couples for their marriages. In the final research report, King listed all the reasons given by the 200 people for their marriages. Professor King is
    a. seeking a probabilistic explanation for marriage
    b. using a nomothetic explanation for marriage
    c. using an idiographic explanation for marriage
    d. committing the error of suppressed evidence
    e. none of the above
       ANS: C
       PG: 90

16. Descriptive studies DO NOT
     a. study relationships between variables
     b. tell why something occurred
     c. use operational definitions
     d. use concepts
     e. descriptive studies DO all of the above
         ANS: B
         PGS: 87-90

17. Which of the following is(are) TRUE regarding the nomothetic model of explanation?
     a. it is inevitably probabilistic
     b. it isolates a few considerations that provide a partial explanation for the phenomenon
         under study
     c. its goal is to provide the greatest amount of explanation with the fewest number of
         variables
     d. it seldom, if ever, provides a complete explanation
     e. all of the above are TRUE
         ANS: E
         PG: 90

18. In Sweden, there is a very strong correlation between the number of storks and the
     number of babies born. However, both of these variables are associated with region (rural
     vs. urban). This illustrates
     a. that the number of storks is causally related to the number of babies born
     b. that the number of babies born precedes the number of storks in time
     c. that there is no causal relationship between the number of storks and the number of
         babies
     d. that storks really do bring babies
     e. none of the above
         ANS: C
         PGS: 91-92

19. A single U.S. Census is a
     a. cross-sectional study
     b. panel study
     c. time series study
     d. trend study
     e. longitudinal study
         ANS: A
         PGS: 101-102

20. There is a strong correlation between the number of firefighters that show up at a fire and the amount of damage produced by the fire. The size of the fire influences both the number of firefighters and the amount of damage. This illustrates that the relationship between the number of firefighters and the amount of damage is:
    a. caused by a third factor
    b. causal
    c. not correlational
    d. a real relationship
    e. cannot tell from the information given
    ANS: A
    PGS: 91-92

21. Which of the following designs uncovers only net changes?
    a. cohort and trend studies
    b. trend and panel studies
    c. cohort and panel studies
    d. cohort and cross-sectional studies
    e. trend and cross-sectional studies
    ANS: A
    PG: 105

22. Professor Willard was interested in examining whether countries with higher GNP's tend to have more gangs than countries with lower GNP's. Willard's unit of analysis was
    a. Gangs
    b. GNP's
    c. Countries
    d. Individuals
    e. Cannot tell from the above information
    ANS: C
    PGS: 94-95

23. Which of the following is NOT an element of a research proposal?
    a. A literature review
    b. A measurement description
    c. A description of data collection methods
    d. A description of the subjects whom you will study
    e. All of the above are elements of a research proposal
    ANS: E
    PGS: 113-114

24. Professor Root was studying the arrest rates for drunken driving in urban and rural areas of Ohio. It was found that the arrest rate was higher in the rural areas. Professor Root concluded that people who live in rural areas are more likely to drive while intoxicated than are people who live in urban areas. Root's conclusion
    a. illustrates the ecological fallacy
    b. illustrates the individualistic fallacy
    c. illustrates good deductive reasoning
    d. illustrates the importance of trend studies
    e. none of the above
        ANS: A
        PG: 100

25. When a researcher is faced with the question from whom or what will the information be gathered, that researcher is dealing with which of the following stages of the research design process?
    a. purposes of research
    b. units of analysis
    c. topics for research
    d. time dimension
    e. motivations for research
        ANS: B
        PGS: 94-95

26. It is possible to draw approximate conclusions about processes that take place over time when using cross-sectional data by
    a. making logical inferences whenever the time order of variables is clear
    b. asking people to report information from their past
    c. examining the data within age groups
    d. all of the above
    e. only a and b are correct
        ANS: D
        PGS: 105-106

27. Committing the error of reductionism is most closely tied to the selection of a(n)
    a. hypothesis
    b. longitudinal study
    c. descriptive study
    d. action focus
    e. theoretical paradigm
        ANS: E
        PG: 101

28. Professor Stone designs a study to examine the effect of a teenage pregnancy on young women's career choices. Stone wants to interview a sample of teenage women during their pregnancy, after the baby's birth, and once a year after that for a ten year period. Stone is using a
   a. cross sectional design
   b. trend study
   c. cohort study
   d. panel study
   e. cannot tell from the given information
      ANS: D
      PG: 104

29. To look at changes in the average age of marriage for men and women in the United States, Professor Torme studied the U.S. Censuses over a period of decades. Torme was doing a
   a. panel study
   b. cross-sectional study
   c. cohort study
   d. trend study
   e. none of the above
      ANS: D
      PG: 103

TRUE-FALSE QUESTIONS

1. Research designs are descriptive, explanatory, or exploratory-never more than one.
   ANS: F
   PG: 87

2. Dr. Jordan chronicles people's attitudes toward an upcoming property tax levy. Jordan is doing explanatory research.
   ANS: F
   PGS: 89-90

3. Panel attrition is comparable to experimental mortality.
   ANS: T
   PG: 105

4. A research proposal describes what you intend to accomplish and how.
   ANS: T
   PGS: 113-114

5. Descriptive research answers the question "What's so?" and explanatory research answers the question "Why?"
    ANS: T
    PG: 89

6. Longitudinal studies may be either trend or cohort studies, but not panel studies.
    ANS: F
    PGS: 102-105

7. A major shortcoming of exploratory studies is that they seldom provide satisfactory answers to research questions.
    ANS: T
    PG: 89

8. Researchers ignore previous work on a topic so that their research can be original.
    ANS: F
    PGS: 109, 113

9. The ecological fallacy refers to drawing conclusions about individuals based solely on the observation of groups.
    ANS: T
    PG: 100

10. Operationalization is the process of clarifying what is meant by the concepts being used in a study.
    ANS: F
    PG: 110

11. The independent (effect) variable must occur later in time than the dependent (cause) variable.
    ANS: F
    PGS: 90-91

12. For a causal relationship to be true, it must apply to a majority of cases.
    ANS: F
    PG: 92

13. If two variables are correlated with each other, there must be a causal relationship between them.
    ANS: F
    PGS: 90-91

14. Being at least 18 years of age is a necessary cause for voting in the United States.
    ANS: T
    PG: 92

15. A necessary condition represents a condition that, if it is present, will pretty much guarantee the effect in question.
    ANS: F
    PG: 92

16. The nomothetic model of explanation is probabilistic in its approach to causation.
    ANS: T
    PG: 90

17. Cohorts are defined only by year of birth.
    ANS: F
    PG: 103

ESSAYS

1. Why is the time element is important in research designs? Describe designs that make different use of the time element. Give examples of research studies employing the different designs.

2. Discuss the three purposes for doing research. Describe a study that illustrates each purpose.

3. Identify and give an example of each of the four units of analysis. Illustrate the ecological fallacy using your examples.

4. What are the two models of explanation? How do they differ from each other? Give examples to support your answer.

5. List and explain the three specific criteria of causality suggested by Babbie. Give an example of a causal statement.

6. What is the difference between a necessary and a sufficient cause? Give an example of each.

CHAPTER 5: CONCEPTUALIZATION, OPERATIONALIZATION, AND MEASUREMENT

OUTLINE

I. Measuring Anything That Exists
    A. Conceptions, concepts and reality
    B. Concepts as constructs

II. Conceptualization
    A. Indicators and dimensions
    B. The interchangeability of indicators
    C. Real, nominal, and operational definitions
    D. Creating conceptual order
    E. An example of conceptualization--anomie

III. Definitions in Descriptive and Explanatory Studies

IV. Operationalization Choices
    A. Range of variation
    B. Variations between extremes
    C. A note on dimensions
    D. Defining variables and attributes
    E. Levels of measurement
        1. Nominal measures
        2. Ordinal measures
        3. Interval measures
        4. Ratio measures
        5. Implications of levels of measurement
    F. Single or multiple indicators
    G. Some illustrations of operationalization choices
    H. Operationalization goes on and on

V. Criteria of Measurement Quality
    A. Precision and accuracy
    B. Reliability
        1. Test-retest method
        2. Split-half method
        3. Using established measures
        4. Reliability of research-workers
    C. Validity
        1. Face validity
        2. Criterion-related validity

3. Construct validity
4. Content validity
   D. Who decides what's valid?
   E. Tension between reliability and validity

BEHAVIORAL OBJECTIVES

Upon completion of this chapter, the student should be able to:

1. Restate the argument that anything that exists can be measured.

2. Define measurement and differentiate it from observation.

3. Link the terms conception, conceptualization, and concepts.

4. Differentiate among the following terms: direct observables, indirect observables, constructs, and concepts.

5. Illustrate reification and explain why it is an error.

6. Show how indicators and dimensions contribute to the conceptualization process.

7. Outline the logic behind the interchangeability of indicators.

8. Describe and compare real definitions, nominal definitions, and operational definitions.

9. Select three concepts and develop both nominal and operational definitions for each.

10. Show how the clarification of concepts is a key element in qualitative research.

11. Explain why definitions are more problematic for descriptive research than for explanatory research.

12. Explain why researchers must be clear about the range of variation in a concept that interests them.

13. Give examples of how the variation between extreme attributes of a variable can affect the operationalization of a concept.

14. Explain why attributes of a variable should be exhaustive and mutually exclusive, and give examples of each.

15. Differentiate the following four levels of measurement and give an example of each: nominal, ordinal, interval, and ratio.

16. Explain why it is important to know the level of measurement for the variables in a study.

17. Explain when single or multiple indicators should be used to reflect a concept.

18. Differentiate precision from accuracy by definition and example.

19. Define reliability and compare these strategies for improving the reliability of measures: test-retest method, split-half method, using established measures, and reliability of research workers.

20. Define validity and compare these types of validity: face validity, criterion-related validity, construct validity, and content validity.

21. Describe the tension between reliability and validity.

TEACHING SUGGESTIONS AND RESOURCES

1. *The Wall Street Journal* (Wed. July 24, 1996) had an article, "Which is the safest airline? It all depends....", that is ideal for this chapter. The reporters describe a major obstacle facing the federal government's proposal to rank airline safety. The obstacle is that a single airline can be considered both the safest and the most dangerous in a single year, depending upon the definition and operationalization of safe.

   Assign the clipping to students and ask them to explain how, from a methodologists viewpoint, a single airline could be considered both the safest and the most dangerous. This analysis should lead into a discussion of conceptualization and operationalization.

2. Tell students to conceptualize and operationalize the concept "love." Give them enough time to do this individually and in small groups.

   Typically, this exercise leads into a discussion of dimensions. As students begin their conceptualizations they frequently ask, "Do you mean the love a parent has for a child or the love I have for a friend?" They will, therefore, raise the dimension issue--romantic, sibling, friendship love, and so on. You may wish to stop and discuss the issue of dimensions at this point. Tell them to focus on romantic love.

   Upon completing this exercise, have students read Rubin, Zick. 1970. "Measurement of Romantic Love." *Journal of Personality and Social Psychology*, 16:265-273.

3. Assign Seeman, Melvin. 1959. "On the Meaning of Alienation." *American Sociological Review*, 24:783-791. The article defines and discusses five dimensions of alienation. After students have read the Seeman article, bring Dean's Alienation Scale to class. Dean's scale was designed to measure three of the five alienation dimensions. Have students determine which items tap the powerlessness dimension, the normlessness dimension, and the social isolation dimension. Use this as a lead into a discussion of face validity.

Below is a keyed copy of one-third of Dean's alienation scale. The letter on the left indicates whether the item taps the powerlessness, normlessness, or social isolation dimension. The scoring of the items has also been included. For additional information, see Dean Dwight. 1961. "Alienation: Its Meaning and Measurement." *American Sociological Review*, 26:753-758, or Miller, Delbert. 1991. *Handbook of Research Design and Social Measurement*. New York: David McKay Company.

Below are some statements regarding public issues with which some people agree and others disagree. Please give us your own opinion about these items (i.e.), whether you agree or disagree with the items as they stand.

Please check the appropriate blank, as follows:

        _A (Strongly Agree)
        _a (Agree)
        _U (Uncertain)
        _d (Disagree)
        _D (Strongly Disagree)

I   1.   Sometimes I feel all alone in the world.

          4 A   3 a   2 U   1 d   0 D

P   2.   I worry about the future facing today's children.

          4 A   3 a   2 U   1 d   0 D

I   3.   I don't get invited out by friends as often as I'd really like.

          4 A   3 a   2 U   1 d   0 D

N   4.   The end often justifies the means.

          4 A   3 a   2 U   1 d   0 D

I   5. Most people today seldom feel lonely.

         4 A   3 a   2 U   1 d   0 D

P   6. Sometimes I have the feeling that other people are using me.

         4 A   3 a   2 U   1 d   0 D

N   7. People's ideas change so much that I wonder if we'll ever have anything to depend on.

         4 A   3 a   2 U   1 d   0 D

I   8. Real friends are as easy as ever to find.

         4 A   3 a   2 U   1 d   0 D

The reliability for the scale was .78. Point out how items 3 and 5, for example, change polarity. To agree with item 3 indicates social isolation, and to agree with item 5 indicates no isolation.

3. FILMS

Intelligence: A Complex Concept
21 min. Color. 1978.
Discusses the concept of intelligence. Explores the definitions of people in the street, Piaget, and Guilford.

POSSIBLE ANSWERS TO STUDY GUIDE QUESTIONS

Exercise 5.1
1. Make sure students go through what Babbie describes as conceptualization--the specification of the concept at a more general level. For example, marital happiness means a state of satisfaction with the various components of being married. Components of such satisfaction might include quality and quantity of communication, shared goals, shared decision making, sexual compatibility, shared activities, and the like.

2. The nominal definition should be relatively brief and reflect the definition assigned to the concept. For example, feminism could be defined as a belief in the equality of men and women. Or it could be defined as support for the feminist movement.

3.   Make sure students list a few indicators of each concept. For example, indicators of religiosity might include questions on the frequency of praying or the frequency of church attendance. Other indicators might include such items as "A supreme being exists"(strongly agree to strongly disagree) and "The Bible is the word of God" (strongly agree to strongly disagree).

Exercise 5.2

GPA as an indicator of intelligence has reliability problems for several reasons. Grades often differ across courses and instructors for the same student. Students of equal intelligence as measured by IQ tests may receive different grades due to such extraneous factors as effort, workload, personality, and so on. Students who retake a course often get different grades. Within one class, a given student may receive different grades on various exams in spite of identical levels of studying and similar extraneous factors due to the vagaries of grading by the instructor, to multiple graders, to variations in the quality of test items, to grading and transcription errors, and so on.

Problems of validity emerge due to several factors. Grades have little relationship to future success, a form of predictive validity. Social scientists are still uncertain as to what intelligence really is and hence do not agree on definitions and measures. Grades tend to be quite global, not allowing for finer distinctions. Also, there is some disagreement about what an A, B, C, or other grade reflects.

Exercise 5.4

2.   A variety of answers are possible. Typical answers include:

Reliability

Test-retest: Respondents answer the same questions at two different points in time. Responses from time 1 are compared to time 2 responses.

Split-half: The four items are randomly split into two halves. Each half contains two items. The results for the two halves are compared.

Using established measures: The results from the four items are compared to an already established measure of attitudes toward pornography.

Research worker: A sample of respondents are randomly called so that their responses can be verified.

Validity

Face: The researcher considers whether each item taps attitudes toward pornography.

Criterion: The researcher may use the responses to predict which respondents would be more likely to attend X-rated movies or read pornography.

Content: The researcher may consider whether different dimensions of attitudes toward pornography are tapped. For example, are values or information tapped?

Construct: The researcher may consider whether the four items relate in a predicted way to such variables as sex, education, or age, as previously indicated in the literature.

Exercise 5.5
1. Nominal--Sue is young and Mary is old.
2. Ordinal--Sue is younger than Mary (or Mary is older than Sue).
3. Interval--Sue is 20 years younger than Mary (or Mary is 20 years older than Sue).
4. Ratio--Mary is twice as old as Sue (or Sue is half as old as Mary).

Exercise 5.6 SPSS Computer Printout

ANOMIA5 LOT OF THE AVERAGE MAN GETTING WORSE * **ANOMIA6** NOT FAIR
TO BRING CHILD INTO WORLD

ANOMIA6 NOT FAIR		TO BRING	CHILD INTO WORLD		
			1 AGREE	2 DISAGREE	Total
ANOMIA5 LOT	1 AGREE	Count	476	419	895
OF THE		% within ANOMIA5	53.2%	46.8%	100.0%
VERAGE MAN		% within ANOMIA6	82.9%	46.9%	61.0%
GETTING	2 DISAGREE	Count	98	475	573
WORSE		% within ANOMIA5	17.1%	82.9%	100.0%
		% within ANOMIA6	17.1%	53.1%	39.0%
Total		Count	574	894	1468
		% within ANOMIA5	39.1%	60.9%	100.0%
		% within ANOMIA6	100.0%	100.0%	100.0%

ANOMIA5 LOT OF THE AVERAGE MAN GETTING WORSE * **ANOMIA7** OFFICIALS
NOT INTERESTED IN AVERAGE MAN

ANOMIA7 OFFICIALS	NOT INTERESTED		IN	AVERAGE	MAN
			1 AGREE	2 DISAGREE	Total
ANOMIA5	1 AGREE	Count	697	197	894
LOT OF THE		% within ANOMIA5	78.0%	22.0%	100.0%
AVERAGE		% within ANOMIA7	69.2%	42.7%	60.9%
MAN	2 DISAGREE	Count	310	264	574
GETTING		% within ANOMIA5	54.0%	46.0%	100.0%
WORSE		% within ANOMIA7	30.8%	57.3%	39.1%
	Total	Count	1007	461	1468
		% within ANOMIA5	68.6%	31.4%	100.0%
		% within ANOMIA7	100.0%	100.0%	100.0%

ANOMIA6 NOT FAIR TO BRING CHILD INTO WORLD * **ANOMIA7** OFFICIALS NOT INTERESTED IN AVERAGE MAN

ANOMIA7	OFFICIALS NOT INTERESTED IN		AVERAGE 1 AGREE	MAN 2 DISAGREE	Total
ANOMIA6 NOT FAIR TO BRING CHILD INTO WORLD	1 AGREE	Count	483	91	574
		% within ANOMIA6	84.1%	15.9%	100.0%
		% within ANOMIA7	47.6%	19.5%	38.7%
	2 DISAGREE	Count	532	376	908
		% within ANOMIA6	58.6%	41.4%	100.0%
		% within ANOMIA7	52.4%	80.5%	61.3%
Total		Count	1015	467	1482
		% within ANOMIA6	68.5%	31.5%	100.0%
		% within ANOMIA7	100.0%	100.0%	100.0%

INFOTRAC EXERCISES

1. Interpreting definitions of public relations: self assessment and a symbolic interactionism-based alternative. Joye C. Gordon. *Public Relations Review*, Spring 1997 v23 n1 p57(10) What are some different conceptualizations of the field of public relations?

2. The test of merit fails that standard. (Scholastic Assessment Test best colleges 1998, cover story). Thomas Toch, Marna Walthall. *U.S. News and World Report*, Sep 1, 1997 v123 n8 p94(2). What evidence is presented to question the effectiveness of SAT scores in predicting college success?

3. Alternative assessment: What, why, how. (Physical education.) Weimo Zhu. *The Journal of Physical Education, Recreation and Dance*, Sep 1997 v68 n7 p17(2). What are the two types of assessment discussed in the article?

4. Using the keyword option, ask students to find a social science article that focuses on conceptualization. Ask students to summarize the article and to describe the author=s point(s) about conceptualization.

5. Using the keyword option, ask students to find a social science article that focuses on reliability and another article that focuses on validity. Ask students to summarize each article and to explain what the author(s) says about reliability and validity in each article.

INTERNET EXERCISES

1. Ask student to conceptualize "race." Then ask students to go to the Census Bureau site to see how the government conceptualized race in 1990 (and in earlier years). Be sure to tell them that they may need to scroll up on the site till they arrive at the definition section and then to click on race.
http://www.census.gov/td/stf3/append_b.html#race

Ask students whether race was conceptualized and operationalized in the same way in 2000. Were the same categories/questions used? If not, what was different? Could the difference in operationalization produce different conclusions?

2. In conjunction with the prior suggestion ask students to go to the Interracial Voice Website. http://www.webcom.com/intvoice/
Ask students to select and summarize an article focusing on racial classification in the U.S. that captures their attention (or select one for the entire class to read and summarize.)

MULTIPLE-CHOICE QUESTIONS

1. The specification of concepts in a scientific inquiry depends on
    a. nominal, operational, and real definitions
    b. real definitions
    c. nominal and operational definitions
    d. nominal and real definitions
    e. operational and real definitions
        ANS: C
        PG: 125

2. Definitions are more problematic for descriptive research than for explanatory research because
    a. the conclusions reached in a descriptive study depend directly on the specific operational definitions employed
    b. changing definitions often results in different descriptive conclusions
    c. explanatory research is more dependent upon patterns of relationships, and these are more consistent than definitions
    d. all of the above are correct
    e. only a and b are correct
        ANS: D
        PGS: 129-131

3. Professor Smith gave an exam on Monday. On Wednesday Smith gave the same class the same exam. Professor Smith was assessing the exam's
   a. reliability
   b. validity
   c. face validity
   d. conceptualization
   e. precision
   ANS: A
   PG: 141

4. Reliability involves
   a. whether a particular technique applied repeatedly to the same object would yield the same results each time
   b. ensuring accuracy
   c. ensuring that your measure measures what you think it should measure
   d. ensuring precision
   e. all of the above
   ANS: A
   PG: 141

5. Which of the following statements is(are) accurate concerning the measurement of concepts?
   a. If there is no clear agreement among social scientists on how to measure a concept, do not use it.
   b. The only justification for giving any concept a particular definition is the truth of that definition.
   c. If the concept has several dimensions, measure them all.
   d. All of the above are accurate statements.
   e. None of the above are accurate statements.
   ANS: C
   PGS: 146-147

6. Professor Spence decided to define socioeconomic status as a combination of income and education. Spence then determined the questions to be asked and the categories of responses. Spence was assigning socioeconomic status
   a. a nominal and an operational definition
   b. an operational and a real definition
   c. a real definition only
   d. a nominal and a real definition
   e. a nominal definition only
   ANS: A
   PG: 125

7. Techniques used to create reliable measures include
   a. asking only about things respondents are likely to know the answer to
   b. using measures that have proved their reliability in previous research
   c. being clear about what you're asking
   d. asking about things relevant to respondents
   e. all of the above
      ANS: E
      PGS: 142-143

8. Most social scientists would not accept the conceptualization of IQ as foot size because such a measurement lacks
   a. precision
   b. reliability
   c. accuracy
   d. validity
   e. all of the above
      ANS: D
      PG: 143

9. Which of the following sequences illustrates the progression of measurement steps?
   a. conceptualization, nominal definition, operational definition, and measurement in the real world
   b. nominal definition, conceptualization, operational definition, and measurement in the real world
   c. operational definition, conceptualization, nominal definition, and measurement in the real world
   d. nominal definition, operationalization, conceptualization, and real-world measurement
   e. conceptualization, operationalization, nominal definition, and real-world measurement
      ANS: A
      PG: 126

10. A researcher must decide in the process of operationalization
    a. the necessary degree of precision
    b. the range of variation
    c. the use of single or multiple indicators
    d. what level of measurement to use
    e. all of the above
       ANS: E
       PGS: 132-139

11. Hudson et al. (1983, *Journal of Sex Research*) developed a series of questions to examine sexual attitudes (SAS). The SAS scores of religious fundamentalists, a group believed to be conservative regarding sexual expression, were compared with the scores of social work graduate students, a group believed to be liberal regarding sexual expression. The researchers were examining the instrument's
    a. split-half reliability
    b. split-half validity
    c. criterion validity
    d. criterion reliability
    e. construct validity
    ANS: C
    PG: 144

12. Troiden and Jendrek used the SAS questions noted in the prior question to examine the link between sexual attitudes and sexual experience. They reasoned that people expressing liberal sexual attitudes would have a wider range of sexual experiences than those expressing conservative attitudes. They were concerned with validating the SAS items using
    a. split-half validity
    b. face validity
    c. criterion-related validity
    d. content validity
    e. construct validity
    ANS: E
    PG: 144

13. Which of the following is FALSE about nominal definitions?
    a. nominal definitions do not claim that the definition represents a "real" entity
    b. nominal definitions typically represent some consensus about how a term is used
    c. nominal definitions allow us to observe some entity
    d. nominal definitions assign a definition to a concept
    e. all of the above are true
    ANS: C
    PG: 125

14. When we fall into the trap of believing that terms have real meanings were are guilty of
    a. Reification
    b. Measurements that lack reliability
    c. Measurements that lack validity
    d. Confusing reliability with validity
    e. Confusing conceptions with conceptualization
    ANS: A
    PG: 122

15. A questionnaire contained the item "educational level completed" with responses of grade school, junior high school, high school, college, graduate degree, and other. A researcher asked subjects to check the appropriate response. The researcher is measuring
    a. direct observables
    b. indirect observables
    c. constructs
    d. a nominal variable
    e. validity
       ANS: B
       PG: 121

16. Because low marital adjustment should lead to divorce, Professor Rogers checked his measure of marital adjustment by examining whether couples with low marital adjustment scores were more likely than couples with high marital adjustment scores to later obtain a divorce. This illustrates the use of
    a. criterion-related validity
    b. face validity
    c. content validity
    d. construct validity
    e. test-retest validity
       ANS: A
       PG: 144

17. When the variable *religious affiliation* is classified as Protestant, Catholic, and Jewish, this variable has the important quality of being
    a. mutually exclusive
    b. exhaustive
    c. interchangeable
    d. ratio scale
    e. ordinal scale
       ANS: A
       PG: 134

18. Which of the following is a nominal variable
    a. Education
    b. Employment status
    c. Age
    d. Occupational prestige
    e. Not enough information to know
       ANS: E
       PGS: 134-136

19. Professor Myth asked respondents whether or not they had ever been divorced. One year later Professor Myth asked respondents the same question. Myth found that with repeated applications of the measure different responses were obtained for the same respondent. This means that the measuring instrument was
    a. unreliable
    b. invalid
    c. unreliable or the value on the variable had changed
    d. lacking face validity
    e. inaccurate
       ANS: C
       PGS: 142-143

20. Professor Miller argues that there are three aspects to the quality of a relationship: 1) belonging/affirmation, 2) interdependence, and 3) intimacy. These "aspects" of quality of a relationship are called:
    a. Variables
    b. Dimensions
    c. Constructs
    d. Indicators
    e. Conceptions
       ANS: B
       PG: 123

21. Miller from question #20 designed an instrument to measure quality of a relationship. In looking at the questionnaire she noticed that there were no items tapping intimacy. Her measure lacks
    a. Reliability
    b. Content validity
    c. Predictive validity
    d. Construct validity
    e. Internal consistency
       ANS: B
       PG: 145

22. What is the lowest level of measurement in which there is an exact difference between attribute values?
    a. nominal
    b. interval
    c. ratio
    d. ordinal
    e. all of the above
       ANS: B
       PG: 135

23. Professor Shipley developed a **NEW** test to measure IQ. He claimed that using his test, someone with an IQ of 180 would be considered twice as intelligent as someone with an IQ of 90 and that someone with an IQ of 90 was three times as intelligent as someone with an IQ of 30. Shipley's test treats IQ as a(n)
    a. nominal variable
    b. interval variable
    c. ratio variable
    d. ordinal variable
    e. none of the above
       ANS: C
       PG: 136

24. Measuring how people feel about proposed income tax hikes when you really want to know how well informed they are on the proposal is a problem of operationalization concerning
    a. the use of single or multiple indicators
    b. how observations are going to be made
    c. the specific dimensions of the variable to be studied
    d. the relevant range of variations
    e. the degree of precision needed between extremes
       ANS: C
       PGS: 123-124

25. Professor Tyler wrote a proposal to study the impact of authoritarianism on child rearing practices. She began her research by reviewing the meaning of *authoritarianism* in the sociological and psychological literature. Based on this review, she formulated her own definition of *authoritarianism*. This process illustrates
    a. Operationalization
    b. The interchangeability of indicators
    c. Conceptualization
    d. Validity assessment
    e. Reliability assessment
       ANS: C
       PG: 122

26. Professor Tyler believes that her measure of authoritarianism is valid after finding that it varies, as predicted by theory, with child rearing practices and voting behavior. Tyler is relying on a _____ approach to validity.
    a. Face validity
    b. Content validity
    c. Predictive validity
    d. Criterion-related validity
    e. Construct validity
       ANS: E
       PG: 144

27. The variable *educational level* was measured as last year in school completed (i.e., none, 1st, 2nd, 3rd, grades, etc.). It is, therefore, measured at the _____ level.
    a. nominal
    b. interval
    c. ratio
    d. ordinal
    e. not enough information to decide
       ANS: C
       PG: 136

28. Professor Tilton measured the variable "feelings toward drafting women" with the categories strongly agree, agree, indifferent, disagree, and strongly disagree. Professor Tilton was using the _____ level of measurement.
    a. nominal
    b. interval
    c. ratio
    d. ordinal
    e. not enough information to decide
       ANS: D
       PG: 135

TRUE-FALSE QUESTIONS

1. Conceptualization is the development of research procedures that will result in empirical observations representing those concepts in the real world.
   ANS: F
   PG: 122

2. If a measure is reliable, it must also be valid.
   ANS: F
   PG: 145

3.   Validity refers to the link between the operational and conceptual definitions.
     ANS: T
     PGS: 143-144

4.   Precision and accuracy are synonyms.
     ANS: F
     PG: 140

5.   Conceptions are mental images that summarize collections of seemingly related
     observations and experiences.
     ANS: T
     PGS: 120, 124

6.   A split-half reliability test taps the idea of the general stability of the instrument over
     time.
     ANS: F
     PGS: 142-143

7.   Predictive validity is another term for criterion-related validity.
     ANS: T
     PG: 144

8.   It is impossible to have several indicators of only one concept.
     ANS: F
     PG: 138

9.   Changing definitions almost inevitably results in different descriptive conclusions.
     ANS: T
     PG: 131

10. Precise measurement is more important than accurate measurement.
     ANS: F
     PG: 140

11. Concepts have a single unambiguous meaning.
     ANS: F
     PG: 119

12. The test-retest method for assessing validity assumes that the phenomena under study
     does not change.
     ANS: T
     PG: 142

13. Exact precision in measurement is always necessary and desirable
    ANS: F
    PG: 140

14. A particular variable can usually be measured in several distinct ways using different sources of information and various observation technique.
    ANS: T
    PGS: 138-139

15. When one's research purposes aren't clear, it is advisable to choose the highest level of measurement possible.
    ANS: T
    PGS: 136-138

ESSAYS

1. Select one of the following concepts. How would you conceptualize it? Are there dimensions to the concept? How would you operationalize the concept? Give examples of some of your indicators and explain its level of measurement.
   a. alienation
   b. poverty
   c. modernization

2. Mr. Isle noticed that several women whom he considers to be very feminine often wear dresses or skirts. He therefore decides that he will determine a woman's degree of femininity by finding out how many times she wears a skirt or a dress during the next month. The women who wear dresses or skirts most frequently will be considered the most feminine; those who rarely wear either will be considered the least feminine. Is Mr. Isle's method of measuring femininity reliable? Why or why not? Is his method of measuring femininity valid? Why or why not? What is the tension that often exists between the criteria of reliability and validity?

3. How would you measure each of the following variables using two different levels of measurement?
   a. Age
   b. Income
   c. Family size

CHAPTER 6: INDEXES, SCALES, AND TYPOLOGIES

OUTLINE

I. Indexes versus Scales

II. Index Construction
   A. Item selection
      1. Face validity
      2. Unidimensionality
      3. General or specific
      4. Variance
   B. Examination of empirical relationships
      1. Bivariate relationships
      2. Multivariate relationships among items
   C. Index scoring
   D. Handling missing data
   E. Index validation
      1. Item analysis
      2. External validation
      3. Bad index versus bad validators
   F. The status of women: an illustration of index construction

III. Scale Construction
   A. Bogardus social distance scale
   B. Thurstone scales
   C. Likert scaling
   D. Semantic differential
   E. Guttman scaling

IV. Typologies

BEHAVIORAL OBJECTIVES

Upon completion of this chapter, the student should be able to:

1. Link the contents of this chapter with the previous discussions on conceptualization and operationalization.

2. List three reasons why composite measures are frequently used in social science research.

3. Differentiate index from scale by definition and example.

4. List two reasons why scales are generally superior to indexes.

5. Describe two misconceptions regarding scaling.

6. List the four steps involved in creating an index.

7. Define and illustrate face validity, unidimensionality, and variance as criteria for selecting items.

8. Describe the rationale and application for employing bivariate relationships among items in index construction.

9. Describe the rationale and application of employing multivariate relationships among items in index construction.

10. Describe how items can be scored in index construction.

11. Describe five strategies for handling missing data in index construction.

12. Compare the rationale and application of item analysis and external validation as strategies for validating an index.

13. Describe the logic and procedures of the Bogardus social distance scale.

14. Describe the logic and procedures of Thurstone scaling.

15. Describe the logic and procedures of Likert scaling.

16. Describe the logic and procedures of the semantic differential.

17. Describe the logic and procedures of Guttman scaling.

18. Explain the coefficient of reproducibility.

19. Explain and illustrate how typologies are used in social science research.

TEACHING SUGGESTIONS AND RESOURCES

1. The following suggestion was given to me by Dr. Theodore Wagenaar, Miami University, Oxford, Ohio.
   Construct a Thurstone scale in class. Select about 30 items, all measuring the same concept. You can either make them up or take them from a scale in Delbert C. Miller's *Handbook of Research Design and Social Measurement*, 5th ed. 1991. Newbury Park, California: Sage Publications. Be sure to include some ambiguous items. Give each student copies of each of the items, preferably one item per index card. Then have each student place each item in one of 11 piles according to how

much the item reflects the concept. Calculate median values. Discuss how the scoring suggests which items to delete. Describe how the completed scale would be administered. This principle can be extended to the other types of scales as well.

2. Divide students into small groups. Ask them to develop an index or scale to measure students' popularity. Leave enough time for them to work together on this project.

   In the discussion that follows, be sure to ask why they selected to use an index or scale. As you ask each group about the items they selected, ask the students to comment on why some items appear in each group (e.g., "Do you date?"—very frequently, frequently, infrequently, never—face validity). Also, ask them if they noticed that there were dimensions to popularity (e.g., popularity with same sex, opposite sex, social, academic).

POSSIBLE ANSWERS TO STUDY GUIDE QUESTIONS

Exercise 6.4
1. Face validity
These items all reflect attitudes about the effects of sexual materials. All three appear to reflect different types of effects and the items seem to have sufficient face validity.
Unidimensionality
Two items reflect the negative effects of looking at or reading sexual materials. The first two items, "lead to breakdown of morals" and "lead people to commit rape," are more negative than the third, "provide information about sex." Hence, the unidimensionality of the items may be problematic.

PORNINF MATERIALS PROVIDE INFO ABOUT SEX

		Frequency	Percent	Valid Percent	Cumulative Percent
Valid	1 YES	899	30.0	65.1	65.1
	2 NO	481	16.0	34.9	100.0
	Total	1380	46.0	100.0	
Missing	0 NAP	1507	50.2		
	8 DK	108	3.6		
	9 NA	5	.2		
	Total	1620	54.0		
Total		3000	100.0		

PORNRAPE MATERIALS LEAD TO RAPE

		Frequency	Percent	Valid Percent	Cumulative Percent
Valid	1 YES	741	24.7	55.8	55.8
	2 NO	588	19.6	44.2	100.0
	Total	1329	44.3	100.0	
Missing	0 NAP	1507	50.2		
	8 DK	158	5.3		
	9 NA	6	.2		
	Total	1671	55.7		
Total		3000	100.0		

PORNMORL MATERIALS LEAD TO BREAKDOWN IN MORALS

		Frequency	Percent	Valid Percent	Cumulative Percent
Valid	1 YES	785	26.2	57.9	57.9
	2 NO	571	19.0	42.1	100.0
	Total	1356	45.2	100.0	
Missing	0 NAP	1507	50.2		
	8 DK	132	4.4		
	9 NA	5	.2		
	Total	1644	54.8		
Total		3000	100.0		

2. Bivariate relationships among PONINF, PORNMORL, and PORNRAPE.

PORNINF MATERIALS PROVIDE INFO ABOUT SEX * **PORNMORL** MATERIALS LEAD TO BREAKDOWN IN MORALS

PORNINF			1 YES	2 NO	Total
MATERIALS 1 YES		Count	447	396	843
PROVIDE		% within PORNINF	53.0%	47.0%	100.0%
INFO ABOUT		% within PORNMORL	59.8%	71.1%	64.6%
SEX 2 NO		Count	300	161	461
		% within PORNINF	65.1%	34.9%	100.0%
		% within PORNMORL	40.2%	28.9%	35.4%
Total		Count	747	557	1304
		% within PORNINF	57.3%	42.7%	100.0%
		% within PORNMORL	100.0%	100.0%	100.0%

PORNRAPE MATERIALS LEAD TO RAPE * **PORNMORL** MATERIALS LEAD
TO BREAKDOWN IN MORALS

		PORNMORL MATERIALS LEAD TO BREAKDOWN IN MORALS		
PORNRAPE		1 YES	2 NO	Total
MATERIALS 1 YES	Count	604	106	710
LEAD TO	% within PORNRAPE	85.1%	14.9%	100.0%
RAPE	% within PORNMORL	83.5%	19.3%	55.9%
2 NO	Count	119	442	561
	% within PORNRAPE	21.2%	78.8%	100.0%
	% within PORNMORL	16.5%	80.7%	44.1%
Total	Count	723	548	1271
	% within PORNRAPE	56.9%	43.1%	100.0%
	% within PORNMORL	100.0%	100.0%	100.0%

PORNINF MATERIALS PROVIDE INFO ABOUT SEX * **PORNRAPE**
MATERIALS LEAD TO RAPE

		PORNRAPE MATERIALS LEAD TO RAPE		
PORNINF		1 YES	2 NO	Total
MATERIALS 1 YES	Count	443	386	829
PROVIDE	% within PORNINF	53.4%	46.6%	100.0%
INFO	% within PORNRAPE	62.8%	68.0%	65.1%
ABOUT SEX 2 NO	Count	262	182	444
	% within PORNINF	59.0%	41.0%	100.0%
	% within PORNRAPE	37.2%	32.0%	34.9%
Total	Count	705	568	1273
	% within PORNINF	55.4%	44.6%	100.0%
	% within PORNRAPE	100.0%	100.0%	100.0%

3. Multivariate relationship among the items using PORNINF as the criterion variable.
Percent saying "yes" on PORNINF.

PORNMORL MATERIALS LEAD TO BREAKDOWN IN MORALS * **PORNRAPE**
MATERIALS LEAD TO RAPE

		PORNRAPE MATERIALS LEAD TO RAPE		
PORNMORL		1 YES	2 NO	Total
MATERIALS 1 YES	Count	355	61	416
LEAD TO	% within PORNMORL	85.3%	14.7%	100.0%
BREAKDOWN	% within PORNRAPE	83.5%	16.5%	52.4%
IN MORALS 2 NO	Count	70	308	378
	% within PORNMORL	18.5%	81.5%	100.0%
	% within PORNRAPE	16.5%	83.5%	47.6%
Total	Count	425	369	794
	% within PORNMORL	53.5%	46.5%	100.0%
	% within PORNRAPE	100.0%	100.0%	100.0%

INFOTRAC EXERCISES

1. The reliability and factor structure of the Global Belief in a Just World Scale. Wendy E. O'Connor, Todd G. Morrison, Melanie A. Morrison. *The Journal of Social Psychology*, Oct 1996 v136 n5 p667(2). What suggestion do the authors make for improving the scale?

2. Predictive validity of the Suicide Probability Scale among adolescents in group home treatment. Robert E. Larzelere, Gail L. Smith,Lisa M. Batenhorst, Douglas B. Kelly. *Journal of the American Academy of Child and Adolescent Psychiatry*, Feb 1996 v35 n2 p166(7). What are some of the indicators used in the scale of suicide probability?

3. Using the keyword option, ask students to select one social science article that focuses on index construction and one that focuses on scale construction. Ask students to summarize each article and to describe why the author thought that either index or scale construction was most appropriate. Ask students whether they agree with the author's choice.

4. Using the keyword option, ask students to select an article that uses the Likert scale. Ask them to summarize the scale, how it was constructed and whether the reliability and validity of the scale was assessed.

INTERNET EXERCISES

Ask students to go to the following website on the Bogardus Social Distance Scale:
http://www.mediajunk.com/public/archives/000007.html
This site reviews the original scale and suggests some new distance measures such as:
I would include a member of group X: a) in my address book, b) in the list of people to whom I mass-send jokey emails, c) as someone I text-message once a week, d) as someone I would allow in my chat group. Ask students what they think about the suggested additions. Have them collect data for the class and see if it scales.

2. Ask students to go to the following website on a variety of composite measures:
http://www.surveyz.com/tutorial/2.html
They can review and see examples of a variety of composite measures by clicking on "Survey Answer Types."

3. Another interesting review site for composite measures is provided at:
http://trochim.human.cornell.edu/kb/scaling.htm
This site enables students to review and see multiple examples of Guttman, Likert, and Thurstone scales.

MULTIPLE-CHOICE QUESTIONS

1. Among the reasons for the frequent use of composite measures is(are) that
   a. the researcher is seldom able to develop in advance single indicators of complex concepts
   b. a single data item might not have enough categories to provide a range of variation
   c. composite measures give a more comprehensive and accurate indication of a given variable
   d. they are efficient data reduction devices
   e. all of the above
      ANS: E
      PG: 151

2. Which of the following do indexes and scales have in common?
   a. They are interval measures.
   b. Their attributes form an intensity structure.
   c. They rank-order the units of analysis in terms of specific variables.
   d. Their scores represent a pattern of response
   e. They are nominal measures.
      ANS: C
      PG: 152

3. When a researcher is selecting items for a composite index, which of the following should be kept in mind?
   a. Each item should have face validity.
   b. A composite measure should be unidimensional.
   c. There should be concern about the amount of variance provided by the items.
   d. All of the above are correct.
   e. Only a and b are correct.
      ANS: D
      PG: 154

4. Which of the following steps in index construction is the first one to be out of sequence?
   a. select items for inclusion
   b. examine the multivariate relationships among the items being considered for inclusion
   c. study the bivariate relationships among the items
   d. assign scores to particular responses
   e. none of the above is out of sequence
      ANS: B
      PGS: 154-161

5. The following items and scoring scheme were taken from the *Minnesota Survey of Opinions*. The four items were part of a series of items designed to assess attitudes toward education. In the index
    SA=strongly agree, A=agree, U=undecided,
    D=disagree, and SD=strongly disagree

    1. A MAN CAN LEARN MORE BY WORKING FOUR YEARS THAN BY GOING TO SCHOOL.
        SA(5) A(4)   U(3)   D(2)   SD(1)

    2. THE MORE EDUCATION A MAN HAS, THE BETTER HE IS ABLE TO ENJOY LIFE.
        SA(1) A(2)   U(3)   D(4)   SD(5)

    3. EDUCATION HELPS A PERSON TO USE HIS LEISURE TIME TO BETTER ADVANTAGE.
        SA(1) A(2)   U(3)   D(4)   SD(5)

    4. EDUCATION IS OF NO HELP IN GETTING A JOB TODAY.
        SA(5) A(4)   U(3)   D(2)   SD(1)

    These items illustrate a _____ question format:
    a. Likert scale
    b. Thurstone scale
    c. Guttman scale
    d. semantic differential scale
    e. Bogardus social distance scale
        ANS: A
        PG: 169

6. The scoring scheme for the items in the previous question illustrate(s) that
    a. item 1 is weighted 5 times items 2 and 3
    b. item 1 is weighted equally to item 4 only
    c. item 2 is weighted equally to item 3 only
    d. all of the items are equally weighted
    e. cannot tell how they were weighted from the given information
        ANS: D
        PGS: 169-170

7. If you were to treat the composite index in question #5 on attitudes toward education as an independent variable and each of the four items as dependent variables, you would be doing
   a. index validation
   b. item analysis
   c. external validation
   d. all of the above
   e. only a and b are correct
      ANS: E
      PGS: 164-165

8. Professor Duncan administered a questionnaire containing the following items: Please tell me how you feel about your supervisor's leadership style on the following three items:

valuable	----:----:----:----:----	worthless
easy	----:----:----:----:----	demanding
critical	----:----:----:----:----	uncritical

   Duncan was using a
   a. Semantic differential scale
   b. Thurstone scale
   c. Bogardus social distance scale
   d. Guttman scale
   e. Likert scale
      ANS: A
      PG: 170

9. The coefficient of reproducibility for a Guttman scale should be at least
   a. 1.00
   b. .90
   c. .8
   d. .70
   e. it doesn't matter
      ANS: B
      PG: 173

10. A friend of yours is trying to develop an index to reproduce respondents' patterns of responses. You tell your friend to
    a. construct a Guttman scale
    b. construct a Likert scale
    c. construct a Thurstone scale
    d. construct any one of the above
    e. it cannot be done
       ANS: E
       PG: 152

11. Professor Thames used a Guttman scale on his data set that he had seen published in a major journal. Thames was upset because the items did not scale on his data. Confused, he asked for your help. You should tell him
    a. the article that appeared in the journal was probably in error
    b. he should recheck his scaling techniques because he probably made an error
    c. items may form a Guttman scale in one sample but not in another
    d. it was probably not a very good scale
    e. none of the above
       ANS: C
       PG: 173

12. Professor Swanson developed an index of marital happiness. Several items in Swanson's questionnaire were not part of the index (i.e., "How many serious quarrels or arguments have you had with your spouse in the last year?" "If you had your life to live over, do you think you would marry the same person?"). Swanson compared the index score of marital happiness with these questions. Swanson was doing
    a. index validation
    b. item analysis
    c. external validation
    d. a and b only are correct
    e. a and c only are correct
       ANS: E
       PGS: 164-165

13. If an index fails to predict strongly the external validation items then
    a. The index does not adequately measure the variable in question
    b. The validation items do not adequately measure the variable
    c. Either a or b are true
    d. A and b are both true
    e. Cannot tell given the above information
       ANS: C
       PG: 166

14. Using Likert-type scale items, Professor Wong developed an index to assess job morale. Wong administered the index to 2,000 workers and found that 1-4 responses were missing on each of the items. Wong could
    a. exclude the cases that contained the missing data from the analysis
    b. assign the middle value to cases with missing data
    c. analyze the cases that had missing data to interpret their meaning
    d. assign values at random
    e. all of the above
       ANS: E
       PGS: 162-163

15.   Given the following patterns for a Guttman scale on life satisfaction, the
       coefficient of reproducibility is: (Note: a + = "Yes" and a - = "No")

                        VARIABLES

	HEALTH	HOBBIES	CITY	Number of Cases
A	+	+	+	100
B	+	+	-	75
C	+	-	-	50
D	-	-	-	25

       a. 1.00
       b. .95
       c. .90
       d. .85
       e. cannot compute from the information given
           ANS: A
           PGS: 171-172

16.   Line A from the previous question is a scale type
       a. 1
       b. 2
       c. 3
       d. 4
       e. cannot compute from the information given
           ANS: C
           PG: 172

17.   The following items measure the extent to which Americans are willing to
       associate with extraterrestrials.
       1. It's OK if my child marries an extraterrestrial.
       2. It's OK to have an extraterrestrial for a friend.
       3. It's OK to have an extraterrestrial living on the block.
       4. It's OK to have an extraterrestrial living in my community.

       These items illustrate a
       a. Guttman scale
       b. Bogardus social distance scale
       c. Thurstone scale
       d. Likert scale
       e. none of the above
           ANS: B
           PG: 168

17.   Which of the following statements is NOT applicable to typologies?
       a. They are nominal composite measures.
       b. It is easy to analyze a typology as an independent variable.
       c. It is easy to analyze a typology as a dependent variable.
       d. They are often used when researchers wish to summarize the intersection of two or more variables.
       e. All of the above apply to typologies.
           ANS: C
           PG: 174

19.   A _____ scale is a measurement technique for determining the willingness of people to participate in social relations - of varying degrees of closeness - with other kinds of people.
       a. Bogardus
       b. Guttman
       c. Thurstone
       d. Semantic differential
       e. Likert
           ANS: A
           PG: 168

20.   Giving a set of judges a large number of items that are thought to be indicators of a given variable and asking them to estimate how strong an indicator of the variable each item is, is a technique used in constructing a _____ scale.
       a. Bogardus
       b. Guttman
       c. Thurstone
       d. Semantic differential
       e. Likert
           ANS: C
           PGS: 168-169

TRUE-FALSE QUESTIONS

1. If two items in an index are perfectly correlated, both of them should be eliminated from the index.
    ANS: F
    PGS: 155-156

2. For an index or scale to be considered unidimensional, its component items should be indicators of only one dimension.
    ANS: T
    PG: 154

3.   An index is constructed by assigning scores to patterns of attributes.
     ANS: F
     PG: 152

4.   Always include at least one item in an index on which all respondents give the
     same answer.
     ANS: F
     PG: 154

5.   Item analysis allows you to examine the extent to which the composite index is
     related to other items in the questionnaire that are not part of the index.
     ANS: F
     PG: 164

6.   The coefficient of reproducibility refers to the ability of a Guttman scale to
     reproduce the pattern of individual responses.
     ANS: T
     PG: 173

7.   A set of questionnaire items that Guttman scaled on one data set will usually
     Guttman scale on another data set.
     ANS: F
     PG: 173

8.   Typologies are nominal composite measures.
     ANS: T
     PG: 174

9.   The purpose of multivariate analysis is to discover the simultaneous interaction of
     the items to determine whether they are all appropriate for inclusion in the same
     index.
     ANS: T
     PGS: 158-160

10. Good indexes provide researchers with a ratio measurement.
     ANS: F
     PG: 152

11. Scales take into consideration the intensity with which different items reflect the
     variable being measured.
     ANS: T
     PG: 152

ESSAYS

1. Choose a topic not discussed in the book or class, and devise a scale using one of the following methods:
   a. Bogardus social distance scale
   b. Guttman scale
   Be sure to discuss all the steps you would go through in constructing your scale.

2. Explain the logic of index validation. What methods are used to validate a composite index? Give examples.

3. Compare scales, indexes, and typologies. Give examples of each.

CHAPTER 7: THE LOGIC OF SAMPLING

OUTLINE

I. A Brief History of Sampling

II. Nonprobability Sampling
   A. Reliance on available subjects
   B. Purposive or judgmental sampling
   C. Snowball sampling
   D. Quota sampling
   E. Selecting informants

III. The Theory and Logic of Probability Sampling
   A. Conscious and unconscious sampling bias
   B. Representativeness and probability of selection
   C. Random selection
   D. Probability theory, sampling distributions, and estimates of sampling error
      1. The sampling distribution of ten cases
      2. Sampling distributions and estimates of sampling error
      3. Confidence levels and confidence intervals

IV. Populations and Sampling Frames

V. Types of Sampling Designs
   A. Simple random sampling (SRS)
   B. Systematic sampling
   C. Stratified sampling
   D. Implicit stratification in systematic sampling
   E. An illustration: sampling university students
      1. Study population and sampling frame
      2. Stratification
      3. Sample selection
      4. Sample modification

VI. Multistage Cluster Sampling
   A. Multistage designs and sampling error
   B. Stratification in multistage cluster sampling
   C. Probability proportionate to size (PPS) sampling
   D. Disproportionate sampling and weighting

VII. Probability sampling in review

BEHAVIORAL OBJECTIVES

Upon completion of this chapter, the student should be able to:

1. Define sampling.

2. Document the historical connection between sampling and political polling.

3. Describe and illustrate each of the following types of nonprobability sampling: reliance on available subject sampling, purposive (judgmental) sampling, quota sampling, and snowball sampling.

4. Describe the role of informants in nonprobability sampling and provide advice on how to select them.

5. Describe the logic of probability sampling, and include heterogeneity and representativeness in your response.

6. List two advantages of probability sampling over nonprobability sampling.

7. Define an EPSEM sample.

8. Define each of the following terms and explain its relevance for random sampling: element, study population, random selection, and sampling unit.

9. Define and differentiate a parameter from a statistic.

10. Define sampling error and show how confidence levels and confidence intervals are used in interpreting sampling errors.

11. Using probability sampling theory, describe the sampling distribution.

12. Explain how to interpret a standard error in terms of the normal distribution using confidence levels and confidence intervals.

13. Present an argument that the survey uses of probability theory are not entirely justified technically.

14. Define sampling frame and restate the cautions regarding making generalizations from sampling frames to populations.

15. Describe simple random sampling and list two reasons why it is seldom used.

16. Summarize the steps in using a table of random numbers.

17. Describe systematic sampling and employ the concepts of sampling interval, sampling ratio, and periodicity in the description.

18. Link stratified sampling with the principle of heterogeneity and describe how this strategy is executed.

19. Identify the major advantage of multistage cluster sampling and describe how this procedure is executed.

20. Present guidelines for balancing the number of clusters and the cluster size in multistage cluster sampling.

21. Explain why a researcher might use probability proportionate to size sampling and explain the logic behind this strategy.

22. Outline the rationale for disproportionate sampling and weighting and note the dangers in using these strategies.

TEACHING SUGGESTIONS AND RESOURCES

1. Announce in class that you are going to do a descriptive study. The people in class will constitute the population. Using a sample drawn from the class, describe the age, sex, major, class standing, etc., distributions.

   The class will serve as the sampling frame. Are there problems with that? People absent? People dropped? Explain how this situation is analogous to using an outdated phone book as a sampling frame.

   After purging the list of absent students, assign each student a number. Decide on a sample size. Select two samples of that size to illustrate that samples will yield different statistics. If you have selected the sample using simple random sampling, have students break into groups to select samples that are stratified, e.g., male-female.

   You may wish to construct confidence intervals around the estimates. Compare the sample statistics with the population parameters.

2. A variation on #1 was suggested to me by Dr. Theodore Wagenaar, Miami University, Oxford, Ohio.

Obtain a standard set of poker chips. There should be 50 white chips, 25 blue chips, and 25 red chips. Mix them up in a bag. Ask several students to draw a sample of five chips, making sure they cannot see the chips during the selection. Then have several other students draw samples of ten chips. On the board, put the percentage distribution of the different colored chips for each sample. Use the results to show that larger samples more closely represent the population than do smaller samples and that the sample values do reflect a sampling distribution around the population value. You can modify this technique by showing the effects of sampling with replacement versus sampling without replacement.

The chips can also be used to demonstrate each of the probability and each of the nonprobability designs.

3. The following tables can be used to illustrate that
    (1) when using SRS, the mean of all possible sample means of a given size is equal to the population parameter; the expected value idea;
    (2) larger samples are more likely to represent the true population parameter than are smaller samples.

This is illustrated in the tables by pointing to the fact that extreme samples are less likely to be selected with large samples and that large samples tend to cluster in the category containing the true population parameter.

Hand out the tables. Explain that Table 1 represents the population and that there are only 12 elements in the population. Tell them that Table 2 represents all samples of sizes 2, 4, and 6 that could have been drawn from the population. The mean for each sample was calculated and coded in the average monthly income categories. Ask the students if they notice anything interesting about the table. They will usually make all the points noted above.

TABLE 1
Hypothetical Data on Monthly Income of 12 Families

FAMILY NUMBER	MONTHLY INCOME
1	$ 500
2	450
3	375
4	475
5	1350
6	900
7	675
8	325
9	550
10	1200
11	225
12	775
Total monthly income	$7800
Mean monthly income	$ 650

TABLE 2
Distribution of Average Monthly Income of
All Possible Samples, by Sample Size 2, 4, 6

Average Monthly Income	n=2	n=4	n=6
Under $300	1	0	0
300-399	7	12	1
400-499	11	67	66
500-599	12	102	193
600-699	9	101	290
700-799	8	103	240
800-899	7	64	122
900-999	6	32	12
1000-1099	3	13	0
1100-1199	1	1	0
1200 or more	1	0	0
Number of samples	66	495	924
Average monthly income			
of all samples	$ 650	$ 650	$650

These tables are from Warwick, Donald P., and Charles A. Linger. 1975. *The Sample Survey: Theory and Practice*. New York: McGraw-Hill.

   4.   FILMS

Against All Odds: Inside Statistics: See preface for a description of each part:
   4. *Normal Distributions*
   13. *Blocking and Sampling*
   14. *Samples and Surveys*
   17. *Binomial Distributions*
   19. *Confidence Intervals*

Inferential Statistics-Part 1: Sampling and Estimation Saves 122,000,000 Dollars!
20 min. Color. 1976. Kent State Univ.
Illustrates a situation in which statistics saves a company from making a costly error. Uses the concepts of population, selecting a random sample, using a random number table, and conducting a survey.

Inferential Statistics-Art 2: Hypothesis Testing, Rats, Robots, and Roller Skates
23 min. Color. 1976. Kent State Univ.
Discusses random sampling, control groups, forming a statistical hypothesis, type I and type II errors.

Populations and Data
30 min. 1990. Insight Media
Introduces the types of problems statisticians deal with and discusses the notions of population and data.

Statistics (4)-Place Your Bets: Probability
30 min. Color. 1985. Indiana Univ. 2" VHS.
Looks at the operation of a gambling casino to analyze how random phenomena that have unpredictable outcomes nevertheless follow a predictable pattern after many repetitions. Introduces the concepts of sampling distribution, normal curves, standard deviations, and expected value.

Statistics: Sampling & Surveys: Sampling and Sampling Distributions
58 min. Color. 1989. Indiana Univ. 2" VHS.
Discusses stratified and multistage sampling designs. Points out practical difficulties in sampling human populations. Introduces the idea of a sampling distribution. Examines the 1936 Gallup election poll.

POSSIBLE ANSWERS TO STUDY GUIDE QUESTIONS

Exercise 7.1
Be sure to go over the concepts of rows and columns with students so that they can tell you the row and column in which they started. Then, you can follow the procedure that they used in selecting the random numbers.

Exercise 7.2
This exercise will create a dilemma as to whether some people are male or female. This can lead into a discussion of the need for accurate prior information on which to stratify. This exercise can also be used to discuss proportionate and disproportionate sampling. If students use k=7 it will produce a proportionate sample. However, if students decide to sample 5 males and 5 females they will need to have a separate k for each strata.

Exercise 7.3
The following answer is only one of several that are acceptable. Stratify colleges by type (public/private) and size for each state and take a random sample. Stratify students by grade level and sex and sample.

INFOTRAC EXERCISES

1. Respondent-driven sampling: a new approach to the study of hidden populations. Douglas D. Heckarthon. *Social Problems*, May 1997 v44 n2 p174(26). What is a "hidden population," and what are some techniques used to reach them?

2. How sampling will help defeat the undercount. Harvey M. Choldin, *Society*, March-April 1997 v34 n3 p27(4). Discuss the problem that sampling is intended to solve.

3. Gummy bears in the White House. Martin Vern Bonsangue, David L. Pagni. *Teaching Children Mathematics*, Feb 1996 v2 n6 p379(3). How were gummy bears used to illustrate sampling?

4. Using the keyword option, ask students to read a social science article that focuses on probability sampling. Ask your students to summarize the article. Did it focus on all forms of probability sampling or only one? If one, which one and why?

INTERNET EXERCISES

1. Ask students to go to the Annenberg Series on-line interactive site on sampling: http://www.learner.org/exhibits/statistics/

Tell them to answer the poll and then to follow the directions. The site enables them to review sampling. Ask them to summarize the site and what they learned by using the site. Ask them to comment on the poll results and why the participants do NOT represent a random sample.

2. Ask students to access the following site:
http://trochim.human.cornell.edu/kb/sampterm.htm
Ask students to read the site and then to apply what they have read to a topic of interest to them. For example, students might decide to do a study on grandparents who raise grandchildren, or do a study on college students who attend state schools. They are then to describe their theoretical population, the study population, the sampling frame, and the sample. Ask students to describe whether they had a problem applying any of the terms to their study. If so, what was the problem?

3. Ask students to access the following Gallup Poll website:
http://www.gallup.com/
Ask students to go the section (at the left) on "how polls are conducted." Then ask them to click on "how does Gallup polling work?" and then to click on "how polls are conducted." Ask them to read this material focusing on sampling. How does Gallup sample? What are the issues that concern the pollsters and how do they "resolve" those issues?
NOTE: This site can also be used to talk about interviews. Also note that this site changes and there are other parts of the site that could be used for class discussion or homework assignments.

MULTIPLE-CHOICE QUESTIONS

1. In general, as sample size increases
    a. the standard error increases in size
    b. the standard error decreases in size
    c. the standard error will remain the same regardless of changes in sample size
    d. the standard error is a constant
    e. the standard error fluctuates in size
        ANS: B
        PG: 197

2. Stratifying a population prior to drawing a sample
    a. eliminates the need for simple random sampling
    b. is most useful for studying a homogeneous population
    c. eliminates the need for probability sampling
    d. is an alternative to either random or systematic sampling
    e. none of the above
        ANS: E
        PGS: 205-206

3. Nonprobability sampling
    a. always produces samples that possess distorted characteristics relative to the population
    b. denies the researcher the use of statistical theory to estimate the probability of correct inferences
    c. should never be used under any circumstances
    d. includes stratified sampling
    e. requires the use of sampling frames
        ANS: B
        PGS: entire chapter

4. The chief purpose of probability sampling is to be able to select
    a. simple random samples
    b. a sample whose statistics will accurately portray an unknown population parameter
    c. a sample whose parameters will accurately portray an unknown population statistic
    d. a sample whose statistics will accurately portray a known population parameter
    e. a sample whose unknown statistics will accurately portray a known parameter
        ANS: B
        PGS: 186, 190

5. Drawing a judgmental sample
    a. allows researchers to use their prior knowledge about the topic
    b. enlists the aid of uninformed respondents
    c. results in a sample that has no researcher bias
    d. ensures a representative sample
    e. requires the development of a quota matrix
        ANS: A
        PG:183

6. Probability theory specifies that
    a. 68% of the samples will fall within about plus or minus one standard error of the population parameter
    b. 95% of the samples will fall within about plus or minus two standard errors of the true value
    c. 99% of the samples will fall within about plus or minus three standard errors of the parameter
    d. 34% of the samples will fall within one standard error increment above the population parameter
    e. all of the above
        ANS: E
        PGS: 197-198

7. Probability samples are advantageous to the researcher because
   a. the method by which they are selected limits conscious and unconscious sampling bias
   b. the accuracy or representativeness of the sample can be estimated
   c. they are perfectly representative of the population from which they are drawn
   d. all of the above
   e. only a and b are correct
      ANS: E
      PG: 189

8. A sampling interval of 5 was used to select a sample from a population of 1000. How many elements are to be in the sample?
   a. 5
   b. 50
   c. 100
   d. 200
   e. 1000
      ANS: D
      PG: 203

9. Using the information in question #8, a researcher should start sampling with
   a. The 5th element on the list
   b. A random start between 1 and 1000, including 1 and 1000
   c. A random start between 1 and 5, including 1 and 5
   d. A random start between 1 and 5, excluding either 1 or 5
   e. It doesn't matter where the researcher starts
      ANS: C
      PG: 204

10. A researcher discovers that in a particular city 10% of the households are headed by a single person and that 90% of the families are husband-wife families. The researcher tells interviewers to conduct 80 interviews. Ten percent of these interviews should be with families that are headed by a single person, and 90% should be with husband-wife families. This research uses
    a. simple random sampling
    b. quota sampling
    c. cluster sampling
    d. stratified sampling
    e. accidental sampling
       ANS: B
       PGS: 184-185

11.   You are doing research on hospital personnel--orderlies, technicians, nurses, and doctors.
       You want to be sure you draw a sample that has cases in each of the personnel categories.
       You want to use probability sampling. An appropriate strategy would be
       a.   simple random sampling
       b.   quota sampling
       c.   cluster sampling
       d.   stratified sampling
       e.   accidental sampling
              ANS: D
              PGS: 205-206

12.   Suppose the researcher in question #11 wanted to use nonprobability sampling. An
       appropriate strategy would be
       a.   simple random sampling
       b.   quota sampling
       c.   cluster sampling
       d.   stratified sampling
       e.   accidental sampling
              ANS: B
              PGS: 184-185

13.   The unit about which information is collected and that provides the basis of analysis is
       called a(n)
       a.   universe
       b.   sampling unit
       c.   unit of analysis
       d.   sampling frame
       e.   element
              ANS: E
              PG: 189

14.   You want to examine the relationship between family size and family cohesion. You use
       as your sample all the students in your research methods class. What kind of sampling
       design are you using?
       a.   simple random sampling
       b.   quota sampling
       c.   cluster sampling
       d.   stratified sampling
       e.   reliance on available subjects
              ANS: E
              PG: 183

15. A summary description of a variable in a sample is called a
    a. variable
    b. parameter
    c. confidence level
    d. confidence interval
    e. statistic
       ANS: E
       PG: 195

16. Every *k*th element in a list is chosen for inclusion in the sample in
    a. simple random sampling
    b. systematic sampling
    c. disproportionate sampling
    d. cluster sampling
    e. stratified sampling
       ANS: B
       PG: 203

17. Statistical computations assume that you have done
    a. simple random sampling
    b. systematic sampling
    c. cluster sampling
    d. stratified sampling
    e. any one of the above is assumed
       ANS: A
       PG: 201

18. If a field researcher wanted to learn a political organization's pattern of recruitment over time, the researcher might begin by interviewing a fairly recent recruit and ask who introduced that person to the organization. Then the researcher might interview the person named and ask who introduced that person to the political organization. This would be an example of
    a. snowball sampling
    b. systematic sampling
    c. deviant cases sampling
    d. accidental sampling
    e. quota sampling
       ANS: A
       PG: 184

19. In terms of probability theory, the standard error is valuable because
     a. it is an estimate of the parameter
     b. it is an estimate of the statistic
     c. it indicates the extent to which the sample estimates will be distributed around the population parameter
     d. only a and b are correct
     e. only b and c are correct
         ANS: C
         PG: 196

20. Disproportionate sampling and weighting are used by the researcher
     a. to ensure a sufficient number of cases in each of the sample subpopulations
     b. to give a proportionate representation to each sample element
     c. to provide a representative picture of the total population
     d. to handle situations involving the errors and approximation that are often inherent in complex, multistage designs
     e. all of the above
         ANS: E
         PGS: 213-214

21. A disadvantage of stratified sampling is that it
     a. denies you the use of probability theory
     b. requires you to have some prior knowledge about the elements in the population prior to drawing the sample
     c. usually increases the standard error
     d. usually requires samples that are larger in size than those required by simple random sampling
     e. none of the above
         ANS: B
         PGS: 205-206

22. Professor Hall was planning to do a field study of hitchhikers. Hall wanted to be sure that persons representing all different age, racial, and sex categories were included in the sample of hitchhikers. What kind of sampling scheme would you recommend?
     a. deviant cases
     b. quota sampling
     c. stratified sampling
     d. snowball sampling
     e. cluster sampling
         ANS: B
         PGS: 184-185

23. A study population is
    a. the hypothetical aggregation of all the elements in a study
    b. the theoretically specified aggregation of study elements
    c. that aggregation of elements from which the sample is actually selected
    d. that aggregation or set of elements considered for selection in some stage of sampling
    e. that aggregation of elements from which information is collected
    ANS: C
    PG: 190

24. After taking a random start between 1 and 20 and then taking every 20th element from the sampling frame, Smith learned that 40% of the sample believed the company's president was doing a good job. The calculated standard error was 3 percent. This means that
    a. between 37% and 43% of the employees believe the president is doing a good job
    b. you are 95% certain that between 37% and 43% of the employees believe the president is doing a good job
    c. you are 68% certain that between 37% and 43% of the employees believe the president is doing a good job
    d. you are 99% certain that between 37% and 43% of the employees believe the president is doing a good job
    e. none of the above
    ANS: C
    PGS: 197-198

25. The sampling scheme used in the prior question is
    a. systematic
    b. stratified
    c. simple random
    d. quota
    e. multistage cluster
    ANS: A
    PGS: 203-204

TRUE-FALSE QUESTIONS

1. The standard error tells us how closely the population parameter is clustered around a single sample statistic.
   ANS: F
   PG: 196

2. In a sample stratified by gender, the sampling error on this variable is reduced to zero.
   ANS: T
   PGS: 205-206

3.   The study of deviant cases is an example of a purposive study.
     ANS: T
     PG: 184

4.   A confidence interval at the 68% confidence level will be larger than one constructed at the 95% confidence level.
     ANS: F
     PG: 198

5.   If two samples of the same size are drawn from the same population using simple random sampling, it follows that they will have the same statistics.
     ANS: F
     PG: 195

6.   Periodicity is a danger involved in the use of stratified sampling.
     ANS: F
     PG: 205

7.   Generally, the more heterogeneous the population, the more beneficial it is to use stratified sampling.
     ANS: T
     PG: 206

8.   Sampling error is typically reduced by either increasing sample size or by increasing the homogeneity of the elements being sampled.
     ANS: T
     PG: 205

9.   The general guideline for the cluster design is to minimize the number of clusters selected while increasing the number of elements within each cluster.
     ANS: F
     PG: 210

10. Stratification represents a modification to rather than an alternative to simple random sampling and systematic sampling.
     ANS: T
     PG: 205

11. Nonprobability sampling is particularly useful in quantitative studies.
     ANS: F
     PG: 186

12. If a household has more than one telephone listed in a directory, both should be included in the sampling frame.
     ANS: F
     PG: 200

13. Findings based on a sample can be taken as representing only the aggregation of elements that compose the sampling frame.
     ANS: T
     PG: 201

14. Taken as a whole, a stratified sample is more likely to be representative on several variables than a single random sample.
     ANS: T
     PG: 206

ESSAYS

1. What is the basic logic of probability sampling? How do such concepts as homogeneity, heterogeneity, sampling bias, representativeness, and probability of selection fit into this logic?

2. Telephone directories are notorious for being inadequate sampling frames. Suppose the population was defined as "all telephone subscribers in the directory's service area." What criticisms could you make of the telephone directory as a sampling frame?

3. Compare probability designs with nonprobability designs. Identify the kinds of sampling designs available within each of these major categories. Explain a situation in which it would be more appropriate to use probability sampling and one where nonprobability sampling would be preferred.

CHAPTER 8: EXPERIMENTS

OUTLINE

I. Topics Appropriate to Experiments

II. The Classical Experiment
   A. Independent and dependent variables
   B. Pretesting and posttesting
   C. Experimental and control groups
   D. The double-blind experiment

III. Selecting Subjects
   A. Probability sampling
   B. Randomization
   C. Matching
   D. Matching or randomization?

IV. Variations on Experimental Design
   A. Preexperimental research designs
      1. One-shot case study
      2. One-group pretest-posttest design
      3. Static-group comparison
   B. Validity issues in experimental research
      1. Sources of internal invalidity
         a. History
         b. Maturation
         c. Testing
         d. Instrumentation
         e. Statistical regression
         f. Selection biases
         g. Experimental mortality
         h. Causal time-order
         i. Diffusion or imitation of treatments
         j. Compensation
         k. Compensatory rivalry
         l. Demoralization
      2. Sources of external invalidity

V. An Illustration of Experimentation

VI. "Natural" Experiments

VII.   Strengths and Weaknesses of the Experimental Method

BEHAVIORAL OBJECTIVES

Upon completion of this chapter, the student should be able to:

1.   Give several examples showing that the experimental mode of observation is particularly appropriate for explanatory purposes.

2.   Describe and illustrate with examples the three major pairs of components in the classical experiment.

3.   Give an example of the double-blind experiment and indicate why such a design would be used.

4.   Contrast the following three strategies for selecting subjects: probability sampling, randomization, and matching.

5.   Note the feature that the preexperimental designs have in common, and define and develop examples of each of the following three designs: one-shot case study, one-group pretest-posttest design, and static-group comparison.

6.   Explain how the following factors may threaten internal validity: history, maturation, testing, instrumentation, statistical regression, selection biases, experimental mortality, causal time-order, diffusion or imitation of treatments, compensation, compensatory rivalry, and demoralization.

7.   Show how the classical experiment handles each of these problems of internal invalidity.

8.   Compare the following true experimental designs: classical design, Solomon four-group design, and posttest-only control group design.

9.   Show how the true experimental designs address the problem of external validity.

10.   Describe how natural experiments occur and give two examples.

11.   Examine the strengths and weaknesses of the experimental method.

TEACHING SUGGESTIONS AND RESOURCES

1. Divide students into small groups. Tell them to design an experimental study to determine whether review sessions affect exam grades. Many issues will come up as students work together on this design-ethics, the effect of the pretest on the posttest, generalizability, and so on.

2. Do a taste test in class. You will need a covered bottle of Coke and a covered bottle of Pepsi. (You can substitute any sodas you wish.) You will also need cups.

   Ask students to volunteer to participate in a soda taste test. Let the volunteers take the test. Always give one brand first and then the next. Do not let anyone repeat the test! Record their preferences. After stating the conclusions of the experiment, discuss the design problems. Issues ranging from the self-selection of participants to the effect of maturation (no longer thirsty after the first drink) will be discussed.

3. FILMS

Against All Odds: Part 12, Experimental Design
See preface for a more complete description

Experimental Studies in the Social Climates of Groups
32 min. B/W. 1940. Iowa Univ.
Presents a study of the effects of types of social organizations upon the attitudes and learning of junior high school children. The social climates developed in the experimental situations are democratic, laissez-faire, and autocratic.

Experiments in Human Behavior
35 min. 1985. Insight Media
Discusses several landmark experiments. Examines experimental design and experimenter bias.

Moral Development
20 min. 1973. Brigham Young Univ.
Presents the Milgram experiments. Illustrates an experiment conducted in a controlled laboratory setting. Also good for a discussion of ethics.

The Social Animal
35 min. B/W. Indiana Univ.
Presents the conformity studies of Schachter, Asch, and so on. Uses actors, not real subjects. This film was reviewed in the ASA publication on films; see Preface. It was suggested that the film be used to show an experiment conducted in a controlled laboratory setting.

Statistics: Experimental Design
58 min. Color. 1989. Indiana Univ. 2" VHS.
Discusses the advantages of planned data collection over anecdotal evidence or available data.
Discusses the idea of an experiment and the basic design principles of comparison, randomization, and replication.

POSSIBLE ANSWERS TO STUDY GUIDE QUESTIONS

Exercise 8.1

1. Select an introductory or some other type of class with at least 100 male students. Or take a random sample of 100 male students from the student directory. Randomly assign the students to the experimental and control groups. Students may suggest including both females and males in the sample, but this is not necessary because females will be confederates.

2. Such tasks as the following are possible: diagnosing a malfunctioning engine, solving an algebraic problem, solving a crime, and the like.

3. Use a few questions, such as:
- - - I would vote for a woman for president.
- - - I support the use of female astronauts.
- - - Men typically make better engineers than do women.

4. Give the answer to the task to the women confederates in the experimental group. Some students may suggest a modification of the classical design by suggesting two experimental groups: one with women who clearly do worse than the men and one with women who clearly do better than the men. The control group in either case will be men who did not work with women.

5. Use the test that was described in part 3.

6. The classical design's control group and random assignment controls for history, maturation, selection biases, testing, instrumentation, statistical regression, experimental mortality, causal time-order.

7. Because the classical design is used, the interaction between testing and the stimulus will be the major threat to invalidity.

8. Results will vary, but they should clearly address the design.

Exercise 8.3

Possible answers are given using gender-role orientation as the dependent variable.
Static-group comparison

Find children who have watched *Sesame Street* and those who have not. Compare the two groups on their views of the appropriate roles of females and males.

This design has no random assignment, and hence there is no way to establish comparability before watching *Sesame Street*. Those who watch *Sesame Street* could easily be different on some other characteristics, such as social class or having been read to a lot.

Advantages: It may be the only appropriate design since it may be difficult to find a group of children with similar characteristics all of whom have not seen *Sesame Street*.

One-group pretest-posttest design
Find some children who have not seen *Sesame Street*. Give them a test on gender-role orientation. Then show *Sesame Street* and retest. Changes could be due to *Sesame Street*.

Advantages: The design is useful when only one group of children can be identified.

Disadvantages: Because there is no control group, it is difficult to make comparisons.

One-shot case study
Find some children who have seen *Sesame Street*. Measure their sex-role orientations. Try to make some conclusions.

Advantages: This type is useful when actual presentation of the stimulus is difficult or too costly.

Disadvantages: It can make no conclusions about the effect of the "stimulus" since there is no pretest and no control group.

All three of these designs share in the problems of internal invalidity.

Classical design
Find 100 children who have not seen *Sesame Street*. Randomly assign them to the experimental and control groups. Pretest on sex-role orientations. Show *Sesame Street* to the experimental group for a couple of weeks. Retest.

Advantages: Causality can be more clearly attributed if scores are significantly different between groups and within the experimental group. The design controls for most sources of internal invalidity.

Disadvantages: It may be hard to find 100 children who have not seen *Sesame Street*. Hence, generalizations may be limited. There could also be an interaction effect with the pretest and the stimulus.

Solomon four-group design
Double sample size and do the same as in #4, but add two groups. Give the same procedures to these two groups except do not give a pretest.

Advantages: It will allow the experimenter to examine the interaction effect, and it controls for most other causes of internal invalidity.

Disadvantages: More children are needed, and more effort and time on the part of the experimenter are required.

Posttest-only control group design
Find 100 children who have not seen *Sesame Street*. Randomly assign them to experimental and control groups. Do not pretest. Show *Sesame Street* to the experimental group for a couple of weeks and measure sex-role orientation.

Advantages: The pretest will not affect posttest scores, nor will pretest scores interact with the stimulus since there is no pretest. It is easier to do and faster since it requires fewer children. It controls for most sources of internal invalidity.

Disadvantages: Without a pretest, actual change due to stimulus cannot be calculated. Generalizability may still be a problem given the requirement for children who have not seen *Sesame Street*.

Exercise 8.4

EVER APPROVE OF MAN PUNCHING ADULT MALE * HAVE GUN IN HOME

| | | | HAVE GUN IN HOME? | | |
			YES	NO	Total
EVER APPROVE OF MAN	YES	Count	195	242	437
		% within HAVE GUN IN HOME	70.1%	64.0%	66.6%
PUNCHING ADULT MALE	NO	Count	83	136	219
		% within HAVE GUN IN HOME	29.9%	36.0%	33.4%
Total		Count	278	378	656
		% within HAVE GUN IN HOME	100.0%	100.0%	100.0%

People who have guns in the home are more likely than people who do not have guns in the home to approve of a man punching an adult male. However, most of the sample approved.

INFOTRAC EXERCISES

1.   Experiments ahoy! (Science students test models to design kayaks.) Karen De Seve. *Science World*, Sept 16, 1994 v51 n2 p8(4). What were the variables students experimented with?

2   Social experiments: some developments over the past fifteen years. Thomas D. Cook, William R. Shadish. *Annual Review of Psychology,* 1994 v45 p545(36). Explain three of the developments in your own words.

3.   Using the keyword option, ask students to read a social science articles that uses an experimental group and a control group. Ask students to summarize the article. Then ask students to: 1) name the type of design used in the research, 2) describe whether the researcher(s) could have arrived at the same conclusion(s) without a control group, and 3) whether another design would have been more appropriate for the research and if so, what design and why.

4.   Using the keyword option, ask students to read a social science article that focuses on internal validity. Ask students to summarize the article and then to answer: 1) how did the researcher(s) assess internal validity?, 2) what type(s) of internal validity was assessed?, 3) does the student agree with the outcome of the assessment?

INTERNET EXERCISES

1.   Ask students to go to the following site:
http://trochim.human.cornell.edu/kb/desexper.html
Ask students to read the segment entitled "experimental design" and to select at least two other links in that site (e.g., introduction to design, internal validity, etc.) Ask students to summarize the material. Did they learn anything new about designs from the site? If yes, what? If no, was all the material covered in Babbie?

2.   Ask students to go to the following tutorial site on internal validity:
http://server.bmod.athabascau.ca/html/Validity/
This tutorial was developed for a psychology class at Athabasca University. This site covers via definition, examples, and a "test" the following threats to internal validity: 1) selection, 2) history, 3) maturation, 4) repeated testing, 5) instrumentation, 6) regression to the mean, 7) experimental mortality, 8) selection-maturation interaction, and 9) experimenter bias. Ask students to "DO" parts 1 and 2. Tell students to indicate their agreement or disagreement with tutorial answers. If they disagree with an answer and believe another threat to internal validity was crucial, ask them to explain their disagreement.
NOTE: The examples used in this site can be used for a class discussion.

MULTIPLE-CHOICE QUESTIONS

1. Among the requirements for the classical experimental design is a posttest measurement of the
    a. dependent variable for both the experimental and control groups
    b. independent variable for both the experimental and control groups
    c. independent variable for the control group only
    d. dependent variable for the experimental group only
    e. independent variable for the experimental group only
        ANS: A
        PGS: 222-223

2. The problem of an interaction between the testing and the experimental stimulus is handled by
    a. the Solomon four-group design
    b. the posttest-only control group design
    c. the classical experimental design
    d. all of the above
    e. only a and b are correct
        ANS: E
        PG: 234

3. In order to ensure that experimental and control groups are similar before the experiment begins, social scientists sometimes
    a. pair subjects who are identical on relevant variables and assign one to the control group and one to the experimental group
    b. create groups that are equivalent in terms of their averages on some relevant variables
    c. assign subjects randomly to the experimental and control groups
    d. match subjects on relevant variables
    e. all of the above
        ANS: E
        PGS: 226-227

4. Which of the following is LEAST suited to providing clear evidence about a causal relationship between the independent and dependent variables?
    a. classical experimental design
    b. Solomon four-group design
    c. posttest-only control group design
    d. one-shot case study
    e. all of the above are equally effective in providing evidence of a causal relationship
        ANS: D
        PGS: 228-230

5. The double-blind experiment is one in which
   a. the experimenters do not know which is the experimental group and which is the control group
   b. the experimental subjects do not know that they are in the experimental group, and the control group subjects know that they are in the control group
   c. neither the subjects in the experimental or control groups nor the experimenters know which are the experimental and control groups
   d. the control group subjects do not know that they are in the control group, and the experimental group subjects know that they are in the experimental group
   e. the experimental and control groups are given placebos
   ANS: C
   PG: 225

6. Experiments are least appropriate for research projects that involve
   a. small-group interaction
   b. hypothesis testing
   c. testing relatively limited and well-defined concepts and propositions
   d. descriptive purposes
   e. explanatory purposes
   ANS: D
   PG: 221

7. Without randomly assigning subjects, a researcher administers the experimental stimulus to the experimental group and then measures the dependent variable in both the experimental and comparison groups. This design is known as the
   a. one-group pretest-posttest design
   b. one-shot case study
   c. static-group design
   d. classical experimental design
   e. posttest-only control group design
   ANS: C
   PG: 228

8. The Solomon four-group design
   a. combines the classical experimental design with the posttest-only control group design
   b. combines the classical experimental design with the pretest-only control group design
   c. combines the classical experimental design with the static-group comparison design
   d. combines the static-group comparison design with the one-group pretest-posttest design
   e. none of the above
   ANS: A
   PGS: 233-234

9. Assume that you have developed a study technique that you believe will result in students scoring higher on research methods exams. You test your study technique with the design diagramed below. Where:

    R=random assignment
    O=observation on the dependent variable
    X= the independent variable

    R O1 X O2
    R O3   O4

    Using the diagramed design, what predictions are correct?
    a. O2 should be greater than O1
    b. the (O2O1) change should be greater than the (O4O3) change.
    c. O4 must equal O3
    d. all of the above are correct
    e. only a and b are correct
       ANS: E
       PGS: 222-224

10. The design diagramed in the prior question
    a. is a static-group comparison design
    b. is the classical experimental design
    c. treats O as the new teaching technique
    d. treats O as the old teaching technique
    e. treats X as the scores on the research methods exam
       ANS: B
       PGS: 222-224

11. An example of a natural experiment would include
    a. exploring the behavioral consequences on families when the breadwinner is killed on the job
    b. doing a comparative analysis of families that choose to stay and those who choose to move out of an ethnically changing neighborhood to find out the underlying causes for the difference in their choices
    c. determining the effects of the preferential hiring of people with disabilities on the morale of people without disabilities
    d. all of the above
    e. only a and b are correct
       ANS: D
       PGS: 237-238

12. A friend of yours, a senior, took the Graduate Record Exam in September and scored in the 99th percentile. In February, your friend took the same exam over again. This time your friend scored in the 84th percentile. As a research methods student, you told your friend that his/her lowered score was most likely due to
    a. testing
    b. differential selection
    c. statistical regression
    d. demoralization
    e. compensation rivalry
       ANS: C
       PG: 231

13. Preexperimental designs
    a. are the weakest experimental designs
    b. control for most sources of internal invalidity
    c. control for most sources of external invalidity
    d. are excellent for drawing causal inferences
    e. are highly recommended by Campbell and Stanley
       ANS: A
       PG: 228

14. An instrumentation effect occurs when
    a. the instrument employed for the pretest has an effect that shows up on the posttest
    b. the measurement instrument is changed from the pretest to the posttest
    c. there is a change on the dependent variable from the pretest score to the posttest score
    d. all of the above
    e. only a and b are correct
       ANS: B
       PG: 230

15. You were asked to participate in an experiment to test the effectiveness of review sessions on exam grades. As a research methods student, you concluded that you had been assigned to the control group because you simply took the scheduled exams. Since you did not want the students in the experimental group to get higher grades than you did on the exams, you organized a review session with other control group subjects. This illustrates
    a. compensation
    b. the testing effect
    c. demoralization
    d. maturation
    e. compensatory rivalry
       ANS: E
       PG: 231

16. The question of internal validity refers to
    a. the comparison of the results obtained for the experimental group with those obtained for the control group
    b. whether the experimental stimulus really affected the dependent variable
    c. the determination of the proper time to do the posttest
    d. the determination of the proper time to do the pretest
    e. generalizability
    ANS: B
    PG: 230

17. The experimental and control groups should be comparable on
    a. variables that are likely to be related to the independent variable under study
    b. variables that are likely to be related to the dependent variable under study
    c. age, education, and ethnicity
    d. all of the above
    e. only b and c are correct
    ANS: B
    PG: 227

18. A researcher administered a math test to a group of 9th graders in September. During the school year the students received an intensive program designed to improve their math skills. In May the math test was again given and the math scores improved. A major problem in this research is that the researcher failed to control for
    a. history
    b. maturation
    c. testing
    d. selection biases
    e. all of the above
    ANS: E
    PGS: 230-231

19. The design used in question #18 is a
    a. Classical experimental design
    b. One-group pre-test post-test design
    c. Static group design
    d. One shot case study
    e. Post-test only control group design
    ANS: B
    PG: 228

20. The classical experimental design (pretest-posttest control group design
    a. helps guard against the sources of internal and external validity
    b. helps guard against the sources of external invalidity
    c. helps guard against the sources of internal invalidity
    d. cannot guard against the sources of either internal or external invalidity
    e. what it helps guard against depends upon the particular experiment
       ANS: C
       PGS: 230-232, 240

TRUE-FALSE QUESTIONS

1. The problem of external validity refers to the generalizability of results.
   ANS: T
   PG: 233

2. Mortality effects only need to be controlled when your research focuses on the elderly.
   ANS: F
   PG: 231

3. In a natural experiment, the researcher does NOT manipulate the independent variable.
   ANS: T
   PGS: 237-239

4. Instrumentation is NOT a threat to internal validity in the one-shot case study.
   ANS: T
   PG: 230

5. The use of an experimental group allows the researcher to detect any effects of the experiment itself.
   ANS: T
   PG: 223

6. Campbell and Stanley suggest that, given proper randomization in the assignment of subjects to experimental and control groups, there is no need for pretesting.
   ANS: T
   PG: 234

7. Randomization is the preferred technique for assigning subjects to experimental and control groups even when you CAN specify in advance the relevant matching variables.
   ANS: T
   PGS: 227-228

8. Questions about the generalizability of findings are more likely to be raised about explanatory studies using college students than on descriptive studies using college students.
    ANS: F
    PG: 225

9. The effectiveness of randomization in experimentation is affected by the number of subjects involved.
    ANS: T
    PG: 228

10. Preexperimental designs do not have control groups.
    ANS: F
    PG: 228

11. The classical experimental design controls for an interaction between the testing and the stimulus.
    ANS: F
    PG: 233

ESSAYS

1. Professor Rose was asked to design an experiment to test whether obese people would lose weight on a new diet plan. Professor Rose was not a methodologist. Rose asked for your help. You immediately told Rose that the selected design would have to be sensitive to the issues of statistical regression, diffusion or imitation of treatment, compensatory rivalry, and demoralization. Rose said, "I don't understand." Explain these issues to Rose. Suggest and explain a design that would control for these problems.

2. Explain the elements of the classical experimental design. Is this design especially useful in dealing with causal relationships? If yes, why? If not, why?

3. Explain what is meant by internal and external validity.

4. What differentiates experimental from preexperimental designs? Give an illustration of a situation in which an experimental design would be preferred and one in which a preexperimental design would be preferred.

CHAPTER 9: SURVEY RESEARCH

OUTLINE

I. Topics Appropriate to Survey Research

II. Guidelines for Asking Questions
   A. Choose appropriate question forms
   B. Make items clear
   C. Avoid double-barreled questions
   D. Respondents must be competent to answer
   E. Respondents must be willing to answer
   F. Questions should be relevant
   G. Short items are best
   H. Avoid negative items
   I. Avoid biased items and terms

III. Questionnaire Construction
   A. General questionnaire format
   B. Formats for respondents
   C. Contingency questions
   D. Matrix questions
   E. Ordering items in a questionnaire
   F. Questionnaire instructions
   G. Pretesting the questionnaire
   H. A composite illustration

IV. Self-administered Questionnaires
   A. Mail distribution and return
   B. Monitoring returns
   C. Follow-up mailings
   D. Acceptable response rates
   E. A case study

V. Interview Surveys
   A. The role of the survey interviewer
   B. General guidelines for survey interviewing
      1. Appearance and demeanor
      2. Familiarity with questionnaire
      3. Follow question wording exactly
      4. Record responses exactly
      5. Probing for responses
   C. Coordination and control

BEHAVIORAL OBJECTIVES

Upon completion of this chapter, the student should be able to:

1. Illustrate how surveys may be used for descriptive, explanatory, and exploratory purposes.

2. Describe how survey are sometimes misused.

3. Outline the conditions under which open-ended and closed-ended questions are used.

4. List and illustrate several guidelines for asking effective questions.

5. Explain why social desirability is a problem in asking questions.

6. List three guidelines for good questionnaire format.

7. Describe the role of contingency questions and list the principles for their use.

8. Describe the role of matrix questions and list the principles for their use.

9. Explain why the order in which questions are asked is important, and describe how this principle is differentially applied in questionnaires and interviews.

10. List three principles for providing instructions for respondents of surveys.

11.   Explain why it is important to pretest a questionnaire.

12.   List three methods for distributing self-administered questionnaires.

13.   List three principles for mail distribution and return of questionnaires.

14.   Present an argument for monitoring returns, and show how this can be done with the return rate graph.

15.   List three principles regarding follow-up mailings.

16.   State the response rates that Babbie considers adequate, good, and very good.

17.   Present four advantages of interviews over questionnaires.

18.   Restate the five general rules for successful interviewing.

19.   Discuss the role of specifications in training interviewers.

20.   List five advantages and three problems with telephone surveys.

21.   Show how random-digit dialing and computer-assisted telephone interviewing overcome some of the weaknesses of the telephone survey.

22.   Describe the several new technologies available for computer-assisted telephone interviewing.

23.   Describe the advantages of online polling and offer some advice for successful online polling.

24.   Contrast questionnaires and interviews, and describe when each is most appropriate.

25.   Assess the strengths and weaknesses of survey design.

26.   Give two examples of secondary analysis and/or data archives, and summarize the advantages and disadvantages of this approach.

TEACHING SUGGESTIONS AND RESOURCES

1. Conduct an interview in class. If possible, record the interview with audio-visual equipment. If this is not possible, record the interview ahead of time. Recording the interview enables you to go back over it with the class noting the good and bad aspects of the interview.

   Select a topic that is of interest to the students, e.g., grading policies, students' use of cars, liquor on campus. Depending upon your questionnaire, conduct the interview with either a student or a colleague. Work with them ahead of time so that you are both prepared to do some superb acting! Include examples of open, closed, and contingency questions.

   In the course of the interview, violate all the general rules that are suggested in Babbie for interviewing.

2. The American Statistical Association has a pamphlet series on surveys which can also be read on-line at: http://www.amstat.org/sections/srms/whatsurvey.html
   Included in the series are the following titles:
   1. "What is a Survey?"
   2. "How to Plan a Survey"
   3. "How to Collect Survey Data"
   4. "Judging the Quality of a Survey"
   5. "How to Conduct Pretesting"
   6. "What are Focus Groups?"
   7. "More About Mail Surveys"
   8. "What is a Margin Of Error?"
   9. "Designing a Questionnaire"
   10. "More About Telephone Surveys"

   To order the series contact the American Statistical Association at:
   1429 Duke Street
   Alexandria, VA 22314-3402 USA
   (703) 684-1221/fax: (703) 684-2037
   E-mail: asainfo@amstat.org

3. Give students the following two questions from the Roper Center's July/August 1994 publication, *The Public Perspective,* that I learned about from John (Jay) Stewart's (University of Hartford) posting on the methods net.
   In November 1992 the Roper Center did a survey for the American Jewish Committee using the following question:

   Does it seem possible or does it seem impossible to you that the Nazi extermination of the Jews never happened?

65%   Impossible it never happened
12%   Don't know
22%   Possible it never happened
In March 1994 the Roper Center asked the following question with the following results:
Does it seem possible to you that the Nazi extermination of the Jews never happened or do you feel certain that it happened?
91%   Certain it happened
  8%   Don't know
  1%   Possible it never happened

Ask students to discuss why the change in response. This should lead students into a discussion of question wording and the use of a negative question (the first version).

3. FILMS

Interviewing Children Sounds Easy, But. . .
24 min. Color. 1979. Washington State Univ.
Provides a detailed guide and demonstration of various techniques useful in an initial assessment of problems. A psychiatrist and a medical student discuss the challenge of interviewing children during psychiatric evaluation.

Interviewing the Abused Child
22 min. Color. 1978.
A series of actual interviews using different techniques demonstrates the skill and sensitivity required of caseworkers, teachers, hospital personnel, police officers, and prosecutors to elicit responses and information from children of various ages.

Leading Questions: Part of a 4-part series, Moyers: The Public Mind.
60 min. PBS Videos.
MPUM-102-CR94
ISBN 0-7936-0037-5
This program examines the power of professional pollsters to influence public opinion. In the hands of campaign consultants, the sophisticated techniques of market research become tools of political persuasion.

Political Polling
ID: 53375, C-SPAN Video. 1993.
Purdue University. Public Affairs Video Archives.
A pollster discusses how survey research fits into the political campaign context. He also presents a sample political poll and analyzes its significance.

Probing Questions (Questioning Skills)
7 min. Color. Univ. of Wisconsin (LaCrosse).
Probing requires the student to go beyond the superficial response. The teacher demonstrates this technique by asking for more information. Part of the Teaching Skills for Elementary and Secondary Education Teachers Series.

Research Interview Module 1
20 min. Color. 1972. Cornell Univ.
Covers basic techniques: how to gain entry, begin the interview, and conduct the actual interview.

Research Interview Module 2
20 min. Color. 1972. Cornell Univ.
How to record information verbatim and how to probe are emphasized. Interviews are analyzed in the program.

Research Interview Module 3
20 min. Color. 1972. Cornell Univ.
Shows how three different interviewers handled three specific problems. Which one was successful?

Statistics (2)-Behind the Headlines: Collecting Data.
30 min. Color. 1985. Indiana Univ.
Takes a look at data collection and explores how surveys and public opinion polls actually work. Explains the difference between a survey and an experiment, pointing out that random sampling is employed to eliminate bias and that experiments are controlled to discover cause-and-effect relationships.

Unmarried Mother Interview, Peters-Browning, Part 2.
17 min. B/W. 1965. Univ. of Calif./Berkeley.
Illustrates how the interviewer's attitudes affect the interviewee.

POSSIBLE ANSWERS TO STUDY GUIDE QUESTIONS

Exercise 9.1

Be sure the return rate graph begins on the first mailing date, March 1, and not March 6th, the date the first returns were received.
Cumulative percents indicate a 49.4% return rate.

Exercise 9.2

1. There is no question
   Attributes are not mutually exclusive
   No boxes are provided for an answer
   No instructions for instrument
2. Respondent is not competent to answer
   Responses are not mutually exclusive
3. Not clear on what is to be included
   May not be relevant for the unemployed
   Respondent cannot answer exactly
   The time frame is not specified
4. Range of variation of responses too limited
   Biased due to social desirability
5. Responses are not exhaustive
   Double barreled question
   Responses reflect social desirability
   Needs to be rewritten as a contingency question
   No instructions for answering the question-check all that apply, rank, or select the most
   important reason
   Not clear
6. Too long
   Double-barreled
   Not exhaustive due to omission of "neutral"
   Limited range of variation in answers
7. Biased due to "with the President"
   Contains a double negative
   Respondent may not be competent to answer, or the item may not be relevant
8. Double-barreled
   Not exhaustive in answers
9. Biased
   Leading
   Ambiguous

Exercise 9.3
You can use several sampling strategies for this assignment. The student directory can be used to take a random sample. The registrar's office may be willing to draw a sample for you and provide the labels. A quota design could be used, using such variables as class level and sex. Or, a convenience sample could be used by having students interview whomever they wish. Be sure to tell the class how to sample. If left to their own devices, students typically select convenience samples.

Exercise 9.4: Examples of possible questions include:
1. What is your class level?
   1. First year
   2. Sophomore
   3. Junior
   4. Senior
   5. Graduate student
   6. Other (please describe)

2. In what college or division are you currently enrolled?
   1. Arts and Sciences
   2. Business
   3. Education
   4. Fine Arts
   5. Applied Science
   6. Other (please describe)

3. What is your sex?
   1. Male
   2. Female

4. Various items are possible. Examples: I tend to vote for candidates who support gun control. (SA to SD) How many guns do you own?

5. Can vary.

6. How many movies have you seen in the last month?
   1. Zero
   2. One
   3. Two
   4. Three
   5. Four
   6. Five
   7. Six
   8. Seven
   9. Eight or more
NOTE: This can be used as a contingency question to #7

7. Overall, how would you rate your enjoyment of attending movies?
   1. Very high
   2. Moderately high
   3. Average
   4. Moderately low
   5. Very low

8. What two issues do you feel are the most serious in America today? Why? (Probe)

9. Can vary.

10. Can vary.

INFOTRAC EXERCISES

1. Survey: Americans are well-informed about AIDS. *AIDS Weekly Plus*, Dec 22, 1997 p10(2). What were some of the opinions and levels of knowledge turned up in this survey?

2. Using the keyword option, ask students to read a social science article that focuses on response rates. Ask students to summarize the article and to state whether the author(s) agreed or disagreed with Babbie's information on response rates.

3. Using the keyword option, ask students read a social science article that focuses on closed-ended questions and one that focuses on open-ended questions. What did they learn from reading these two articles?

4. Using the keyword option, ask students to read a social science article that focuses on secondary analysis. Ask students to summarize the article. Why was secondary analysis used/recommended? Would original data collection be more appropriate for the topic under investigation?

INTERNET EXERCISES

1. Ask students to access the following tutorial site on survey research:
http://www.statpac.com/surveys/
This site addresses such issues as: cost considerations, the advantages and disadvantages of written questionnaires, questionnaire design considerations, pre-notification letters, cover letters, response rates, nonresponse bias, the order of the questions, anonymity and confidentiality, questionnaire length, reply envelopes and postage, the "Don't Know", "Undecided", and "Neutral" response options, sponsorship, sampling methods, etc.

Ask students to access one or more of these topics and summarize that part of the tutorial. What did they learn from this site that they did not learn from Babbie? What did they learn from this site that supports or varies from Babbie?

2. Ask students to access the following site which is produced by a company called the Business Research Lab:

http://www.busreslab.com/tips/tipsgen.htm

This site gives tips on such things as leading questions, minimizing non-response, questionnaire length, doing mall samples, etc. Ask students to summarize three of the topics (you can select the topics ahead of time or ask students to select the topics that interest them) and to indicate whether this company agrees or disagrees with Babbie on how to handle the selected issues.

3. Ask students to read and summarize one (or more) of the American Statistical Association's brochures noted in the teaching suggestions and resources section of this chapter.

MULTIPLE-CHOICE QUESTIONS

1. Professor Smidlapp mailed a questionnaire to students on the issue of academic dishonesty. Smidlapp planned to use inferential statistics in the analyses and was concerned about the response rate. You tell Smidlapp that technically the use of inferential statistics assumes that
   a. all members of the population complete and return the questionnaire
   b. all members of the initial sample complete and return the questionnaire
   c. at least 50% of the members of the initial sample complete and return the questionnaire
   d. at least 50% of the population complete and return the questionnaire
   e. the overall response rate exceeds 75%
   ANS: B
   PG: 261

2. Monitoring questionnaire returns may enable you to detect which of the following threats to internal validity?
   a. standard errors
   b. statistical regression
   c. compensatory rivalry
   d. instrumentation
   e. history
   ANS: E
   PG: 260

3. The primary function of the probe is to
    a. loosen up the respondent
    b. get the correct answer from the respondent
    c. get the respondent to answer a question more fully
    d. indicate an understanding and interest in the respondent
    e. all of the above
        ANS: C
        PG: 266

4. One of the most important **natural abilities** of good interviewers is their ability to
    a. dress in a fashion similar to that of the people being interviewed
    b. determine very quickly the kind of person the respondent will feel most comfortable with
    c. rephrase questions in their own words
    d. probe for responses
    e. pry into the respondent's personal life
        ANS: B
        PG: 265

5. Working with a **very limited budget**, Professor Jenner undertook a national survey of 3,000 households. Jenner felt that the topic under investigation would produce a low response rate. What advice would you give Jenner?)
    a. Use postage stamps for both the outgoing and the return mail.
    b. Use postage stamps for the outgoing mail and business reply permits for the return mail.
    c. Use bulk rate for the outgoing mail and business reply for the return mail.
    d. Use bulk rate for the outgoing mail and postage stamps for the return mail.
    e. Use bulk rate for both the outgoing and the return mail.
        ANS: C
        PG: 259

6. Which of the following lists the three main methods of administering survey questionnaires to a sample of respondents?
    a. Self-administered questionnaires, telephone interviews, and mail surveys
    b. Face-to-face interviews, CATI surveys, and telephone surveys
    c. Face-to-face interviews, telephone interviews, and electronic surveys
    d. Telephone interviews, electronic surveys, and self-administered questionnaires
    e. Face-to-face interviews, self-administered questionnaires, and telephone surveys
        ANS: E
        PG: 256

7.   In general, survey research is an appropriate observational method for
     a.   describing a population too large to observe directly
     b.   descriptive, exploratory, and explanatory purposes
     c.   the measurement of attitudes prevalent in a larger population
     d.   studies that have individual people as the unit of analysis
     e.   all of the above
          ANS: E
          PG: 243

8.   When follow-ups are planned with mail surveys
     a.   the anonymity of respondents can no longer be guaranteed
     b.   more thoughtful answers are usually provided by those who wait until the follow-up to respond
     c.   response rates typically increase
     d.   response bias can no longer be estimated
     e.   all of the above
          ANS: C
          PGS: 260-261

9.   Professor Donnelly wants to conduct a training session for new interviewers working on his project. Donnelly asks you to review his plan for the training session. After reviewing the plan you should tell Donnelly to exclude _____ from the session?
     a.   A discussion of specifications
     b.   Practice interviews where the interviewers interview each other
     c.   A description of what the study is about
     d.   Practice interviews on people that Donnelly's selected for the sample
     e.   You should tell Donnelly to include ALL of the above in the training session
          ANS: D
          PG: 267

10. Which of the following statements is(are) INCORRECT?
     a.   Closed-ended questions should limit respondents to three or four choices.
     b.   Closed-ended questions should have response categories that are mutually exclusive and exhaustive.
     c.   Closed-ended questions should provide uniformity of response.
     d.   Closed-ended questions should cover the range of likely responses.
     e.   Closed-ended questions are appropriate when relevant answers to questions are relatively clear.
          ANS: A
          PG: 245

11.   A return rate graph
       a. begins on the day the questionnaires were mailed
       b. begins on the day the first response is received
       c. begins on the day when at least ten responses are received
       d. begins on the day the second mailing is planned
       e. varies as to when it should begin depending on the nature of the project
           ANS: A
           PG: 260

12.   A key problem of secondary analysis is
       a. cost
       b. validity
       c. sample selection
       d. data collection strategies
       e. questionnaire construction
           ANS: B
           PG: 276

13.   In general, survey research is
       a. strong on reliability and strong on validity
       b. strong on reliability and weak on validity
       c. weak on reliability and strong on validity
       d. weak on reliability and weak on validity
       e. reliability and validity are not issues that concern researchers who use the survey
           technique
           ANS: B
           PG: 275

14.   Assume that the following four questions appear in a survey. Which of the questions
       is(are) a contingency question?
       Q1: Are you married? (Yes, No)
       Q2: How old was your spouse on his/her last birthday?
       Q3: What is your spouse's current employment status?
       Q4: What is your current employment status?
       a. Q1 is a contingency question and the rest are not
       b. Q1, Q2, and Q3 are contingency questions and Q4 is not
       c. Q2 and Q3 are contingency questions and Q1 and Q4 are not
       d. Q2, Q3, and Q4 are contingency questions and Q1 is not
       e. All of the questions are contingency questions
           ANS: C
           PG: 251

15. Interview surveys have a number of advantages over mail surveys; which of the following is NOT one of those advantages?
    a. higher response rates
    b. there is generally a smaller number of "don't knows" and "no answers"
    c. there is a smaller number of relevant responses given to a question
    d. observations can be made
    e. all of the above are advantages of the interview
       ANS: C
       PGS: 263-264

16. Babbie recommends that the interviewer training session begin with
    a. a discussion of general guidelines and procedures
    b. a description of the specifications
    c. a demonstration interview
    d. a description of what the study is about
    e. a description of the questionnaire
       ANS: D
       PG: 266

17. Which of the following is NOT an advantage of interviews as compared to self-administered questionnaires?
    a. Interviews are more effective in dealing with complicated issues
    b.. Interviews produce fewer incomplete questions
    c. Interviews have higher response rates
    d. Interviews handle sensitive issues more effectively
    e. All of the above ARE advantages of the interview
       ANS: D
       PG: 273

18. During an interviewer training session, Jones, a trainee, asks you, "What should I do if. . . ?" You tell Jones
    a. check the specifications
    b. do whatever you think is most appropriate in that situation
    c. it will not happen
    d. call me, if it happens
    e. jot down problems and skip that part of the interview
       ANS: A
       PG: 267

19.   Which of the following is NOT an example of an electronic survey?
      a. CATI (computer assisted telephone interviewing)
      b. CASI (computer assisted self-interviewing
      c. TDE (touchtone data entry)
      d. VR (voice recognition)
      e. All of the above are examples of electronic surveys
          ANS: E
          PG: 271

20.   According to Babbie, the minimum level for an **adequate** response rate for analysis and
      reporting is:
      a. 30 percent
      b. 40 percent
      c. 50 percent
      d. 60 percent
      e. 70 percent
          ANS: C
          PG: 261

21.   Assume that the following would be reasonable conversational questions/statements
      based on a subject's previous statement. Which is(are) the best probe(s)?
      a. "In what way is that a better job?"
      b. "How is that a better job?"
      c. "Tell me more about why that's a better job."
      d. "Can you tell me more about how that's a better job?"
      e. All of the above are good probes.
          ANS: E
          PG: 266

22.   Contingency questions are used to
      a. increase the likelihood of responses from those for whom the questions are relevant
      b. spare respondents the frustration of reading and puzzling over questions that are
          irrelevant to them
      c. enable the researcher to ask several questions that have the same set of answer
          categories
      d. all of the above
      e. only a and b are correct
          ANS: E
          PGS: 251-252

23. Which guideline does the following questionnaire item violate? "Would you not say that crime is not a serious problem in the U.S.?"
    a. Avoid double-barreled questions.
    b. Avoid short items.
    c. Avoid leading the respondent.
    d. Avoid meaningful questions.
    e. Avoid negative items.
    ANS: E
    PG: 249

24. The questionnaire item "Did you file federal and state income tax reports last year?" with a response set of yes, no, can't remember, other, is an example of a(n)
    a. open-ended question
    b. ordinal question
    c. double-barreled question
    d. negative item
    e. ratio variable
    ANS: C
    PG: 246

25. Which of the following techniques does Babbie recommend as the "best" for the presentation of response categories to the respondent?
    a. A code number
    b. Brackets
    c. Boxes
    d. Parentheses
    e. All of the above are equally good
    ANS: C
    PG: 251

26. Which of the following is NOT an advantage of the telephone interview as compared to the face-to-face interview?
    a. Saves time
    b. Less expensive
    c. Safer
    d. No interviewer bias
    e. All of the above are advantages of the telephone interview
    ANS: D
    PG: 268

27. Which of the following advantages of the interview may raise ethical issues?
    a. its higher response rate
    b. its fewer number of "don't knows"
    c. the ability of interviewers to clarify questions
    d. the ability of interviewers to observe respondents as well as ask questions
    e. none of the above raise ethical issues
       ANS: D
       PG: 264

28. Bias in a questionnaire item
    a. encourages respondents to answer questions in a particular way
    b. helps reveal the respondents' true feelings about a topic
    c. is usually obvious to both the respondents and the researcher
    d. occurs only when questions are negatively worded
    e. helps develop rapport between researcher and subject
       ANS: A
       PG: 249

TRUE-FALSE QUESTIONS

1. The higher the response rate, the less likely the chance of a significant response bias.
   ANS: T
   PG: 261

2. Whenever the interview contains open-ended questions, it is important that the interviewer summarize and paraphrase what has been said so that a more meaningful interpretation can be given to the data.
   ANS: F
   PG: 265

3. To overcome the effect of the order of questions on respondent's answers, it is important to randomize the order of the items.
   ANS: F
   PG: 254

4. Open-ended questions are analogous to multiple choice questions and closed-ended questions are analogous to essay questions.
   ANS: F
   PG: 245

5.   Always try to "squeeze" questions together so that the questionnaire looks shorter to the respondent.
     ANS: F
     PGS: 250-251

6.   Probes are used more frequently in open-ended questions than in closed-ended ones.
     ANS: T
     PG: 266

7.   The standardization of the data collected represents a special strength and weakness of survey research.
     ANS: T
     PG: 274

8.   Secondary analysis refers to research in which the data collected and processed by one researcher are reanalyzed by another researcher, often for a different purpose.
     ANS: T
     PG: 276

9.   The use of inferential statistics in survey analysis assumes that at least 55% of the initial sample completed and returned their questionnaires.
     ANS: F
     PG: 261

10. The use of computer-assisted telephone interviewing (CATI) enables a researcher to begin analyzing data before the interviewing is complete.
     ANS: T
     PG: 271

11. Surveys are excellent devices for studying the context of social life.
     ANS: F
     PG: 275

12. A demonstrated lack of response bias is more important that a high response rate.
     ANS: T
     PG: 261

13. The interviewer should be a neutral medium through which questions and answers are transmitted.
     ANS: T
     PG: 264

14. Response sets are more likely to occur with matrix questions than with other types of questions.
    ANS: T
    PG: 254

15. Babbie suggests beginning a questionnaire with interesting items (e.g., questions about sexual practices or deviant behaviors) so that respondents glancing over the first few items will want to answer.
    ANS: F
    PG: 254

ESSAYS

1. Give a comparative analysis of the strengths and weaknesses of survey research.

2. Describe three research questions for which survey research is an appropriate technique of observation. Describe whether and why these three topics are better suited to an interview or a mailed questionnaire.

3. What guidelines would you suggest adhering to in designing a questionnaire?

CHAPTER 10: QUALITATIVE FIELD RESEARCH

OUTLINE

I. Topics Appropriate to Field Research

II. Special Considerations in Qualitative Field Research
    A. The various roles of the observer
    B. Relations to subjects

III. Some Qualitative Field Research Paradigms
    A. Naturalism
    B. Ethnomethodology
    C. Grounded theory
    D. Case studies and the extended case method
    E. Institutional ethnography
    F. Participatory action research

IV. Conducting Qualitative Field Research
    A. Preparing for the field
    B. Qualitative interviewing
    C. Focus groups
    D. Recording observations

V. Research Ethics in Qualitative Field Research

VI. Strengths and Weaknesses of Qualitative Field Research
    A. Validity
    B. Reliability

BEHAVIORAL OBJECTIVES

Upon completion of this chapter, the student should be able to:

1. Define qualitative field research and compare it with other methods of observation.

2. Identify the key strengths of field research.

3. Define and give examples of each of the following elements of social life appropriate for qualitative field research: practices, episodes, encounters, roles, relationships, groups, organizations, settlements, social worlds, and lifestyles (or subcultures).

4. Give three examples of research topics particularly appropriate for qualitative field research.

5. Compare the various roles the field researcher can assume, ranging from complete participant to complete observer.

6. Explain how people who are being studied might modify their behavior if they knew that they were being studied.

7. Compare the postures of fully accepting the beliefs, attitudes, and behaviors of those under study versus remaining more "objective."

8. Define and illustrate the following paradigms: naturalism, ethnomethodology, grounded theory, case studies and extended case method, institutional ethnography, and participatory action research.

9. Provide advice on each of the following steps in preparing for the field: review of the relevant literature, use of informants, and establishing initial contacts.

10. Provide advice for asking questions in qualitative field research, and compare a field research interview with normal conversation.

11. Describe the stages in a complete interviewing process: thematizing, designing, interviewing, transcribing, analyzing, verifying, and reporting.

12. Define and illustrate focus groups.

13. List advantages and disadvantages of the focus group technique.

14. Show how focus groups are relevant in qualitative field research.

15. Provide advice for recording observations in qualitative field research.

16. Identify the ethical issues that emerge in qualitative field research.

17. Address the strengths and weaknesses of qualitative field research.

18. Describe how reliability and validity relate to qualitative field research.

TEACHING SUGGESTIONS AND RESOURCES
1. The following technique generates a lively discussion on participant-observer roles. It also forces students to think about the implications of assuming the complete participant role.

    During your in-class discussion of the roles assumed by field researchers, mention that a new member of your faculty is completing research on student interaction patterns. State that your colleague assumed the role of the complete participant and lived in one of your college's dormitories. Student interest will immediately pick up! Students will begin to ask such questions as—what dorm? What's the person's major? Did the person take tests? Date? Have a roommate? Be prepared for many questions. Some students will begin to express their distaste for the study—"My privacy has been invaded." Their comments and questions can be used to lead into a discussion of the ethical considerations facing researchers undertaking participant-observation studies. It can also lead into a discussion of whether and how observers can affect what they observe.

    After discussion has "died down," and before class ends, debrief your students. Let them know that no such study is being done. I tell them that I had no desire to trick them, but only to get them to think about the roles that a researcher can assume. Tell them to take a look at their reactions to learning about such a study—these would be the reactions of people actually being observed.

2. FILMS

The Pilgrim Must Embark: Living in Community
25 min. 1993.
Contact: Larry Frey, Dept. of Communication, Loyola University, Chicago. Phone: (312)508-3733
An ethnographic film that examines community practices in a residential facility for people with AIDS. An instructional guide is also available.

INFOTRAC EXERCISES

1. Electronic grassroots organizing. Michele Adrisin Wittig, Joseph Schmitz. *Journal of Social Issues*, Spring 1996 v52 n1 p53(17). How did the researchers engage in participant observation in this study?

2. Sacrifice of praise: emotion and collective participation in an African-American worship service. Timothy J. Nelson. *Sociology of Religion*, Winter 1996 v57 n4 p379(1). Describe the "feeling rules" discussed by the author.

3.   Using the "KEYWORD" option, ask students to read a social science article that discusses or uses focus groups. Ask your students to summarize the article.

4.   Using the "KEYWORD" option, ask students to read a social science article that focuses on grounded theory and one that focuses on case studies. Ask students to summarize each article and to explain how these articles link to the area of qualitative field research.

INTERNET EXERCISES

1.   Ask students access the University of Michigan's Center for Ethnography of Everyday Life web site at:
http://www.ethno.isr.umich.edu

Ask students to click on the "centers research projects" and to then summarize the types of projects currently underway. Then ask students to click on "working papers" and to select and read one paper that interests them (or you can select one article for the entire class). Ask students to summarize the paper and to explain why it is an ethnography.

2.   Ask students to access the following site to learn more about grounded theory:
http://dir.lycos.com/Science/Social+Sciences/Methodology/Grounded+Theory/

Ask students to select one of the areas that focuses on grounded theory and to summarize the listing.

3.   Ask students to access a discussion of the qualitative/quantitative debate at:
http://trochim.human.cornell.edu/kb/qualdeb.htm
Ask students what they learned about the interplay between qualitative and quantitative analyses from this discussion. At the same site ask them to click on "qualitative approaches" and "qualitative methods." What did they learn from these two summaries?

POSSIBLE ANSWERS TO STUDY GUIDE QUESTIONS

Exercises 10.1 and 10.2

Students should include the location, day, and time for each observation. Emphasize that field notes should be as detailed as possible.

MULTIPLE-CHOICE QUESTIONS

1. An example(s) of the complete participant role is(are)
   a. joining a sorority or fraternity to study initiation rituals without revealing your identity as a researcher
   b. standing at a street corner and watching whether males or females are more likely to jay-walk
   c. telling a motorcycle gang that you are a researcher and would like to ride with them for a year to understand their interaction patterns
   d. being a newspaper reporter who interviews union workers to learn about recent strike efforts
   e. all of the above are examples of the complete participant role
   ANS: A
   PG: 286

2. An advantage(s) of field research is(are)
   a. it enables the researcher to draw statistical conclusions about the population
   b. the researcher can control the variables under study
   c. social processes can be studied over time
   d. hypotheses can be rigorously tested
   e. all of the above
   ANS: C
   PG: 307

3. In comparison to experiments and surveys, field research has
   a. greater reliability and greater validity
   b. greater reliability and less validity
   c. less reliability and greater validity
   d. less reliability and less validity
   e. can't tell without more information about the particular study
   ANS: C
   PGS: 307-308

4. Among the advantages of field research is(are) that it
   a. yields precise descriptive statements about a large population
   b. involves the uniform application of precise operational definitions
   c. allows for the modification of research design
   d. produces definitive conclusions
   e. is an extremely reliable technique
   ANS: C
   PG: 307

5. The field researcher
   a. seldom approaches the task with precisely defined hypotheses to be tested
   b. attempts to make sense out of an ongoing process that cannot always be predicted in advance
   c. alternates between induction and deduction
   d. makes initial observations, develops tentative conclusions that suggest further observation, and revises the conclusions
   e. all of the above
      ANS: E
      PG: 282

6. Which of the following statements is TRUE?
   a. grounded theorists enter the field with clear cut ideas about what they'll find
   b. extended case study theorists enter the field without preconceptions about what they'll find
   c. grounded theorists seek to know all the literature before entering the field
   d. extended case study theorists seek to know all the literature before entering the field
   e. all of the above are TRUE
      ANS: D
      PG: 293

7. Professor Milne was preparing to do some qualitative interviewing in a field research project. Milne knew that you were a research methods student and asked for your advice. You told Milne
   a. try not to alter the specific wording of questions
   b. try to use the same probes with the same wording for each respondent
   c. try not to alter the sequence of questions
   d. all of the above
   e. none of the above
      ANS: E
      PGS: 300-302

8. Which of the following is POOR advice about recording observations in the field?
   a. Don't trust your memory anymore than you have to
   b. Always take notes during the observation
   c. Take notes in stages
   d. Advance preparation on recording anticipated observations better enables you to record unanticipated observations
   e. All of the above is good advice
      ANS: B
      PGS: 304-306

9. Dr. Fielding is interested in the stratification system in the United States and how it is perpetuated through time. Fielding decides to examine the experiences of minority students who seek college counseling in high school. He interviews minority students in four high schools. Fielding then conducts interviews with the school administrators, guidance counselors, teachers, parents, and social workers at those high schools.. Fielding is probably using a/an _____ approach.
    a. participatory action research
    b. ethnomethodology
    c. ethnography
    d. case study
    e. institutional ethnography
        ANS: E
        PG: 295

10. Grounded theory begins with
    a. Patterns
    b. Hypothesis
    c. Key variables
    d. Data collection
    e. Any one of the above
        ANS: D
        PG: 291

11. Which of the following is POOR advice for a qualitative field interviewer?
    a. Learn to listen, think, and talk almost at the same time
    b. Be more interested than interesting
    c. Do not deviate from your schedule of preestablished questions
    d. Don't try to halt your respondents line of discussion even if it's not on topic
    e. All of the above is GOOD advice
        ANS: C
        PGS: 300-302

12. Professor Miller taped eight focus groups to examine citizens' attitudes toward park development. As a research methods student, you told her that an advantage of the focus group is(are)
    a. moderators need little skill
    b. moderators can easily control the focus group's discussion
    c. data tapes are easily analyzed
    d. high face validity
    e. all of the above
        ANS: D
        PG: 303

13. Sara wanted to learn about battered women. She lived in a battered women's shelter in order to fully learn about the views of these women. She wanted to write a detailed and accurate description of the lives that the women report. Which of the following approaches best describes Sara's research paradigm?
    a. Naturalist
    b. Ethnomethodology
    c. Grounded theory
    d. Institutional ethnography
    e. Participatory action research
       ANS: A
       PG: 28

14. Sara, from the prior question, was trying to write a:
    a. Structured interview
    b. Unstructured interview
    c. Ethnography
    d. Case study
    e. None of the above
       ANS: C
       PG: 289

15. An ethnomethodologist reviewing Sara's work (from the previous question) would say that the women in the shelter were:
    a. Describing their socially constructed reality
    b. Reporting their world as they made sense of it
    c. Describing their world "as it really is"
    d. Telling us how and why the world made sense to them
    e. A and b only are true
       ANS: E
       PG: 290

16. Jenny wants to do research that tells the stories of rape victims. She wants to tell "their stories" the way they "really are." Jenny is using a _____ paradigm.
    a. Naturalist
    b. Ethnomethodology
    c. Grounded theory
    d. Case study
    e. Participating action research
       ANS: A
       PG: 289

17. As noted by Kvale, in a complete interviewing process a researcher will
    a. Thematize
    b. Design
    c. Transcribe
    d. Verify
    e. All of the above
       ANS: E
       PG: 302

18. A(n) _____ focuses on giving a detailed and accurate description rather than explanation
    a. Ethnomethodology
    b. Naturalism
    c. Ethnography
    d. Grounded theory
    e. Case study
       ANS: C
       PG: 289

19. Which of the following exemplifies a breaching experiment?
    a. Walking into an elevator and turning to face the door.
    b. Opening an umbrella on a beautiful day.
    c. Closing an umbrella after the rain ends.
    d. Looking at the sky when birds fly by.
    e. None of the above are examples of breaching experiments.
       ANS: B
       PG: 290

20. Jamie is interested in uncovering the institutional practices that create sexism in politics. She will probably use the _____ paradigm.
    a. Naturalism
    b. Ethnomethodology
    c. Grounded theory
    d. Institutional ethnography
    e. Participatory action research
       ANS: D
       PG: 295

21. Which of the following is not part of grounded theory?
     a. Analyses of patterns
     b. Analyses of themes
     c. Analyses of common categories
     d. All of the above are part of grounded theory
     e. Only a and b are part of grounded theory
         ANS: D
         PG: 291

22. Which of the following is NOT a disadvantage of focus groups?
     a. Focus group moderators require special skills.
     b. Focus group data are easy to analyze.
     c. Focus groups are often difficult to assemble.
     d. Focus groups afford the researcher less control than individual interviews.
     e. All of the above are disadvantages of focus groups.
         ANS: E
         PG: 303

23. The qualitative field research interview is typically
     a. Unstructured
     b. Structured
     c. Similar to the survey interview
     d. A and c are correct
     e. B and c are correct
         ANS: A
         PGS: 300-302

24. Case studies should NOT be used for
     a. Descriptive purposes
     b. Explanatory purposes
     c. Idiographic purposes
     d. Nomothetic purposes
     e. Case studies can be used for any of the above purposes
         ANS: E
         PG: 293

25. Which of the following is FALSE regarding qualitative field research?
    a. Field research is well suited to studying social processes over time
    b. Field research is well suited to studying behaviors within their natural setting
    c. Field research is well suited to studying attitudes within their natural setting
    d. Field research is well suited for quantitative analysis
    e. All of the above statements are true about qualitative field research
    ANS: D
    PGS: 282-283

TRUE-FALSE QUESTIONS

1. Unstructured interviews are less appropriate for field designs than structured interviews.
   ANS: F
   PG: 300

2. The complete participant must always be a genuine member and participate in what he or she is studying.
   ANS: F
   PGS: 285-286

3. Your field notes should record what you *know* happened NOT what you *think* happened.
   ANS: F
   PG: 304

4. Qualitative field researchers must always participate in what they are studying.
   ANS: F
   PG: 286

5. The extended case study approach is a valuable technique for deciding whether to reject or approve a theory.
   ANS: F
   PG: 293

6. Researchers who assume the role of the complete participant are unlikely to affect what they are studying.
   ANS: F
   PG: 286

7. The "Convert" is more likely to run the risk of "going native" than the "Martian."
   ANS: T
   PG: 286

8. An informant is one of your colleagues who attempts to gain membership into the group being studied.
    ANS: F
    PG: 289

9. Qualitative field researchers should wait to record observations until enough time has passed to put the events in a proper perspective.
    ANS: F
    PGS: 303-304

10. Qualitative field research differs from other forms of observation in that it is both a data-collecting and a theory-generating activity.
    ANS: T
    PG: 282

11. The terms field research and participant observation are synonyms.
    ANS: F
    PG: 285

12. Specific methods do not link to specific paradigms.
    ANS: T
    PG: 289

13. Case studies may be descriptive or explanatory.
    ANS: T
    PG: 293

14. Focus group participants are typically selected via probability samples.
    ANS: F
    PG: 303

15. Field researchers are like journalists; the two share a similar relationship to data.
    ANS: F
    PG: 284

ESSAYS

1. Select a topic. Describe how a complete participant and a complete observer might study that subject.

2. In comparison to other types of research, what are the major strengths and weaknesses of qualitative field research?

3. Although there are no clear guidelines to follow, what ethical considerations should a researcher take into account when choosing which role to assume in the field?

CHAPTER 11: UNOBTRUSIVE RESEARCH

OUTLINE

I. Types
    A. Content analysis
    B. Analysis of existing statistics
    C. Historical/comparative analysis

II. Content Analysis
    A. Topics appropriate to content analysis
    B. Sampling in content analysis
        1. Units of analysis
        2. Sampling techniques
    C. Coding in content analysis
        1. Manifest and latent content
        2. Conceptualization and the creation of code categories
        3. Counting and record keeping
        4. Qualitative data analysis
    D. An illustration of content analysis
    E. Strengths and weaknesses of content analysis

III. Analyzing Existing Statistics
    A. Durkheim's study of suicide
    B. The consequences of globalization
    C. Units of analysis
    D. Problems of validity
    E. Problems of reliability
    F. Sources of existing statistics

IV. Historical/Comparative Analysis
    A. Examples of historical/comparative analysis
        1. Weber and the role of ideas
        2. Japanese religion and capitalism
    B. Sources of historical/comparative data
    C. Analytical techniques

BEHAVIORAL OBJECTIVES

Upon completion of this chapter, the student should be able to:

1. Describe and compare the three unobtrusive research designs: content analysis, analysis of existing statistics, and historical/comparative analysis.

2. Give three examples of artifacts that content analysts might study.

3. Give three examples of content analysis in which the unit of observation differs from the unit of analysis.

4. Show how the unit of analysis influences sample selection in content analysis.

5. Illustrate how a researcher might employ each of the following sampling techniques in content analysis: simple random sampling, systematic sampling, stratified sampling, and cluster sampling.

6. Differentiate manifest content from latent content by definition and example.

7. Present advice for the development of code categories in content analysis.

8. Present advice for counting and record keeping in content analysis.

9. Outline the strengths and weaknesses of content analysis.

10. Explain how analytic induction is used in qualitative content analysis.

11. Summarize the difficulties with units of analysis in existing statistics.

12. Explain why validity is a problem with existing statistics, and present two strategies for resolving this problem.

13. Explain why reliability is a problem with existing statistics, and present two strategies for resolving this problem.

14. List three sources of existing statistics.

15. List three sources of data for historical/comparative analysis.

16. Discuss the role of corroboration in enhancing the quality of existing statistics.

17. Discuss the role of verstehen and ideal types in the analysis of existing statistics.

TEACHING SUGGESTIONS AND RESOURCES

1. An exercise that enables students to combine doing content analysis with issues of conceptualization, operationalization, and sampling involves the analysis of singles columns in newspapers or magazines.

    Provide students with ads from two of the following possibilities: 1) women seeking men, 2) men seeking women, 3) women seeking women, or 4) men seeking men. Ask students to develop hypotheses about the qualities that individuals either provide about themselves or want in the person they seek. Students usually hypothesize that men are more likely to describe their appearance than are females or that females are more likely to talk about romance than males.

    Once you select a hypothesis to test, students will need to conceptualize and operationalize the terms. For example, what does "romantic" mean and how will you know if an ad is "romantic?" Then discuss how to sample the ads using probability sampling. You are now ready to do content analysis!

2. Bring the FBI Uniform Crime Statistics to class. Ask students to estimate the amount of crime that has occurred in the area containing your school. Compare their responses to those listed. Use this comparison to lead into a discussion on the issues of validity and reliability in analyzing existing statistics.

3. Bring population pyramids to class for different countries using the pyramids produced at: www.census.gov/ipc/www/idbpyr.html Be sure to select countries at different stages of development and/or with different issues. For example, ask students to compare the pyramids for the U.S., Mexico, and China. Ask what these pyramids may indicate about the countries/cultures.

INFOTRAC EXERCISES

1. Herrnstein and Murray, Inc. (Race and intelligence, The Bell Curve: Laying Bare the Resurgence of Scientific Racism.) Leonard Lieberman. *American Behavioral Scientist*, Sept-Oct 1995 v39 n1 p25(10). What are some of the objections raised regarding the use of IQ tests to measure intelligence?

2. Sexual bondage: a review and unobtrusive investigation. Kurt E. Ernulf, Sune M. Innala. *Archives of Sexual Behavior*, Dec 1995 v24 n6 p631(24). Describe the study design and key variables in this study.

3. Using the "KEYWORD" option, ask students to read a social science article that uses content analysis. Ask students to: 1) summarize the article, 2) discuss whether the analysis uses manifest or latent content analysis, and 3) describe the process that was used to do the content analysis.

4. Using the "KEYWORD" option, ask students to read a social science article that discusses content analysis and to: 1) summarize the article, 2) describe the content of the article that "duplicated" Babbie, and 3) describe what they learned about content analysis that adds to the discussion in Babbie.

INTERNET EXERCISES

1. Ask students to access the Content Analysis Resources site at: http://www.car.ua.edu/ Ask students to click on "publication alerts" and to locate and read two of the publications. Ask students to: 1) summarize the content of the publication, 2) how does the publication link to content analysis, and 3) was content analysis properly used?

2. Ask students to access the Media and Communications Site via: http://www.aber.ac.uk/media/Sections/textan01.html Ask students to read one article and to: 1) summarize the article, 2) explain how content analysis was used, 3) discuss any concerns they have about the use of content analysis in that article.

3. Ask students to access the Qualitative Data Archival link via: http://www.qualidata.essex.ac.uk/ Ask students to click on "QUALICAT," the qualitative catalogue. Tell them to select a primary discipline such as law, crime and justice or psychology or sociology or social anthropology. Ask students to 1) summarize the types of studies that are retrieved, and, 2) select three of the studies and summarize what the study was about and the type of data that was collected.

4. If you did not use the population pyramids in the "teaching suggestions" section, you can use that for a class assignment. You can either pre-select the countries or allow the students to select countries that interest them. Ask students to describe what they learn about the country from an examining its population pyramid.

MULTIPLE-CHOICE QUESTIONS

1. If we wanted to determine whether states that pass clean air legislation (no smoking in public areas) are more likely to enact laws requiring motorcyclists to wear helmets than are states that had not passed clean air legislation, the unit of analysis would be
    a. the individual states
    b. the individual act of legislation
    c. passage or nonpassage of the clean air legislation
    d. laws distinguishing between motorcyclists and auto drivers
    e. states that had passed clean air legislation
       ANS: A
       PGS: 315-318

2. Which of the following is(are) illustrative of unobtrusive observations?
    a. examining the floor tiles at a museum to determine which exhibits are the most popular
    b. examining the number of beer cans in the university garbage collections to determine beer consumption patterns
    c. examining the wear on the tires of squad cars to determine the extent of police patrols
    d. all of the above
    e. only a and c are correct
       ANS: D
       PGS: 313-314

3. In comparison to coding the manifest content of communication, coding the latent content
    a. has a disadvantage in terms of validity
    b. has an advantage in terms of reliability
    c. is better designed for tapping the underlying meaning of communication
    d. has an advantage in terms of specificity
    e. all of the above
       ANS: C
       PG: 319

4. Which of the following levels of measurement(s) may be employed in content analysis?
    a. nominal
    b. ratio
    c. interval
    d. ordinal
    e. all of the above
       ANS: E
       PG: 320

5. Which of the following modes of observation does NOT require the researcher to intrude to some degree on whatever he or she is studying?
    a. Experiments
    b. Survey
    c. Complete participant observation
    d. Complete observer
    e. All of the above require the researcher to intrude
        ANS: D
        PG: 313

6. Professor Perlman was interested in comparing two textbooks to determine whether one used more sexist language than the other. Perlman counted the number of times a gender reference (ex: "he," "she," "chairman," etc.) appeared in each book. Perlman was doing
    a. latent content coding
    b. manifest content coding
    c. quota sampling
    d. the ecological fallacy
    e. base counting
        ANS: B
        PG: 319

7. Professor Perlman, from the previous question, found that textbook A contained the word *he* 80 times and that textbook B contained it 20 times. In addition, textbook A used the word *chairman* 16 times, and textbook B used it only 4 times. Perlman was correct in concluding that
    a. textbook A was four times as sexist as textbook B
    b. textbook B was one-fourth as sexist as textbook A
    c. the words *he* and *chairman* appeared four times more in textbook A than in textbook B
    d. textbook A was more sexist than textbook B
    e. all of the above
        ANS: C
        PG: 320

8. A friend of yours is doing a term paper to compare the infant mortality rates in the United States, Japan, Bolivia, and Pakistan. You tell your friend that a good source to check is
    a. *Common Cause*
    b. the *Demographic Yearbook*
    c. the *Statistical Abstract of the United States*
    d. the Gallup poll
    e. the *Almanac*
        ANS: B
        PG: 330

9. A friend of yours was interested in determining whether the news media picked up on campus events. Your friend decided to do a content analysis of the local paper. Your friend counted each story that mentioned his university's name. At the end of two months, 136 events had been counted. Your friend asked for your comments on his research. You told your friend
    a. he did manifest coding
    b. he did latent coding
    c. he should have recorded the base
    d. only a and c are correct
    e. only b and c are correct
        ANS: D
        PGS: 319-320

10. You are interested in doing a content analysis of the types of merchandise listed in the garage sale classifieds. Your unit of analysis is
    a. the newspaper
    b. the type of merchandise
    c. the individual garage sale ad
    d. the classified section of the paper
    e. the reader
        ANS: C
        PGS: 315-317

11. Coding in content analysis DOES NOT involve
    a. conceptualization
    b. operationalization
    c. selecting a level of measurement
    d. deductive methods
    e. it involves all of the above
        ANS: E
        PGS: 318-320

12. The adage that you must walk a mile in another person's shoes before judging the person is similar to the sociological concept(s) of
    a. verstehen
    b. historical/comparative analysis
    c. ideal types
    d. the ecological fallacy
    e. content analysis
        ANS: A
        PG: 336

13. After examining the FBI Crime Reports for a 30-year period, Professor Hall claimed that the incidence of rape has increased. After examining the same reports, Professor Shine claimed that the reporting of rape, not the incidence of rape, has increased. This illustrates
     a. the problem of reliability in using existing statistics
     b. the problem of validity in using existing statistics
     c. the need to replicate existing statistics
     d. the ecological fallacy
     e. pre-testing
         ANS: A
         PGS: 327-328

14. The categories used in content analysis codes should be:
     a. Mutually exclusive
     b. Exhaustive
     c. Nominal
     d. All of the above
     e. A and b only are correct
         ANS: E
         PG: 320

15. An example of unobtrusive data collection is(are)
     a. an interview with college freshmen to determine why they selected a particular school
     b. a laboratory experiment designed to determine whether people really prefer Pepsi or Coke
     c. a mailed survey designed to discern students' attitudes toward a planned change in the school's calendar
     d. a researcher who joins a fraternity to understand its rituals
     e. none of the above are unobtrusive
         ANS: E
         PGS: 313-314

16. Professor Jenner was interested in using Census Bureau data to examine the trend in unemployment rates in the United States. However, Jenner's definition of unemployment did not match the one used by the Census Bureau. Jenner was dealing with the issue of
     a. reliability
     b. validity
     c. the ecological fallacy
     d. ideal types
     e. verstehen
         ANS: B
         PG: 327

17. The possibility that patterns of behavior at a group level do not reflect corresponding patterns on an individual level is known as
     a. an ecological fallacy
     b. replication
     c. verstehen
     d. unobtrusive measurement
     e. hermeneutics
         ANS: A
         PG: 327

18. In which of the following analyses is content analysis LEAST likely to be useful?
     a. themes in newspaper editorials
     b. the wording of this exam
     c. topics covered in class lectures
     d. the theme of love as discussed in song
     e. dating patterns among high school seniors
         ANS: E
         PGS: 313-314

19. Unobtrusive measures can reduce the problem(s) of
     a. the researcher's impact on the phenomenon being studied
     b. invalid operationalization of concepts
     c. unreliable measurements
     d. corroboration
     e. the ecological fallacy
         ANS: A
         PG: 313

20. Using existing statistics, Professor Ford finds that towns with low median incomes tend to have higher crime rates than towns with high median incomes. Ford concludes that poor people are more likely to commit crimes than people with high incomes. Ford is
     a. Committing the ecological fallacy
     b. Using verstehen
     c. Doing content analysis
     d. Developing ideal types
     e. Doing replication
         ANS: A
         PG: 327

21. Joe thinks that men who place classified ads seeking women are more likely to describe probability sampling for his research. He should use
    a. Simple random sampling
    b. Cluster sampling
    c. Quota sampling
    d. Stratified sampling
    e. Any one of the above is okay
    ANS: D
    PG: 318

22. Weaknesses of content analysis is(are)
    a. If you make an error in coding, you must recode all of your data
    b. A researcher cannot use it to study change over time
    c. Its use influences that which is being studied
    d. All of the above are weaknesses of content analysis
    e. None of the above are weaknesses of content analysis
    ANS: A
    PG: 323

23. Existing statistics can be used
    a. As the main data for social scientific inquiry
    b. To provide a historical context for research
    c. To provide a conceptual context for research
    d. As a supplemental source of data for social scientific inquiry
    e. To do any of the above
    ANS: E
    PG: 324

TRUE-FALSE QUESTIONS

1. Unobtrusive measures reduce the impact of the researcher on the phenomena being studied.
   ANS: T
   PG: 313

2. Content analysis can be done on newspaper materials and government documents but NOT on diaries and letters.
   ANS: F
   PG: 314

3.   Logical reasoning and replication are used to handle the problem of validity in the
      analysis of existing statistics.
      ANS: T
      PG: 327

4.   As a mode of observation, content analysis is essentially a coding operation.
      ANS: T
      PG: 318

5.   A researcher using official government documents need not be concerned about the
      reliability of those records.
      ANS: F
      PGS: 327-328

6.   An ideal type is a conceptual model composed of the essential characteristics of social
      phenomena.
      ANS: T
      PG: 336

7.   In content analysis the units of observation and the unit of analysis are the same.
      ANS: F
      PGS: 315-316

8.   Many existing statistics can be found on the World Wide Web.
      ANS: T
      PGS: 329-330

9.   In data collection and analysis, the determination of the unit of analysis occurs after
      sampling.
      ANS: F
      PG: 315

10.   Standard probability sampling techniques should NOT be used in content analysis.
      ANS: F
      PG: 318

11.   All content analysis involves counting.
      ANS: F
      PG: 321

12. Unobtrusive research cannot be quantitative research
    ANS: F
    PG: 313

13. Sample selection depends on what the unit of analysis is
    ANS: T
    PG: 315

14. Secondary analysis is synonymous with the analysis of existing statistics.
    ANS: F
    PG: 324

ESSAYS

1. What is the difference between the unit of observation and the unit of analysis in content analysis? Give an example of a research study in which the two are different, and give an example of another study in which they are the same.

2. Describe a study for which content analysis is the appropriate research method. Discuss how you would use manifest and latent coding. Discuss the advantages and disadvantages of the two coding schemes.

3. Describe a study for which the analysis of existing statistics is the appropriate research method. What source would you use? What problems might you encounter, and how would you resolve them?

CHAPTER 12: EVALUATION RESEARCH

OUTLINE

I. Topics Appropriate To Evaluation Research

II. Formulating the Problem: Issues of Measurement
   A. Specifying outcomes
   B. Measuring experimental contexts
   C. Specifying interventions
   D. Specifying the population
   E. New versus existing measures
   F. Operationalizing success/failure

III. Types of Evaluation Research Designs
   A. Experimental designs
   B. Quasi-experimental designs
      1. Time-series designs
      2. Nonequivalent control groups
      3. Multiple time-series designs
   C. Qualitative evaluations

IV. The Social Context
   A. Logistical problems
      1. Motivating sailors example
      2. Administrative control
   B. Some ethical issues
   C. Use of research results
      1. Rape reform legislation
      2. Preventing wife battering

V. Social Indicators Research
   A. The death penalty and deterrence example
   B. Computer simulation

BEHAVIORAL OBJECTIVES

Upon completion of this chapter, the student should be able to:

1. Identify the purposes of evaluation research.

2. Identify three factors influencing the growth of evaluation research.
3. Define and illustrate social intervention.

4.   Describe why it is important to identify the purpose of an intervention.

5.   Define and illustrate the outcome (or response) variable.

6.   Give three examples of experimental contexts that may influence specific evaluation research studies.

7.   Describe two problems with specifying interventions.

8.   Explain why it is important to define the population of possible subjects for whom the program is appropriate.

9.   Compare the two options for measuring variables.

10.   Provide advice for operationalizing success or failure of an intervention.

11.   Apply the classical experimental design to an evaluation research study.

12.   Define quasi-experimental designs.

13.   Define and illustrate time-series designs.

14.   Define and illustrate nonequivalent control group designs.

15.   Define and illustrate multiple time-series designs.

16.   Define and illustrate cost-benefit analysis.

17.   Show how evaluation research can be less structured and more qualitative.

18.   Discuss why evaluation research is particularly subject to problems in the actual execution of the research.

19.   Summarize three reasons why the implications of evaluation research are not always put into practice.

20.   Define and illustrate social indicators research.

21.   Define and illustrate computer simulation.

TEACHING SUGGESTIONS AND RESOURCES

1. Because the end product of evaluation research is typically a final report, invite a technical writing expert to speak to your class about the format for technical reports. To locate such a person, check the English department.

2. Divide students into small groups and ask them to design a study to assess the effectiveness of this class. This will lead quite naturally into a discussion of the intended results of the course, designs, and so on.

3. Ask students to critique an article which appeared on June 9, 1996 in the *Boston Globe* that reported on how the state of New Jersey stopped giving additional welfare payments to women who had more than one child while they were on welfare. State that the new policy started for women going onto the welfare roles as of August 1993 and that it attempted to reduce the number of births for women on welfare. Tell students that the state data showed a 12% reduction in birthrate for welfare mothers. However, social researchers reported no difference in the birthrate of welfare mothers who were subjected to the new policy and those who were not. Ask students:
    1. What design was used?
    2. Was this the best design under the circumstances?
    3. Did the program work?
    4. What additional information is needed to evaluate the findings?
    5. What ethical considerations does this raise?

4. FILMS

Dimensions of Applied Sociology
34 min. Color. 1983. Dept. of Sociology, Univ. of Minnesota.
Available in beta, VHS, and 3/4" U-matic cassette.
Focuses on people who are employed as sociologists in private and public agencies. Each participant describes the role of his or her employer in the community, examines the role(s) of sociologists in the employing organization, and is shown working on one or more specified projects.

POSSIBLE ANSWERS TO STUDY GUIDE QUESTIONS

Exercise 12.1
1. The intervention can be measured in terms of how much of the workbook was used. For each section, an average score could be determined for the proportion of items completed. Or the analysis could be limited to only one or a few chapters.

Outcomes might include ability to define terms, ability to apply concepts and principles, ability to design a study, ability to critique a study, and the like. Such outcomes could be measured in a test situation or by completing exercises similar to those in the workbook.

Contexts might include whether the exercises (and other sections) were assigned or not, whether the instructor provided practice in class with similar questions or exercises, whether completion of the exercises factored in the grades assigned, the size of the class, the level of individual feedback provided, whether the questions and exercises were completed individually or in groups of students, and so on.

2.   Most students will probably select the classical design or approximations to it. Randomly assign students to two groups. Give a pretest on knowledge to be obtained from two chapters. Include both factual and applied questions (make sure students supply examples). For the experimental group, have students complete all questions and exercises. The control group only reads the chapters. Give a posttest and analyze results. Students may decide to use the static group comparison design if two preestablished classes of students are used. In either case, make sure students explain how some of the experimental context variables will be controlled. This can be accomplished most easily by the instructions given by the instructor.

3.   Logistical problems might include unknown levels of cooperation among students in completing the exercises and questions, one class complaining when they find out that the other class does not have to do the extra work (although the design could provide for similar but equivalent interventions, itself a contaminating factor), inability to assign students randomly, interference from administrators, overwork on the instructor's part, having to use two classes with different instructors, and so on.

Ethical problems might include giving differential amounts of work for the same credit, altered grades due to the extra work (some students may get higher grades and some lower grades as a result of being in the experimental group), the change in the grading curve the experiment may produce, the control group may be deprived of a more complete educational experience, the experiment may encourage some students to cheat, lack of voluntary participation and informed consent, and so on.

4.   Results will vary.

Exercise 12.3
1.   Answers will vary. Students may note the following indicators: number of books in the library; average salary of professors; percentage of faculty with terminal degree; number of student organizations; level of student involvement in decision making; availability of legal, medical, and counseling services; proportion of graduates who go on to graduate or professional school; number of parking spots reserved for students, and so on.

INFOTRAC EXERCISES

1.   Can teacher evaluation reflect holistic instruction? Lyndon W. Searfoss, Billie J. Enz. *Educational Leadership*, March 1996 v53 n6 p38(4). What are some of the non-scientific factors involved in the evaluation of teaching quality, reflected in this paper?

2. Ranking research doctorate programs in political science. Includes ranking, departmental rankings: much ado about something? *Political Science and Politics*, June 1996 v29 n2 p 144(2). What were some of the dimensions of quality used in ranking doctoral programs?

3. Using the "KEYWORD" option, ask students to read a social science article on evaluation research. Ask students to: 1) summarize the article, 2) discuss why evaluation research was used, 3) describe the type of design that was used, 4) discuss whether the researcher(s) encountered any logistical or ethical problems and if so, how these were resolved.

4. Using the "KEYWORD" option, ask students to read a social science article that focuses on social indicators. Ask student to: 1) summarize the article, 2) describe the social indicator(s) that were used, 3) describe whether the author(s) discussed the reliability and validity of the indicators and if, so how the reliability and validity of the indicators were assessed.

INTERNET EXERCISES

1. Ask students to access the American Evaluation Association's website via:
http://www.eval.org/EvaluationDocuments/aeaprin6.html
This is the address for the AEA Guiding Principles for Evaluators. Ask students to comment on the major categories used in the guidelines. What obstacles might they encounter in following these guidelines while trying to do a valid and reliable evaluation?

2. Ask students to access the Bureau of Justice Assistance Evaluation Web Site at:
http://www.bja.evaluationwebsite.org/
Ask students to click on the "electronic roadmap for evaluation" and ask them to "go through" the roadmap. Ask students to summarize: 1) what new information they obtained from the site, and 2) what information confirmed that which they learned from Babbie.

3. Ask students to go to the Harvard Family Research Project site using:
http://gseweb.harvard.edu/~hfrp/index.html
Ask students to click on "research areas" and to select one of the listed areas. Ask students to 1) describe the selected project, and 2) describe why the selected project is an applied project.

MULTIPLE-CHOICE QUESTIONS

1. Which of the following would NOT be appropriate for measurement in evaluation research?
   a. dependent variable(s)
   b. the experimental context
   c. the outcome(s) of the experiment
   d. the independent variable(s)
   e. all of the above should be measured
      ANS: E
      PGS: 345-347

2. Which of the following is(are) FALSE regarding time-series designs?
   a. They enable detection of whether a process of maturation could be at work.
   b. Regular fluctuations that occur apart from the experimental stimulus can be identified.
   c. They protect against the possible influence of some extraneous factor.
   d. They involve multiple observations at different points in time.
   e. All of the above are true.
      ANS: C
      PG: 350

3. After the delivery of their baby, new parents in hospital A were given a poison control test. While at the hospital they attended a training session on poison control. At the end of a week, they were given the poison control test again. After the delivery of their baby, new parents in hospital B were given the poison control test. One week later they were given the test again. What kind of design is being used?
   a. pretest-posttest control group
   b. time-series
   c. nonequivalent control group
   d. cross-sectional design
   e. multiple time-series
      ANS: C
      PGS: 350-351

4. Creating new measures for variables in evaluation research has the advantage of
   a. greater possible relevance and validity to the study
   b. having known degrees of reliability
   c. enabling comparisons with other measures
   d. being less time-consuming than using an already devised measure
   e. more precision
      ANS: A
      PG: 347

5. One of the exciting prospects for social indicators research is in the area of computer simulation because
    a. one day it will be possible to test the implications of specific social changes by computer rather than real life
    b. when contemplating the introduction of an intervention, it will be possible to get a description of all the direct and indirect consequences of it
    c. it provides a means for us to know whether or not a specific alteration may make life better
    d. planners can quickly examine different plans
    e. all of the above
        ANS: E
        PGS: 363-364

6. Although some research indicates that the depiction of violence on TV has no effect on children, many parents still screen their children's TV selections to prevent the selection of violent programs. From a methodologists perspective, parents probably ignore the implication of this research because
    a. they may not understand the research
    b. the research may contradict deeply held beliefs
    c. logistical problems enter
    d. administrative control interferes
    e. only a and b are correct
        ANS: E
        PG: 357

7. Producers of TV shows that depict violence often ignore the studies that indicate that children who watch violence are more likely to be aggressive, have fewer friends, and have poorer relationships with their parents than children who do not watch violent shows. The producers of the violent TV shows are most likely to ignore the implications because
    a. they did not understand the researcher
    b. the findings contradict deeply held beliefs
    c. the findings conflict with the producers' vested interests
    d. logistical problems
    e. administrative control interferes
        ANS: C
        PG: 357

8. A friend of yours was asked to evaluate the effect of an advertisement campaign designed to get people to have their blood pressure checked. After examining the records kept by the blood pressure units in the target area, your friend showed you the following graph where X indicates an observation.

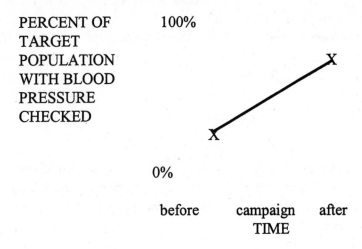

PERCENT OF TARGET POPULATION WITH BLOOD PRESSURE CHECKED

What will you tell your friend?
a. The ad campaign is producing the intended effect.
b. The independent variable, the campaign, is having an effect on the dependent variable, the percent having their blood pressure checked.
c. More observations are needed to determine whether the independent variable is having the intended effect.
d. The ad campaign has no effect.
e. only a and b are correct.
    ANS: C
    PGS: 349-350

9. The denominator in a per capita rate is
a. 1,000
b. the size of the population
c. the size of the sample
d. the GNP
e. the number of households in the population
    ANS: B
    PG: 362

10. If gun control legislation were passed to reduce the number of homicides, which of the
     following graphs would be most likely to convince you that the legislation was producing
     the intended effect? Note that in all graphs the horizontal axis (*x* axis) is time, the vertical
     axis (*y* axis) is number of homicides, and the □ indicates an observation.

a. Hi

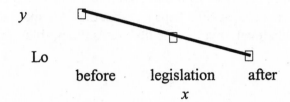

b. Hi

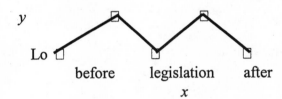

c. Hi

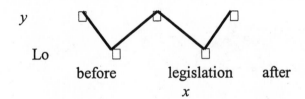

d. Hi

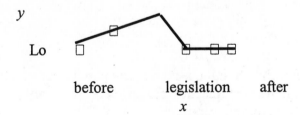

e. none of the above
    ANS: D
    PGS: 349-350

11.   You examined the IQ scores of children at several high schools. You finally select two high schools where the children appear similar in terms of IQ scores, family income, family religion, and the like. You then matched two classes from each grade (9 to 12) from each high school. In one high school you plan to offer a course on study skills in the selected classes and in the other high school you plan to have students follow their "normal" curriculum. After obtaining permission from the principals, parents, and children to do your research, you arrive at the first school to begin the study skills class. You find that the classes you had selected are on field trips and that the principal has assigned another class of the same grade level to you. This illustrates the problem(s) of
    a.   logistics
    b.   administrative control
    c.   ethics
    d.   all of the above
    e.   only a and b are correct
       ANS: D
       PGS: 355-357

12.   The design being used in the previous question is
    a.   the time-series
    b.   the multiple time-series
    c.   the nonequivalent control group design
    d.   the posttest-only control group design
    e.   the one-shot case study
       ANS: C
       PGS: 350-351

13.   The experimental stimulus in the prior question is
    a.   The selected high schools
    b.   The selected classes within each high school
    c.   The similarity of the schools on family income and religion
    d.   IQ
    e.   The study skills class
       ANS: E
       PG: 346

14.   Professor Simon was asked to evaluate the effectiveness of a new parenting seminar. After accepting the job, Professor Simon's first question(s) was(were) probably
    a.   "What is the intended result of the parenting seminar?"
    b.   "What are the anticipated outcomes of the parenting seminar?"
    c.   "What are the unanticipated outcomes of the parenting seminar?"
    d.   All of the above are correct.
    e.   only a and b are correct.
       ANS: E
       PG: 344

15. The national speed limit in the United States was reduced to 55 mph in 1974. Proponents
     and critics of this legislation have looked at the number of traffic fatalities on each of the
     major U.S. highways (e.g., I-90, I-65, I-75) for the years preceding and following this
     legislation. The examination of traffic fatalities on various highways illustrates the use of
     a. pretest-posttest one-group design
     b. the time-series design
     c. the multiple time-series design
     d. the nonequivalent control group design
     e. the one-shot case study
         ANS: C
         PGS: 351-352

16. Professor Henley is interested in comparing the use of the legal system in different
     countries. Henley examines the number of arrests per 1,000 population, the number of
     jury trials per 1,000 court cases, the number of lawyers per capita, and the number of
     people incarcerated per 1,000 population. Henley is doing
     a. social indicator research
     b. cost/benefit analysis
     c. time-series designs
     d. computer simulations
     e. intervention analysis
         ANS: A
         PG: 362

17. Which of the following topics would be appropriate for evaluation research?
     a. Examining whether fee reductions at the local swimming pool increases pool use.
     b. Examining whether women who get mammograms detect breast cancer earlier than
         women who do not.
     c. Examining whether changes in speed limits influence traffic fatalities.
     d. Examining whether the use of mediation in divorces results in "fairer" settlements.
     e. All of the above are appropriate topics for evaluation research
         ANS: E
         PG: 343

18. Social indicators research combines
     a. Evaluation research with interviewing
     b. Evaluation research with the analysis of existing data
     c. The analysis of existing data with questionnaires
     d. The analysis of existing data with the historical/comparative approach
     e. Evaluation research with the historical/comparative approach
         ANS: B
         PG: 362

19. In a study that examined whether the use of mediation in divorces results in "fairer" settlements, the intervention is
    a. The use of mediation
    b. The "fairer" settlement
    c. The actual divorce
    d. The judge's decision
    e. Cannot tell from the given information
    ANS: A
    PGS: 345-346

20. Using the information in question #19, the "outcome" is
    a. The use of mediation
    b. The "fairer" settlement
    c. The actual divorce
    d. The judge's decision
    e. Cannot tell from the given information
    ANS: B
    PGS: 345-346

TRUE-FALSE QUESTIONS

1. Only quasi-experimental designs should be used in evaluation research.
   ANS: F
   PG: 348

2. Evaluation research as a scientific undertaking is a matter of finding out whether something happened or didn't happen.
   ANS: T
   PGS: 343-344

3. Computer simulations are based on mathematical equations describing the relationships that link variables.
   ANS: T
   PG: 363

4. Operationalization is not necessary in evaluation research.
   ANS: F
   PG: 344

5. Cost/benefit analysis is an easy way to assess whether a program succeeded or failed.
   ANS: F
   PGS: 347-348

6. Social indicators research often uses existing statistics.
    ANS: T
    PG: 362

7. Intersocietal comparisons are facilitated by calculating per capita rates.
    ANS: T
    PG: 362

8. Applied research is a form of evaluation research.
    ANS: F
    PG: 343

9. Another name for the experimental stimulus in evaluation research is program intervention.
    ANS: T
    PG: 346

10. Although quasi-experimental designs do not randomly assign subjects to experimental and control groups, they do have control groups.
    ANS: F
    PGS: 349-350

ESSAYS

1. Evaluation research, because it occurs within real life, has special problems. What are some of these problems?

2. What is meant by social indicators research? Give an outline of an original study showing how this type of research would be used.

3. What makes formulating the problem especially difficult in evaluation research? What suggestions are offered for dealing with this issue?

4. If you did not use the teaching suggestion from the *Boston Globe* listed earlier in this chapter, you could use it as an essay question.

CHAPTER 13: QUALITATIVE DATA ANALYSIS

OUTLINE

I.   Linking Theory and Analysis
    A. Discovering patterns
    B. Grounded theory method
    C. Semiotics
    D. Conversation analysis

II. Qualitative Data Processing
    A. Coding
        1. Coding units
        2. Coding as a physical act
        3. Creating codes
    B. Memoing
    C. Concept mapping

III. Computer Programs for Qualitative Data
    A. Leviticus as seen through NUD*IST
    B. Sandrine Zerbib: Understanding women film directors

IV. The Qualitative Analysis of Quantitative Data

BEHAVIORAL OBJECTIVES

1. Define and illustrate qualitative analysis.

2. Compare the connection between data analysis and theory in both qualitative research and quantitative research.

3. Illustrate these ways of looking for patterns in a particular research topic: frequencies, magnitudes, structures, processes, causes, and consequences.

4. Compare the two strategies of cross-case analysis: variable-oriented analysis and case-oriented analysis.

5. Describe the four stages of the constant comparative method used in the grounded theory method.

6.   Define and illustrate semiotics.

7.   Define and illustrate conversation analysis.

8.   Show how coding works in qualitative analysis.

9.   Explain why standardization is a key principle in quantitative analysis but not so in qualitative analysis.

10. Define open coding.

11. Summarize the role of memoing in qualitative data analysis and compare these types: code notes, theoretical notes, and operational notes.

12. Compare these types of memos: elemental, sorting, and integrating.

13. Explain the role of concept mapping.

14. Show how computers can be used in qualitative data analysis.

15. Illustrate how the qualitative analysis of quantitative data is useful.

TEACHING SUGGESTIONS AND RESOURCES

1. Assign Gregory M. Matoesian's article, (1995) "Language, Law, and Society: Policy Implications of the Kennedy Smith Rape Trial" *Law and Society Review*: 29 (4): 669-701. In this article Matoesian does conversation analysis of "trial talk."

2. Have students examine U.S. Supreme Court rulings. They can use these decisions to practice coding, and memoing.

INFOTRAC EXERCISES

1. Using the "KEYWORD" option, ask students to read an article that interests them that uses semiotics. Ask students to: 1) summarize the article, 2) indicate what signs were analyzed, and 3) how the researchers learned about the meanings attached the signs.

2. Using the "KEYWORD" option, ask students to read a social science article that interests them that uses or describes conversation analysis. Ask students to: 1) summarize the article, 2)

describe how conversation analysis was used, and 3) discuss whether other techniques of analysis were used.

3. If you have not used INFOTRAC Exercise #1 suggested in Chapter 1, you could assign it here.

INTERNET EXERCISES

1. Ask students to go to the following site on concept mapping:
http://trochim.human.cornell.edu/kb/conmap.htm
After reading the material on the site, ask students to: 1) summarize what they read, and 2) apply it to an area that interests them.

2. See the INTERNET exercises that were suggested for Chapters 10 and 11. Several of these might be useful here, if you have not already used them.

MULTIPLE-CHOICE QUESTIONS

1. Professor Wang is interested in looking at the grandparent – grandchild relationship. Wang wonders whether grandparents assume different roles when providing care to grandchildren. That is, are some grandparents very distant from the grandchildren while others become surrogate parents? According to the Lofland's scheme, Wang is focusing on:
   a. Frequencies
   b. Causes
   c. Processes
   d. Structures
   e. Magnitudes
      ANS: E
      PG: 371

2. If Wang from the previous question decided to look at whether grandparents who have grandchildren living with them later obtain custody of the grandchildren and then later adopt the grandchildren, Wang would be looking at:
   a. Frequencies
   b. Causes
   c. Processes
   d. Structures
   e. Magnitudes
      ANS: C
      PG: 371

3. Which of the following is TRUE of variable-oriented analysis?
    a. It is similar to the idiographic model of explanation
    b. It assumes that the researcher can predict every individual's behavior
    c. It assumes that the researcher can explain one person's motivations in full
    d. It provides a partial explanation of overall orientations and actions
    e. All of the above are true
        ANS: D
        PG: 371

4. Which of the following statements is TRUE about the grounded theory method?
    a. It is similar to case-oriented analysis
    b. It is similar to variable-oriented analysis
    c. It is similar to cross-case analysis
    d. Depending upon the topic of study it could be similar to either a, b, or c
    e. None of the above is true
        ANS: C
        PG: 372

5. The grounded theory method begins with
    a. Hypotheses
    b. Patterns
    c. Observations
    d. Theory
    e. Any one of the above
        ANS: C
        PG: 372

6. Professor Dahl was using a computer program to help analyze his data. Dahl created a node called "friendship" and then created a node called "same-sex" and another node called "opposite-sex" under "friendship." Dahl was creating
    a. Tree nodes
    b. Free nodes
    c. Memoing
    d. Concept mapping
    e. Semiotic
        ANS: A
        PGS: 388-389

7. Professor Cay notes that respondent Mary Ginger is a 54 year old grandmother who has two grandchildren living in her household. Neither of the grandchildren's parents live with them although Mary is the maternal grandmother. Cay also learns that Ginger had to quit her job in order to stay home with the young grandchildren because Ginger feared leaving the two youngsters with a baby-sitter or in child care. Two of Ginger's friends were dealing with similar situations and a third friend was considering whether to obtain custody of her grandchild. Thus, Cay learned that Ginger wasn't feeling "alone" in caring for her grandchildren. Using this information alone, it sounds like Professor Cay is doing
   a. A case-oriented nomothetic analysis
   b. A case-oriented idiographic analysis
   c. A variable-oriented nomothetic analysis
   d. A variable-oriented idiographic analysis
   e. A cross-case analysis
      ANS: B
      PG: 371

8. If Cay from the previous question began to look at other grandparent respondents to examine their child care and employment concerns, Cay would be doing
   a. semiotics
   b. variable-oriented analysis
   c. case-oriented analysis
   d. theory
   e. cross-case analysis
      ANS: E
      PG: 372

9. Semiotics is a social science because
   a. Meanings are inherent in signs
   b. Meanings reside in people's minds
   c. A particular sign may have a particular meaning to a particular person
   d. We have agreements about the meanings associated with particular signs
   e. All of the above is true
      ANS: D
      PG: 373

10. Qualitative research may be undertaken for
   a. Descriptive purposes
   b. The construction of an ethnography
   c. Explanatory purposes
   d. All of the above are correct
   e. A and b only are correct
      ANS: D
      PG: 370

11.   The following exemplifies:

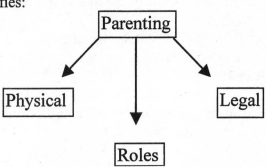

a. Memoing
b. Concept mapping
c. Grounded theory
d. Semiotic
e. Coding
      ANS: B
      PGS: 380-381

12.   Jeremy was born in 1948 and grew up during the 1960's. He was sent to Viet Nam in 1967. In Viet Nam he was horrified by what he saw and when he returned home he suffered sleepless nights and nightmares. He began to work at a bank but often fell asleep during the day. He met Mary, another bank employee, in 1980 and they married in 1981. They divorced in 1983. Mary could not cope with Jeremy's nightmares, bouts of depression, and bouts with alcohol. After the divorce, Jeremy's depression increased and began to drink even more heavily. He was fired from his job in the latter part of 1983. As an explanation for Jeremy's job loss, this could be termed
a. Idiographic and case-oriented analysis
b. Idiographic and variable-oriented analysis
c. Nomothetic and case-oriented analysis
d. Nomothetic and variable-oriented analysis
e. Cannot tell from the given information
      ANS: A
      PG: 371

13.   If a researcher examined Jeremy's story (from the prior question) and then looked at other people "like" Jeremy in order to develop a theory about job loss and veterans, the researcher would be
a. Using inductive reasoning
b. Using a cross-case method approach
c. Developing grounded theory
d. All of the above
e. Only b and c are correct
      ANS: D
      PG: 372

14. Which of the following is NOT one of the four stages of the constant comparative method?
    a. Comparing incidents applicable to each category
    b. Integrating categories and their properties
    c. Delimiting the theory
    d. Writing theory
    e. All of the above are stages in the constant comparative method
    ANS: E
    PGS: 372-373

15. Professor Lip was interested in why grandparents went to court to obtain custody of their grandchildren. One of the grandparents that Lip talked with commented on the issue of "parental neglect" of the grandchild. Once the issue of neglect had been identified, Lip began to notice that other grandparents also used the concept of "parental neglect" to explain why they had a legal relationship with their grandchild. Lip was
    a. Comparing incidents applicable to each category
    b. Integrating categories and their properties
    c. Delimiting the theory
    d. Writing theory
    e. All of the above
    ANS: A
    PG: 372

16. In the Lofland's terms, Professor Lip, from the prior question, was interested in examining which of the following ways of looking for patterns?
    a. Frequencies
    b. Magnitudes
    c. Causes
    d. Consequences
    e. Processes
    ANS: C
    PGS: 370-371

17. In reading Court decisions, Professor Wofford notices that the decisions typically discuss the "rational male." Wofford begins to write notes in which she ruminates about the notion of the rational male as well as why the concept of the rational female is not mentioned. Wofford's memos are
    a. Code notes
    b. Operational notes
    c. Theoretical notes
    d. Integrating memos
    e. All of the above
    ANS: C
    PG: 380

18. Which of the following statements is (are) FALSE regarding semiotic analysis?
    a. There is no meaning inherent in any sign
    b. Language is the only sign system of interest to those doing semiotic analysis
    c. Meanings reside in minds
    d. Semiotics is concerned with our agreements about meanings
    e. All of the above are true regarding semiotic analysis
       ANS: B
       PGS: 373-375

19. Code notes
    a. Cover reflections about the dimensions of concepts
    b. Cover relationships among concepts
    c. Identify the code labels and their meanings
    d. Discuss the deeper meanings of concepts
    e. Do all of the above
       ANS: C
       PG: 380

20. Which of the following statements is (are) TRUE?
    a. Concept mapping is appropriate for qualitative analysis only
    b. Concept mapping can be used for either quantitative or qualitative analysis
    c. Concept mapping is appropriate for quantitative analysis only
    d. Computers cannot be used for qualitative research
    e. Memos should only be used in qualitative research
       ANS: B
       PGS: 380-381

21. Qualitative researchers DO NOT use the computer to
    a. Record and store data
    b. "Find" or "search" text for passages containing key words
    c. Typing code words alongside passages in your notes so that they can later search for those keywords.
    d. Analyze data
    e. Qualitative researchers use the computer to do all of the above
       ANS: E
       PGS: 381-382

TRUE FALSE QUESTIONS

1. Qualitative and quantitative analyses are incompatible
    ANS: F
    PG: 391

2. Data collection, analysis, and theory are more intimately intertwined in qualitative analysis than in quantitative analysis.
    ANS: T
    PG: 370

3. Qualitative research is undertaken for descriptive purposes never for explanatory purposes.
    ANS: F
    PG: 370

4. Variable-oriented research is similar to the nomothetic model of explanation.
    ANS: T
    PG: 371

5. The utility of case-oriented analysis is the fact that one case can make theory.
    ANS: F
    PG: 372

6. Conversational analysts look only at the structure of communication.
    ANS: F
    PG: 375

7. Qualitative data processing is both a science and an art.
    ANS: T
    PG: 375

8. It is as important to identify the standardized unit for coding in qualitative analysis as it is in quantitative analysis.
    ANS: F
    PG: 376

9. Concept mapping is appropriate for both qualitative and quantitative analysis.
    ANS: T
    PG: 381

10. The search for the intentional or unintentional meanings attached to signs is called semiotics.
ANS: T
PG: 373

Essays

1. Define what is meant by variable-oriented analysis and what is meant by case-oriented analysis. Give an example of a research project in which you would use variable-oriented analysis and one where you would use case-oriented analysis.

2. Define what is meant by qualitative analysis and what is meant by quantitative analysis. What are the differences between the two forms of analysis? Are there similarities between the two? If so, describe some of the similarities. If no, why not?

3. Describe how coding, memoing, and concept mapping are used in qualitative analysis.

CHAPTER 14: QUANTITATIVE DATA ANALYSIS

OUTLINE

I. Quantification of data
    A. Developing code categories
    B. Codebook construction
    C. Data Entry

II. Univariate Analysis
    A. Distributions
    B. Central tendency
    C. Dispersion
    D. Continuous and discrete variables
    E. Detail versus manageability

III. Subgroup Comparisons
    A. "Collapsing" response categories
    B. Handling "don't knows"
    C. Numerical descriptions in qualitative research

IV. Bivariate Analysis
    A. Percentaging a table
    B. Constructing and reading bivariate tables

V. Introduction to Multivariate Analysis

BEHAVIORAL OBJECTIVES

Upon completion of this chapter, the student should be able to:

1. Define quantitative analysis.

2. Describe the coding process and compare two approaches to developing code categories.

3. Offer some advice for coding a set of data.

4. Identify two functions of codebooks.

5.   Present some of the common elements in codebook formats.

6.   Describe several ways for entering data.

7.   Define and give examples of univariate analysis.

8.   Define and explain the utility of frequency distributions and marginals.

9.   Explain how to calculate percentages.

10. Define central tendency.

11. Compare the mode, mean, and median in terms of calculation and interpretation.

12. Describe the information provided by measures of dispersion.

13. Compare the range, standard deviation, and interquartile range in terms of calculation and interpretation.

14. Distinguish continuous variables from discrete variables by definition and example.

15. Provide guidelines for balancing the demands of detail versus manageability of data presentation.

16. Differentiate the goals of univariate, bivariate, and multivariate analyses.

17. Identify the goal of subgroup comparisons.

18. Explain two techniques for handling the "don't know" response.

19. Differentiate dependent variable from independent variable by definition and example.

20. Describe how bivariate tables are presented and analyzed.

21. Explain how multivariate tables are presented and analyzed.

TEACHING SUGGESTIONS AND RESOURCES

1. Distribute the following table and ask students to interpret it. The table is from Bullock, Henry Allen. 1961. "Significance of the Racial Factor in the Length of Prison Sentences." *Journal Of Criminal Law And Criminology And Police Science*, 52:411-417. For a comment

on the article's error, see Hagan, John. 1974. "Criminal Sentencing: An Assessment of a Sociological Viewpoint." *Law And Society Review*, 8:357-383.

The students should notice that the table has been percentaged in the wrong direction. That is, instead of percentaging within categories of the independent variable, race, the table was percentaged within the categories of the dependent variable, offense. Use this to illustrate that errors do appear in journals. Students must read both the text and the tables to evaluate the study.

Percent Distribution of 3,644 Prisoners According to Type of Offense, Length of Sentence, and Race

SHORT SENTENCE

OFFENSE	PERCENT NEGRO	PERCENT WHITE	TOTAL
Burglary	35.9	64.1	1141
Rape	36.3	63.7	135
Murder	62.1	37.9	702
Total	45.2	54.8	1978

LONG SENTENCE

OFFENSE	PERCENT NEGRO	PERCENT WHITE	TOTAL
Burglary	47.5	52.5	341
Rape	29.3	70.7	239
Murder	55.3	44.7	1086
Total	50.0	50.0	1666

2. FILMS

Against All Odds: Inside Statistics: see Preface for a full description.
Part 1. What is Statistics
Part 2. Picturing Distributions
Part 3. Describing Distributions: Examine the difference between mean and median and learn about quartiles, box-plots, interquartile range, and standard deviation.
Part 8. Describing Relationships
Part 9. Correlation: How to derive and interpret the correlation coefficient using the relationship between a baseball player's salary and his home run statistics.

Mode, Median and Midrange
30 min. 1990. Insight Media
Demonstrates theoretically and through sample problems the computation of the mode, median and midrange for data and populations.

Statistics
13 min. B/W. 1970. Univ. of Wisconsin (LaCrosse).
Describes how statistics are gathered and used. Considers, for example, why the statistics from a survey conducted in one part of a city may differ from the statistics gathered in another part of the city.

Statistics at a Glance
28 min. Color. 1972. Univ. of Conn.
Focuses on descriptive statistics. Discusses frequency distributions, normal and skewed curves, measures of central tendency, measures of variability, and correlations.

Statistics (1) - Overview
30 min. Color. 1985. Univ. of Indiana. ½" VHS.
Introduces the major themes of statistics, collecting data, organizing and picturing data, and drawing conclusions from data. Explains bias and randomness by looking at formal and informal public opinion polls and by examining a medical experiment.

Statistics (3) - Picture This: Organizing Data
30 min. Color. 1985. Univ. of Indiana. ½" VHS.
Focuses on exploratory data analysis—the art of looking for unanticipated patterns in data. Uses baseball batting averages to illustrate means, medians, quartiles, outliers, and the use of histograms in a one-variable situation. Explains the use of scatterplots and box plots in two-variable situations with examples.

Statistics: For All Practical Purposes
5 segments, 30 min. each. Annenberg/CPB Collection.
Insight Media. Phone: (212)-721-6316
This five-part series provides an overview of how data are collected, organized, and analyzed, and demonstrates the use of random sampling methods.

POSSIBLE ANSWERS TO STUDY GUIDE QUESTIONS

Exercise 14.2
1. Mean is 7.1. This value is obtained by dividing the sum of all scores by the number of cases. This is the value everyone would have if everyone had to have the same value.

2. Median is 6. This is the value that cuts the distribution in half.

3. Mode is 2. This is the most frequently appearing value.

4. The mean includes ALL scores. It can, therefore, be affected by extreme scores, and hence it can be skewed. The median is not affected by extreme scores. It indicates only the middle value and nothing about the range above and below that point. The mode is not as useful, particularly when the modal category is not significantly larger than some other categories. The three values can differ in a distribution.

5. The range is 26 (0-26). This value indicates the distance between the highest and lowest scores. Some people subtract the lowest value from the highest value and add 1 to reflect the true upper and lower limits.

Exercise 14.3

1.

		GENDER	
		Male	Female
CHURCH ATTENDANCE	Yes	28%	76%
	No	72%	24%
	TOTAL	100% (25)	100% (25)

2. Slightly more than half the sample attends church. However, almost three times as many females (76%) attend church as compared to males (28%). This may be due to socialization differences, greater need for social interaction and recognition, greater importance placed on religion as a source of family integration, and so on.

Exercise 14.4

1. The table is constructed to show the effect of two independent variables, age and sex, on the dependent variable, percentage in favor of gun control.

2. (a) Among both men and women, older people are more supportive of gun control than younger people.
   (b) Within each age group, women are more supportive of gun control than men.

Exercise 14.5

REGION OF INTERVIEW

		Frequency	Percent	Valid Percent	Cumulative Percent
Valid	1 NEW ENGLAND	171	5.7	5.7	5.7
	2 MIDDLE ATLANTIC	493	16.4	16.4	22.1
	3 E. NOR. CENTRAL	593	19.8	19.8	41.9
	4 W. NOR. CENTRAL	229	7.6	7.6	49.5
	5 SOUTH ATLANTIC	533	17.8	17.8	67.3
	6 E. SOU. CENTRAL	158	5.3	5.3	72.6
	7 W. SOU. CENTRAL	266	8.9	8.9	81.4
	8 MOUNTAIN	146	4.9	4.9	86.3
	9 PACIFIC	411	13.7	13.7	100.0
	Total	3000	100.0	100.0	

REGION OF INTERVIEW

		Frequency	Percent	Valid Percent	Cumulative Percent
Valid	1 East	664	22.1	22.1	22.1
	2 North Central	822	27.4	27.4	49.5
	3 South	957	31.9	31.9	81.4
	4 West	557	18.6	18.6	100.0
	Total	3000	100.0	100.0	

INFOTRAC EXERCISES

1. Americans lag in safer sex. (Survey shows that US ranks fourth worldwide in using condoms although Americans are internationally renowned for promoting safe sex, brief article.) *USA Today* (magazine) Dec 1996 v125 n2619 p5(1). Identify and report a bivariate analysis from this article.

2. Gender differences, but no racial group differences, in self-reported psychiatric symptoms in adolescents. Regina C. Casper, Joseph Belanoff, Daniel Offer. *Journal of the American*

Academy of Child and Adolescent Psychiatry. April 1996 v35 n4 p500(9). What does Table 1 tell you about the impact of race and gender on depression in adolescents?

3. Sexual harassment in the U.S. military: individualized and environmental contexts. Juanita M. Firestone, Richard J. Harris. *Armed Forces and Society: An Interdisciplinary Journal,* Fall 1994 v21 n1 (p25(19). What were some of the differences discovered in the sexual harassment experiences of men and women in the armed services?

4. Using the keyword option, ask students to read two social science articles that focus on measures of central tendency. Ask students to: 1) summarize the articles, 2) describe the measures of central tendency that were discussed/used, and 3) comment on whether other measures of central tendency could have been used and why.

5. Using the keyword option, ask students to read one social science article that focuses on bivariate analysis and one that focuses on multivariate analysis. Ask students to: 1) summarize each article, 2) describe why one article was "labeled" bivariate and the other multivariate, and 3) describe the analysis that was done in each article.

INTERNET EXERCISES

1. Ask students to go to the following Census Bureau site: http://factfinder.census.gov
After accessing the site tell the students to go to the "Start with Basic Facts Box" and to click on "Population, Race, Hispanic or Latin., and Age (2000)." Ask students to select two states for comparative purposes and to construct a bivariate table that compares the two states in terms of racial composition for "all ages." This site provides students with the needed frequencies and percents. You can either allow the students to decide on categories for race or you can set these up before giving the assignment so that there's comparability across student responses.

2. Ask students to access the FEDSTATS homepage which is a "gateway to statistics from over 100 federal agencies via: http://www.fedstats.gov/
This is a "fun site" to browse. You can either ask students to select a topic or you can select a topic for the entire class using the TOPIC LINKS section. For example, you might ask the class to select AIDS/HIV and ask students to examine under "GENERAL INFORMATION" the "fact sheets." Students could select and report on whatever "facts" were of interest to them. For example, they could report on the statistics associated with the use of condoms and HIV/AIDS. Or, students could select the "Surveillance" fact sheets and report the data on African Americans and HIV/AIDS or minority youth and HIV/AIDS.

Or, assign a topic, such as Divorce, and see what students report. Ask them to also go to at least one additional link mentioned on this site and to summarize what they found on that link.

MULTIPLE-CHOICE QUESTIONS

1. Certain guidelines should be kept in mind when coding. Among these is(are) the following:
   a. The coding scheme should be appropriate to the analysis intended in the study.
   b. The coding scheme should be appropriate to the theoretical concepts being examined.
   c. The reliability of the coder(s) should always be verified.
   d. All of the above are correct.
   e. Only a and b are correct.
   ANS: D
   PGS: 396-398

2. An example of multivariate analysis would be
   a. an examination of the ages of all women who are corporate executives
   b. an analysis of the relationship between age, sex, and type of nightspot frequented in a given city in the Midwest
   c. an analysis of the relationship that exists between types of undergraduate major and positions held in business
   d. an analysis of the relationship between type of offense and length of prison sentence for those who had a jury trial
   e. all of the above
   ANS: B
   PG: 416

3. Which of the following statements is(are) FALSE about coding
   a. codes should be mutually exclusive
   b. it's a good idea to code data in more detail than you plan to use
   c. code categories can always be collapsed for more detail
   d. code categories should be exhaustive
   e. all of the above are true
   ANS: C
   PGS: 397-398

4. In reading a table that someone else has constructed, the rule of thumb is
   a. if the table is percentaged down, read across, and if the table is percentaged across, read down
   b. if the table is percentaged down, read down
   c. if the table is percentaged across, read across
   d. all of the above
   e. only b and c are correct
   ANS: A
   PG: 412

5. A codebook contains the following information:

COLUMNS	DESCRIPTION
1-3	Respondent's I.D. #
4	SEX: Respondent's sex
	1=Male
	2=Female
5	CLASS: Respondent's class standing
	1=freshman
	2=sophomore
	3=junior
	4=senior
	5=transfer
	7=don't know
	8=no answer
	9=refused

Which of the following statements is(are) TRUE concerning the codebook?
a. The variables in this codebook are ID number, sex, and class standing.
b. ID number has been coded so that the categories are mutually exclusive but not exhaustive.
c. Class standing has been coded so that the categories are mutually exclusive and exhaustive.
d. The codebook contains two variables.
e. All of the above are true.
ANS: A
PGS: 399-400

6. The following data applies to the codebook given in the prior question —13228. This data
a. represents the 132nd person selected using a stratified sampling technique who is female
b. represents the 132nd person selected using simple random sampling who is female
c. represents a female whose ID number is 132
d. represents the 132nd person selected using simple random sampling who is male
e. represents a male whose ID number is 132
ANS: C
PGS: 399-400

7. The College of Arts and Science at Delta University has nine departments. The number of faculty in each department is shown below. What is the median number of faculty in the College of Arts and Science?   8, 12, 9, 15, 17, 11, 13, 14, 7
    a. 12
    b. 17
    c. 4.5
    d. 5
    e. there is no median in these data
        ANS: A
        PGS: 403-405

8. Using the data from the prior question, the mean number of faculty in the College of Arts and Science at Delta University is:
    a. 12
    b. 17
    c. 10.7
    d. 11.8
    e. There is no mean for these data
        ANS: D
        PGS: 402-403

9. A codebook
    a. Describes the locations of variables
    b. Lists the codes assigned to the attributes on each variable
    c. Gives an identifier to each variable
    d. Should contain the full definition of the variable
    e. A codebook should do all of the above
        ANS: E
        PGS: 399-400

10. The most frequent attribute, in either grouped or ungrouped data, is the
    a. mean
    b. median
    c. mode
    d. range
    e. marginal
        ANS: C
        PG: 403

11. A friend of yours assigned a code of 1 to "male" and a code of 2 to "female" on the variable *sex*. Your friend asked the computer to compute the average score on sex. The computer printout contained the following information: mean=1.38, standard deviation=.43, median=1.4, and mode=1.0. You advise your friend that the best measure(s) of central tendency to report is(are) the
    a. mean
    b. standard deviation
    c. median
    d. mode
    e. a, c, and d are appropriate measures to report
       ANS: D
       PG: 406

12. If the standard deviation equals 0, we may conclude that
    a. there is no dispersion in the data
    b. the mean is a good measure of the average
    c. the data are homogeneous
    d. all of the above are correct
    e. only a and c are correct
       ANS: D
       PG: 405

13. A measure of dispersion describes
    a. where the data are clustered
    b. which data are the most important
    c. how spread out the data are
    d. which data are appropriate for analysis
    e. discrete data only
       ANS: C
       PG: 405

14. Subgroup comparisons are done by
    a. dividing cases into the appropriate subgroups, describing each subgroup in terms of a given variable, and comparing those descriptions across subgroups
    b. dividing, describing, and comparing subgroups on independent and dependent variables
    c. analyzing the simultaneous relationships among several variables among subgroups
    d. all of the above
    e. only a and b are correct
       ANS: A
       PG: 407

15. Professor Wilton decided to test whether blondes have more fun. Wilton surveyed 600 people and obtained the following results:

HAIR COLOR

FUN	Blondes	Nonblondes	Total
Report fun	250	50	300
Report no fun	150	150	300
Total	400	200	600

The BEST way(s) to percentage this table is(are)
a. within columns, down
b. within rows, across
c. divide each cell by 600
d. within columns, across
e. within rows, down
   ANS: A
   PGS: 412-415

16. Using the data from the prior question, the univariate distribution for the variable *fun* includes the values
a. 250, 150
b. 50, 150
c. 300, 300
d. 400, 200
e. 250, 50
   ANS: C
   PGS: 401,411-412

17. Which of the following is(are) aimed primarily at explanation?
a. univariate analysis
b. multivariate analysis
c. bivariate analysis
d. all of the above
e. only b and c are correct
   ANS: E
   PGS: 407,411,416

18. A friend showed you the following table:

Total Arrests by Type of Crime and Sex

	SEX	
Type of Crime	Male	Female
Violent	20%	30%
Property	80%	70%
Total	100%	100%
	(800)	(400)
No answer =	(20)	(20)

Your friend asked you what to do to improve the table. Your best answer would be
a. nothing, the table is fine
b. add frequencies to each cell
c. omit the "no answer" category since these cases are not included in the analysis
d. the table should be percentaged within categories of type of crime
e. the base for the percentages should be included
   ANS: A
   PG: 415

19. Using the data from the prior question, what percentage of males committed a violent crime?
a. 20
b. 30
c. 80
d. 70
e. not enough information to calculate
   ANS: A
   PGS: 414-415

20. Which of the following statements is(are) TRUE concerning the data presented in the table in the prior question?
a. The cases were divided into groups according to their attributes on sex.
b. Males are more likely to commit property crimes than violent crimes.
c. Females are more likely to commit property crimes than violent crimes.
d. Males are more likely than females to commit property crimes.
e. All of the above are true.
   ANS: E
   PG: 414

21.   Which of the following statistics can be calculated on continuous data?
      a.   mean
      b.   median
      c.   standard deviation
      d.   all of the above
      e.   only a and c are correct
            ANS: D
            PG: 406

22.   Which of the following measures of central tendency can be used at any level of
      measurement?
      a.   mean
      b.   mode
      c.   median
      d.   standard deviation
      e.   all of the above can be used
            ANS: B
            PG: 406

23.   Given the following age distribution, the mean is
            18, 33, 7, 32, 6, 5, 4
      a.   4
      b.   7
      c.   15
      d.   32
      e.   cannot compute from the information given
            ANS: C
            PGS: 402-403

24.   Given the following age distribution, the range is
            12, 15, 8, 17, 34, 43, 2, 16, 43, 3

      a.   12, 3
      b.   17
      c.   2, 17
      d.   2, 43
      e.   cannot compute from the information given
            ANS: D
            PG: 405

25. A description of the number of times that the various attributes of a variable are observed is called a
    a. frequency distribution
    b. mean
    c. measure of dispersion
    d. contingency table
    e. multivariable table
      ANS: A
      PG: 401

TRUE-FALSE QUESTIONS

1. Coding should always begin with a relatively well-developed coding scheme derived from your research purpose.
   ANS: F
   PG: 397

2. A codebook is a guide for locating variables and interpreting codes in one's data file.
   ANS: T
   PG: 399

3. If you do ALL your own coding then you do not need to verify your reliability as a coder.
   ANS: F
   PG: 398

4. The number of cases omitted from a bivariate analysis because of missing data should be included in the table.
   ANS: T
   PG: 415

5. Whereas univariate analysis and subgroup comparisons focus on the descriptions of the people under study, the focus of bivariate analysis is on the relationships among the variables themselves.
   ANS: T
   PGS: 407, 410-411

6. A univariate analysis examines the distribution of cases on one or more variables.
   ANS: F
   PG: 400

7. The mean is a particularly useful statistic when there is great disparity in a distribution.
    ANS: F
    PGS: 404-405

8. A nominal variable is a discrete variable.
    ANS: T
    PG: 406

9. In multivariate analysis a second dependent variable is added.
    ANS: F
    PG: 416

10. The range is larger than the interquartile range.
    ANS: T
    PGS: 405-406

11. Half the cases are above the mode and half the cases are below the mode.
    ANS: F
    PG: 403

12. A bivariate table is read by comparing the independent variable subgroups with one another in terms of a given attribute of the dependent variable.
    ANS: T
    PGS: 412-415

13. The "don't know" category should always be excluded from analysis.
    ANS: F
    PGS: 409-410

14. Frequency distributions indicate the number of times that variables are observed.
    ANS: F
    PG: 401

15. Bivariate and multivariate analyses are aimed primarily at explanation.
    ANS: T
    PG: 407

ESSAYS

1. What is a codebook? Construct a codebook for the following questionnaire items.
    a. Sex
        ( ) Male
        ( ) Female

    b. Age at last birthday?

    c. How many brothers and sisters do you have? (Count only those who are now alive. Include stepbrothers and stepsisters and children adopted by your parents.)

    d. What is your marital status?
        ( ) Married
        ( ) Widowed
        ( ) Divorced
        ( ) Separated
        ( ) Never married

2. A researcher believes that a person's occupation affects his or her political party preference. Given the following data on occupation and political party preference, construct a contingency table. Percentage the table and interpret your results.

Semiskilled	Republican
Unskilled	Republican
Semiskilled	Democrat
Skilled	Other
Semiskilled	Other
Unskilled	Other
Semiskilled	Democrat
Semiskilled	Democrat
Unskilled	Other
Skilled	Republican
Unskilled	Other
Skilled	Democrat
Skilled	Other
Skilled	Republican
Semiskilled	Democrat
Skilled	Other
Skilled	Other
Unskilled	Republican
Semiskilled	Democrat
Skilled	Other

3. Why do percentages allow us to compare two or more frequency distributions? Give an example.

4. A random sample of sociology majors at the University of Methods were asked a series of questions about their major advisor. Interpret their answers to the following question: "My advisor encourages me to see him/her."

Level of Agreement	f
Strongly agree	19
Agree	29
Undecided	34
Disagree	13
Strongly disagree	14
No answer	44

CHAPTER 15: THE ELABORATION MODEL

OUTLINE

I.   The Origins of the Elaboration Method

II. The Elaboration Paradigm
    A. Replication
    B. Explanation
    C. Interpretation
    D. Specification
    E. Refinements to paradigm

III. Elaboration and Ex Post Facto Hypothesizing

BEHAVIORAL OBJECTIVES

Upon completion of this chapter, the student should be able to:

1.   Describe the goal of the elaboration model.

2.   Summarize the historical origins of the elaboration model.

3.   Define and illustrate control variables.

4.   Define partial tables and partial relationships.

5.   Differentiate antecedent from intervening variables by definition and example.

6.   Differentiate the following outcomes of the elaboration model by definition and example: replication, explanation, interpretation, and specification.

7.   Differentiate a suppressor variable from a distorter variable by definition and example.

8.   Discuss the positive and negative features of ex post facto hypothesizing.

TEACHING SUGGESTIONS AND RESOURCES

1. Divide students into small groups. Distribute the following tables, and ask the students which aspect of the elaboration model these tables illustrate.

A researcher believed that father's occupational prestige influenced the number of children in the family.

FATHER'S OCCUPATIONAL PRESTIGE
(in percent)

# OF SIBLINGS	Low	Moderate	High
0-2	40.4%	25.0%	42.9%
3-5	32.7	39.1	31.4
6 or more	26.9	35.9	25.7
TOTAL	100.0%	100.0%	100.0%
	(52)	(64)	(35)

Chi square = 4.51 $p = .3403$

FOR PEOPLE LIVING IN THE FARM OR COUNTRY:
FATHER'S OCCUPATIONAL PRESTIGE
(in percent)

# OF SIBLINGS	Low	Moderate	High
0-2	66.7%	14.6%	33.3%
3-5	0.0	41.5	33.3
6 or more	33.3	43.9	33.3
TOTAL	100.0%	100.0%	99.9%
	(9)	(41)	(3)

Chi square = 12.23 $p = .0157$

FOR PEOPLE LIVING IN A SMALL CITY OR TOWN:
FATHER'S OCCUPATIONAL PRESTIGE
(in percent)

# OF SIBLINGS	Low	Moderate	High
0-2	52.6%	33.3%	33.3%
3-5	26.3	44.4	46.7
6 or more	21.1	22.2	20.0
TOTAL	100.0%	99.9%	100.0%
	(19)	(9)	(15)

Chi square = 2.05 p = .7265

FOR PEOPLE LIVING IN A MEDIUM-SIZED CITY:
FATHER'S OCCUPATIONAL PRESTIGE
(in percent)

# OF SIBLINGS	Low	Moderate	High
0-2	11.1%	44.4%	62.5%
3-5	55.6	33.3	12.5
6 or more	33.3	22.2	25.0
TOTAL	100.0%	99.9%	100.0%
	(9)	(9)	(8)

Chi square = 5.53 p = .2368

FOR PEOPLE LIVING IN A LARGE CITY:
FATHER'S OCCUPATIONAL PRESTIGE
(in percent)

# OF SIBLINGS	Low	Moderate	High
0-2	26.7%	60.0%	44.4%
3-5	46.7	20.0	22.2
6 or more	26.7	20.0	33.3
TOTAL	100.1%	100.0%	99.9%
	(15)	(5)	(9)

Chi square $= 2.80$ $p = .5913$

2. An old and excellent source for numerous examples of the elaboration method is Rosenberg, Morris. 1968. *The Logic Of Survey Analysis*. New York: Basic Books.

POSSIBLE ANSWERS TO STUDY GUIDE QUESTIONS

Exercise 15.1
1. Bivariate table to test hypothesis

		COLLEGE	
		North	South
	Low	66.7%	34.0%
PREJUDICE			
	High	33.3%	66.0%
	TOTAL	100.0%	100.0%
		(300)	(250)

The results indicate that those who graduated from colleges in the North are more likely to score low on prejudice and that those who graduated from colleges in the South are more likely to score high on prejudice.

2. Other two bivariate tables

		CHILDHOOD	
		North	South
	Low	90.0%	20.0%
PREJUDICE			
	High	10.0%	80.0%
	TOTAL	100.0%	100.0%
		(250)	(300)

Those who were raised in the North are much more likely to score low on prejudice, and those who were raised in the South are more likely to score high on prejudice.

		CHILDHOOD	
		North	South
	North	80.0%	33.3%
COLLEGE			
	South	20.0%	66.7%
	TOTAL	100.0%	100.0%
		(250)	(300)

Those who were raised in the North are much more likely to attend college in the North, and those who were raised in the South are more likely to attend college in the South.

3. Trivariate table

		CHILDHOOD			
		NORTH		SOUTH	
		College		College	
		North	South	North	South
	Low	90.0%	90.0%	20.0%	20.0%
PREJUDICE					
	High	10.0%	10.0%	80.0%	80.0%
	TOTAL	100.0%	100.0%	100.0%	100.0%
		(200)	(50)	(100)	(200)

The original hypothesis suggesting that region of college attended influences prejudice is not supported. In fact, in both partials there is no difference between those attending college in the North and those attending college in the South regarding their level of prejudice. But most of those raised in the North score low on prejudice, and most of those raised in the South score high on prejudice. Hence, region of childhood is a critical factor, and region of college attended plays no role.

4. The explanation form of the elaboration model best represents the pattern of results because the partials are completely reduced from the original relationship and because the control variable is antecedent to the two variables in the original table.

Exercise 15.2
1. Bivariate table to test hypothesis

		SEX	
		Male	Female
	Few	34.0%	66.7%
ACCIDENTS			
	Many	66.0%	33.3%
	TOTAL	100.0%	100.0%
		(250)	(300)

Results indicate that two-thirds of the males have many accidents and only one-third of the females have many accidents.

2. Other bivariate tables

		SEX	
		Male	Female
	Few	20.0%	66.7%
MILES			
	Many	80.0%	33.3%
	TOTAL	100.0%	100.0%
		(250)	(300)

Results indicate that the vast majority of the males drive many miles, and only a third of the females drive many miles.

		MILES	
		Few	Many
	Few	90.0%	20.0%
ACCIDENTS			
	Many	10.0%	80.0%
	TOTAL	100.0%	100.0%
		(250)	(300)

Results indicate that almost all of those who drive few miles also have few accidents, and only a fifth of those who drive many miles have few accidents.

3. Trivariate table

		MILES			
		FEW		MANY	
		Sex		Sex	
		Male	Female	Male	Female
ACCIDENTS	Few	90.0%	90.0%	20.0%	20.0%
	Many	10.0%	10.0%	80.0%	80.0%
	TOTAL	100.0%	100.0%	100.0%	100.0%
		(50)	(200)	(200)	(100)

Results indicate no difference between men and women in terms of accidents when number of miles driven is controlled. In fact, those who drive few miles have few accidents, and those who drive many miles have many accidents. Hence, sex makes no difference, but miles driven is the important variable.

4. The interpretation form of the elaboration model best represents the pattern of results because the partials are completely reduced from the original table and the control variable (miles driven) is intervening between sex and number of accidents.

INTERNET EXERCISES

1. Ask students to go the the following site:
http://www-iea.fmi.uni-sofia.bg/Module7/typesof.htm
This module reviews the concepts of the independent, dependent, and control variables. The module ends with an example. Students are asked to name the different types of variables and the answers are provided.

2. A second site for reviewing hypothesis formulation and types of variables is:
http://www.psy.pdx.edu/PsyTutor/Tutorials/Research/Elements/P1.htm
Students can use this site as a review of many aspects of the research process. However, if they go to: http://www.psy.pdx.edu/PsyTutor/Tutorials/Research/Overheads/3rdVarExplain0.htm
the issue of a control variable is addressed via an example.

MULTIPLE-CHOICE QUESTIONS

1. Professor Smith found a relationship between education and occupation. However, when age was introduced as a test factor, the relationship between education and occupation disappeared in the partials. This illustrates
    a. specification
    b. explanation
    c. interpretation
    d. replication
    e. spurious relationship
        ANS: B
        PGS: 427-430

2. Whenever the partial relationships are essentially the same as the original relationship, the term assigned to the result, regardless of whether the test variable is antecedent or intervening, is a(an)
    a. spurious relationship
    b. explanation
    c. specification
    d. replication
    e. interpretation
        ANS: D
        PGS: 427-428

3. For a spurious relationship to occur, which of the following condition(s) is(are) required?
    a. The partial relationships must be significantly less than the original.
    b. The test variable must be antecedent to the dependent variable.
    c. The test variable must be antecedent to the independent variable.
    d. All of the above are correct.
    e. Only a and c are correct.
        ANS: D
        PG: 428

4. The difference between interpretation and explanation is
    a. a logical difference
    b. a statistical difference
    c. that the partials are reduced in explanation but not in interpretation
    d. that the partials are reduced in interpretation but not in explanation
    e. all of the above
        ANS: A
        PG: 427

5. Suppose we observed that the more firefighters there were at a fire site, the greater the amount of fire damage. Suppose we also observed that the size of the fire was related to both the amount of damage and the number of firefighters present. In this case, we would call size of fire the
    a. independent variable
    b. dependent variable
    c. intervening test variable
    d. antecedent test variable
    e. cannot tell from the information given
        ANS: D
        PGS: 427, 429

6. The relationship between numbers of firefighters and the amount of fire damage described in question #5 illustrates that:
    a. The relationship between the two variables is causal
    b. That the number of firefighters causes the damage
    c. That the relationship between firefighters and the amount of damage is spurious
    d. That the number of firefighters at a fire may cause the amount of damage
    e. That the amount of damage at a fire causes firefighters to appear at the fire
        ANS: C
        PGS: 428-430

7. According to the following model
    $$X \varpi \quad Y \varpi Z$$

    a. X is the dependent variable
    b. X is the independent variable
    c. Z is the independent variable
    d. X is the intervening variable
    e. Y is the dependent variable
        ANS: B
        PG: 427

8. Using the model in the previous question, which of the following statements is (are) FALSE about Y? Y is the
    a. Test variable
    b. Intervening variable
    c. Antecedent variable
    d. Y helps us interpret the relationship between X and Z
    e. All of the above are TRUE about Y
        ANS: C
        PG: 427

Use the following four tables for Questions 9-11.

TABLE A: WOMEN'S MARITAL STATUS BY THEIR LABOR FORCE PARTICIPATION

		CURRENTLY MARRIED	
		YES	NO
IN LABOR FORCE	Yes	48%	75%
	No	52%	25%
	Total	100%	100%
		(500)	(500)

TABLE B: FOR WOMEN UNDER 35 YEARS OF AGE: MARITAL STATUS BY LABOR FORCE PARTICIPATION

		CURRENTLY MARRIED	
		YES	NO
IN LABOR FORCE	Yes	50%	80%
	No	50%	20%
	Total	100%	100%
		(200)	(200)

TABLE C: FOR WOMEN 35-65: MARITAL STATUS BY LABOR FORCE PARTICIPATION

		CURRENTLY MARRIED	
		YES	NO
IN LABOR FORCE	Yes	45%	70%
	No	55%	30%
	Total	100%	100%
		(200)	(200)

TABLE D: FOR WOMEN 65 & OLDER: MARITAL STATUS BY LABOR FORCE PARTICIPATION

		CURRENTLY MARRIED	
		YES	NO
IN LABOR FORCE	Yes	47%	75%
	No	53%	25%
	Total	100%	100%
		(100)	(100)

9. Using the previous tables, which of the following are partials?
   a. tables A, B, C, D
   b. tables A, B, C
   c. tables A, C, D
   d. tables A, B, D
   e. tables B, C, D
   ANS: E
   PGS: 426-427

10. The control variable(s) in the prior tables is(are)
    a. marital status
    b. labor force participation
    c. age
    d. a and b are control variables
    e. there is no control variable
    ANS: C
    PG: 426

11. Your friend asks for your methodological opinion on what the preceding four tables indicate. You should tell her
    a. replication
    b. specification
    c. explanation
    d. interpretation
    e. none of the above
    ANS: A
    PGS: 427-428

12. Suppose there is a relationship between variables A and B. You introduce variable C as a control variable, and the relationship between A and B disappears in the partials. Then
    a. the relationship between A and B was clearly spurious
    b. this is clearly an example of explanation
    c. variable C is clearly an antecedent variable
    d. variable C is clearly a distorter variable
    e. none of the above
    ANS: E
    PG: 427

13. You notice a positive relationship between the number of children in a family and father's occupational prestige. When you control for mother's occupational prestige, the partials become negative in sign. This illustrates
    a. specification
    b. a distorter variable
    c. a suppressor variable
    d. explanation
    e. interpretation
       ANS: B
       PGS: 434-435

14. Professor Rumpler found a relationship between age at marriage and marital happiness. Rumpler introduced sex, race, number of years married, and income as test variables. In all partials, the relationship between age at marriage and marital happiness held. Rumpler probably
    a. concluded that the relationship between age and marital happiness was most likely a genuine one
    b. decided that replication had increased his confidence that there was a relationship between age and marital happiness
    c. now knew why age and marital happiness were related
    d. all of the above
    e. only a and b are correct
       ANS: E
       PG: 428

15. Deciding whether the partials are significantly different from the original table is(are)
    a. an arbitrary decision
    b. based on your judgment
    c. follows a rigorous procedure
    d. requires additional testing
    e. only a and b are correct
       ANS: E
       PG: 434

16. A zero-order relationship means that
    a. There is no relationship between the variables
    b. The partials have been reduced
    c. No test factors have been controlled for
    d. The partials have remained the same as the original relationship
    e. There is one independent variable
       ANS: C
       PG: 427

17.   A relationship was found between education and income. Tables A and B are the partials controlling for sex. What do these tables indicate?

	TABLE A MALES		TABLE B FEMALES	
	EDUCATION		EDUCATION	
INCOME	No H.S.	H.S.	No H.S.	H.S.
Less than $10,000	70%	40%	70%	70%
More than $10,000	30%	60%	30%	30%
Total	100%	100%	100%	100%

    a. replication
    b. specification
    c. explanation
    d. distorter
    e. interpretation
      ANS: B
      PG: 431

18.   Which of the following statements is FALSE concerning the table in the prior question?
    a. The partials specify the conditions under which the original relationship holds
    b. Among women there is no relationship between education and income
    c. Among men there is a relationship between education and income
    d. Sex is an intervening variable
    e. All the statements are true
      ANS: D
      PGS: 427, 431-434

19.   A relationship was found between variables A and B. Variable C was introduced, and the relationship between A and B was still strong in the partials. This illustrates
    a. that the relationship between A and B is nonspurious
    b. that the relationship between A and B is spurious
    c. replication
    d. only a and c are correct
    e. only b and c are correct
      ANS: D
      PGS: 427-428

TRUE-FALSE QUESTIONS

1.   An antecedent control variable is one that occurs between the independent and the dependent variable in time.
    ANS: F
    PG: 427

2.   When using the elaboration paradigm, you should always begin with an observed
     relationship.
     ANS: F
     PG: 434

3.   A partial relationship cannot be stronger than the original relationship.
     ANS: F
     PG: 434

4.   The elaboration model can only be used on dichotomous variables.
     ANS: F
     PG: 436

5.   The acceptance of a hypothesis is really a function of the extent to which it has been
     tested and not disconfirmed.
     ANS: T
     PG: 437

6.   Ex post facto hypothesizing refers to the development of hypotheses "predicting"
     relationships that have already been observed in the data.
     ANS: T
     PG: 436

7.   Explanation is the term used to describe a spurious relationship.
     ANS: T
     PG: 428

8.   The elaboration model is NOT a simple set of procedures for analyzing data.
     ANS: T
     PGS: The entire chapter

9.   The term *specification* is used in the elaboration model regardless of whether the test
     variable is antecedent or intervening.
     ANS: T
     PGS: 427, 434

10. Good researchers avoid ex post facto hypothesizing.
     ANS: F
     PGS: 436-437

11. The terms "test factor" and control variable are synonyms.
     ANS: T
     PG: 426

ESSAYS

1. Having observed an empirical relationship between two variables, we seek to understand the nature of that relationship through the effects produced by introducing other variables. In view of this, what is the basic form of the elaboration model?

2. What is meant by ex post facto hypothesizing? Why does it sometimes mislead inexperienced researchers?

CHAPTER 16: SOCIAL STATISTICS

OUTLINE

I. Introduction

II. The Danger of Success in Math

III. Descriptive Statistics
   A. Data reduction
   B. Measures of association
      1. Nominal variables
      2. Ordinal variables
      3. Interval or ratio variables
   C. Regression analysis
      1. Linear regression
      2. Multiple regression
      3. Partial regression
      4. Curvilinear regression
      5. Cautions in regression analysis

IV. Other Multivariate Techniques
   A. Path analysis
   B. Time-series analysis
   C. Factor analysis

V. Inferential Statistics
   A. Univariate inferences
   B. Tests of statistical significance
   C. The logic of statistical significance
   D. Chi square
      1. Degrees of freedom
      2. Some words of caution

BEHAVIORAL OBJECTIVES

Upon completion of this chapter, the student should be able to:

1. Differentiate descriptive statistics from inferential statistics.

2. Define raw-data matrix.

3. Define data reduction.

4. Define measures of association and explain the logic behind such measures, using the proportionate reduction of error principle.

5. Describe the logic and calculation of lambda, gamma, and Pearson's *r*.

6. Describe the relationship between levels of measurement and measures of association.

7. Briefly describe regression analysis as an analytical technique.

8. Summarize and note the utility of each of the following types of regression analysis: linear regression, multiple regression, partial regression, and curvilinear regression.

9. Summarize the cautions that should be applied when using regression analysis.

10. Define and note the utility of time-series analysis.

11. Define and note the utility of path analysis.

12. Define and note the utility of factor analysis.

13. Outline the logic, the calculation, and the interpretation of the standard error.

14. Define and state the relationship between confidence level and confidence interval, and give an example.

15. List three assumptions underlying inferential statistics.

16. Define tests of significance, and link this concept to that of standard error.

17. Show how the level of significance is interpreted.

18. Using the null hypothesis, describe how chi square is calculated and interpreted.

19. Summarize three dangers in interpreting the results of tests of significance.

TEACHING SUGGESTIONS AND RESOURCES

1. To illustrate the notion of a relationship, the following three tables are suggested.

TABLE 1: A PERFECT RELATIONSHIP

		VARIABLE X		
VARIABLE Y	X_a	X_b	X_c	Total
Y_a	60	0	0	60
Y_b	0	60	0	60
Y_c	0	0	60	60
Total	60	60	60	180

TABLE 2: A MODERATE RELATIONSHIP

		VARIABLE X		
VARIABLE Y	X_a	X_b	X_c	Total
Y_a	40	10	10	60
Y_b	10	40	10	60
Y_c	10	10	40	60
Total	60	60	60	180

TABLE 3: NO RELATIONSHIP

		VARIABLE X		
VARIABLE Y	X_a	X_b	X_c	Total
Y_a	20	20	20	60
Y_b	20	20	20	60
Y_c	20	20	20	60
Total	60	60	60	180

Point out that the number of cases and the marginals are the same in all three tables.

Ask students to predict the case value on Y when they are told the case is an X_a. In Table 1 they will be able to predict perfectly, the case is a Y_a. In Table 2 they would make the same prediction, but some cases would be misclassified ($n=20$). In Table 3, however, any prediction would be equally likely.

2. To illustrate the importance of understanding the basis of a statistic, have the students analyze the following table. Use this opportunity to review percentaging tables and the interpretation of those percentages. Then calculate and interpret chi square. Finally, calculate lambda. Ask if there are any questions. One student will usually ask, "Why is lambda = 0 when both the percentages and chi square indicate a statistically significant relationship?" If nobody asks, puzzle over it in class. Point out that in a case such as this, lambda will always equal 0 since the modal categories are the same on the dependent variable for each attribute of the independent variable. Point out that lambda is not a good measure of association to use in this case, and briefly explain how other nominal measures of association overcome this difficulty.

RACE OF OFFENDER

TYPE OF LAWYER	White	Nonwhite	Total
Private	95	25	120
	(47.5%)	(8.3%)	
Court appointed	105	275	380
	(52.5%)	(91.7%)	
Total	200	300	500

Chi square = 100.92 with 1 degree of freedom
Lambda = 0

3. To illustrate that chi square is NOT a measure of association, show students the following two tables. Percentage the tables and then calculate chi square. Point out that although the percentages are the same, chi square is twice as large in the table with twice as many cases, Table B.

	TABLE A					TABLE B		
		Total					Total	
	30	20	50			60	40	100
	20	30	50			40	60	100
Total	50	50	100		Total	100	100	200

Chi square = 4.0   Chi square = 8.0

4. Present the following path models in class. They are two of the four models presented in Lin, Nan, and Daniel Yauger. 1975. "The Process of Occupational Status Achievement: A Preliminary Cross-National Comparison." *American Journal of Sociology*, 81:543-562.

PATH MODEL OF OCCUPATIONAL STATUS
ACHIEVEMENT: COSTA RICA

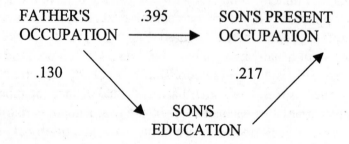

PATH MODEL OF OCCUPATIONAL STATUS
ACHIEVEMENT: U.S.

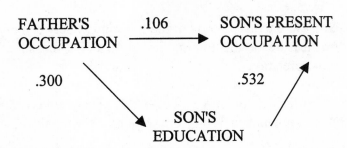

FATHER'S   .106   SON'S PRESENT
OCCUPATION   ——————→   OCCUPATION

.300   .532

SON'S
EDUCATION

Ask the students to interpret the models. Ask them if the differences between Costa Rica and the United States could be used to generate an empirical generalization using inductive reasoning. They may note that the more industrialized a society, the greater the emphasis upon education or achievement rather than parental status or ascribed status.

6. FILMS
Against All Odds: Inside Statistics
See preface for a complete description of each part:
20.Significance Tests
25.Inferences for Relationships

Confidence Intervals and Significance Tests
2 parts, 30 min. each, 1989. Insight Media
Using population surveys to show how margin of error and confidence levels are interpreted, this video explains what a confidence interval is. Also illustrates the basic reasoning behind tests of significance.

Correlation
2 parts, 30 min. each, 1989. Insight Media
Using the relationship between baseball player=s salary and his home run statistics, this program describes how to calculate and interpret a correlation coefficient.

Hypothesis Testing
3 volumes, 30 min. each, 1990. Insight Media
Explains the purpose of hypothesis testing. Examines Type I and Type II errors, the null hypothesis and levels of significance.

Linear Regression
30 min. 1990. Insight Media
Teaches how to create and read scatter diagrams. Discusses the least squares method for fitting a straight line that relates to variables.

POSSIBLE ANSWERS TO STUDY GUIDE QUESTIONS

Exercise 16.1
1. Lambda is an appropriate measure to use to look at the association between two nominal variables. Race and party were measured at the nominal level. As a PRE measure, lambda also has a strict reduction in error interpretation.

2. Lambda with political party as the dependent variable = .297. There were 185 errors made if only the distribution on party was known, and 130 errors were made when the distribution on race was also known.

3. A lambda of .297 indicates that there is a 29.7% reduction in error in predicting political party when we know race.

Exercise 16.2
1. Gamma was selected because both education and religiosity were measured at the ordinal level. Gamma is an appropriate PRE measure of association for two ordinal variables.

2. Gamma = .512. Point out to students that there are two ways to do the calculation depending upon which corner cell they select. The answers will, however, be identical. This is one calculation:

Same order pairs = 70(90 + 20 + 30 + 60) + 25(20 + 60) + 50(30 + 60) + 90(60) = 25900

Different order pairs = 20(90 + 50 + 20 + 30) + 25(50 + 20) + 20(20 + 30) + 90(20) = 8350

(25900 8350)/(25900 + 8350) = .512

3. A gamma of .512 indicates that there is a 51.2% reduction in error in predicting one variable from the other and that the relationship is positive. As education increases, so too does religiosity.

Exercise 16.3

Cell #	Observed frequency	Expected frequency	Ob-Ex	(Ob-Ex)^2	(Ob-Ex)^2/E
1	70	38	32.0	1024	26.9
2	35	38	.3	9	.2
3	10	38	.28	784	20.6
4	20	37	.17	289	7.8
5	50	37	13.0	169	4.6
6	40	37	3.0	9	.2
7	10	25	.15	225	9.0
8	15	25	.15	100	4.0
9	50	25	.25	625	25.0

SUM = 98.3

1. Chi square = 98.3

2. 4 degrees of freedom

3. *p* less than .001

4. Chi square = the overall difference between the observed and expected frequencies. The significance level indicates that there is a less than 1 chance in 1000 that the results are due to sampling error.

Exercise 16.5
1. $X = 3$, $Y = 7.5$
    $X = 2.4$, $Y = 6.6$
    $X = 4.6$, $Y = 9.9$

2. In the plot of the regression line, students should plot the point through the Y axis. When $X = 0$, $Y = 3$. They should also plot thepoints from part 2.

INFOTRAC EXERCISES
1. A statistics primer: hypothesis testing. John E. Kuhn, Mary Lou V.H. Greenfield, Edward M. Wojtys. *The American Journal of Sports Medicine*, Sept-Oct 1996 v24 n5 p702(2). What is meant by "Type I" and "Type II" errors?

2. Using statistics in HRD. (Includes glossary of terms.) Joseph T. Martelli. *Training and Development*, Feb 1997 v51 n2 p62(2). What is the difference between descriptive and inferential statistics?

INTERNET EXERCISES

1. An interesting site for students to review and learn more about factor analysis is R.J. Rummel's site: http://www.hawaii.edu/powerkills/UFA.HTM
This site has many examples for students to examine.

2. An interactive site for students that review regression analysis is:
http://www.ruf.rice.edu/~lane/stat_sim/reliability_reg/
This site enables students to work with scatterplots, standard deviations, pearon's r, etc. via interactive exercises.

MULTIPLE-CHOICE QUESTIONS

1. Which of the following hypotheses assumes that there is no relationship between two variables?
   a. research
   b. null
   c. alternate
   d. secondary
   e. substantive
   ANS: B
   PG: 464

2. The formulas for some measures of association can result in coefficients with either positive or negative signs. Under which of the following circumstances can those signs be meaningfully interpreted?
   a. whenever the data are expressed as frequencies
   b. when the data are measured at the nominal level
   c. when the data are measured at the ordinal level
   d. whenever the data have a modal category
   e. whenever the data are expressed as percentages
   ANS: C
   PG: 446

3.   Professor Doner asked you to interpret a gamma of 1.3. You told Doner
     a.   it indicated an exceedingly strong relationship
     b.   it indicated a moderate relationship
     c.   it indicated a positive relationship
     d.   it indicated an error in calculations
     e.   none of the above
          ANS: D
          PG: 446

4.   Which of the following statistics can be used to determine whether or not there is a
     statistically significant relationship between two variables in a contingency table?
     a.   gamma
     b.   chi square
     c.   lambda
     d.   Pearson's product moment correlation coefficient
     e.   all of the above
          ANS: B
          PG: 464

5.   Jeff thinks that market sales are influenced by the preceding year's unemployment rate.
     Jeff should use a ____ for his analysis.
     a.   time-series analysis
     b.   path analysis
     c.   factor analysis
     d.   time-lagged regression analysis
     e.   regression analysis
          ANS: D
          PG: 454

6.   An appropriate measure of association for determining the strength of the relationship
     between religious affiliation (Protestant, Catholic, Jewish, Other) and sex (male, female)
     is
     a.   gamma
     b.   lambda
     c.   chi square
     d.   Pearson's product moment correlation
     e.   all of the above
          ANS: B
          PGS: 444-445

7. Given the following table of hypothetical data relating age to employment status, which of the following conclusion(s) can be drawn?

EMPLOYMENT STATUS

AGE	High	Medium	Low
31-40	100	300	800
41-50	300	700	500
51-60	600	200	100

    a. There is a negative association between age and employment status.
    b. As age increases so does the employment status.
    c. There is a positive association between age and employment status.
    d. Only a and b are correct.
    e. Only b and c are correct.
        ANS: E
        PGS: 445-447

8. An appropriate measure(s) of association for the data presented in the prior question is(are)
    a. gamma
    b. lambda
    c. chi square
    d. Pearson's product moment correlation
    e. all of the above
        ANS: A
        PG: 445

9. How many degrees of freedom exist in the prior table?
    a. 9
    b. 8
    c. 3
    d. 4
    e. Not enough information to calculate
        ANS: D
        PG: 466

10. Given the following table relating the social class of husband with the social class of wife, which of the following computations would equal the number of pairs with the same ranking?

SOCIAL CLASS OF HUSBAND

SOCIAL CLASS OF WIFE	Working	Middle	Upper	Total
Working	10	25	50	85
Middle	20	30	10	60
Upper	30	10	15	55
Total	60	65	75	200

a. 200(199)/2
b. 50(20+30+30+10) + 25(20+30) + 10(30+10) + 30(30)
c. 10(30+10+15+10) = 25(10+15) + 20(10+15) + 30(15)
d. 60(65+75) + 85(60+55)
e. none of the above
ANS: C
PG: 446

11. Suppose you had calculated gamma for the previous table, and it was .36. This means that
a. husband's social class is positively associated with wife's social class
b. 36% more of the pairs examined had the same ranking than had the opposite ranking
c. 36% more of the pairs examined had the opposite ranking than had the same ranking
d. only a and b are correct
e. only a and c are correct
ANS: D
PG: 446

12. Using simple random sampling, 100 males were drawn from a population and asked their age. The mean age for these men was 22. The standard error for the sample was 5. We are 68% confident that the population parameter is
a. 22
b. between 19.5 and 24.5
c. between 17 and 27
d. between 12 and 32
e. not enough information to calculate
ANS: C
PG: 458

13. Given the following bivariate matrix, which of the following statements is(are) INCORRECT?

Variable	Y	X_1	X_2	X_3	X_4
	Y_1	12	24	38	41
	Y_2	18	14	16	12
	Y_3	4	8	17	42

Variable X (spanning X_1 through X_4)

a. X is the column variable.
b. Fourteen cases have the pattern X_2Y_2.
c. There are three different variables on Y.
d. Four cases are located at Y_3X_1
e. All of the above are accurate.
    ANS: C
    PGS: 443-444

14. Which of the following is(are) an assumption(s) underlying the use of inferential statistics?
a. sample must be drawn from the population about which inferences are to be made
b. simple random sampling
c. 100% completion rate
d. sampling with replacement
e. all of the above
    ANS: E
    PG: 459

15. Faced with data that do not support an assumption of independence between two variables in a population, a researcher
a. immediately rejects the assumption of independence
b. may attribute this discrepancy to an unrepresentative sample or reject the assumption of independence
c. needs to retest the data in order to confirm these initial findings
d. can immediately assume that the sample was unrepresentative of the population
e. none of the above
    ANS: B
    PG: 464

16. Which of the following is(are) considered to be inferential statistics?
    a. computing a mean
    b. setting up a frequency table
    c. testing the significance of a correlation coefficient
    d. calculating gamma
    e. calculating Pearson's *r*
       ANS: C
       PGS: 458-459

17. A .05 level of significance means that
    a. there is only a 5% chance that the statistic's value could be obtained as a result of sampling error only
    b. one is 50% certain that the sample value is representative of the population
    c. there is only a 5% chance that the variables tested are not independent
    d. the results can be accepted because the sampling error is only 5%
    e. the level of confidence is only 5%
       ANS: A
       PG: 464

18. Professor Smigel calculated a chi square of 83.26 on a set of data. The value for chi square in the table at the .05 level was 16.91. Smigel concluded that
    a. it is improbable that the observed relationship could have resulted from sampling error alone
    b. the null hypothesis was rejected
    c. there is a statistically significant relationship at the .05 level
    d. all of the above
    e. only b and c are correct
       ANS: D
       PGS: 466-467

19. Which of the following regression equations represents the strongest relationship between *X* and *Y*?
    a. $Y = 2 + .3X$
    b. $Y = 2 + 1.3X$
    c. $Y = 2 + 1.8X$
    d. $Y = 2 + 3X$
    e. the strength of the relationship cannot be determined from the regression equation
       ANS: E
       PGS: 448-449

20. The regression model can be used to
    a. summarize a relationship between variables
    b. predict a value of one variable from its relationship to another related variable
    c. analyze a relationship between two variables
    d. determine the specific function relating the two variables
    e. all of the above
       ANS: E
       PG: 448

21. If one wished to examine the relationship between education and income with age held constant, an appropriate technique would be
    a. multiple regression
    b. partial regression
    c. curvilinear regression
    d. factor analysis
    e. time-series analysis
       ANS: B
       PG: 450

22. Given that $X = 1.50 + .50Y$, what is the predicted value for a Y value of 6?
    a. 3.00
    b. 3.50
    c. 4.00
    d. 4.50
    e. cannot compute from the given information
       ANS: D
       PG: 448

23. Using the following regression equation, which of the following statements is false?

    $$Y = b_0 + bX_1 + bX_2 + bX_3$$

    a. It treats b as the independent variable.
    b. There are three independent variables.
    c. There is one dependent variable.
    d. It predicts Y from the X's.
    e. It treats Y as the dependent variable.
       ANS: A
       PG: 450

24. In path analysis, the statistic measuring the strength of a relationship between pairs of variables with the effect of other variables held constant is called
     a. a path coefficient
     b. a partial epsilon
     c. a coefficient of alienation
     d. residual variance
     e. a variance coefficient
         ANS: A
         PG: 453

25. Factor analysis attempts to
     a. analyze interrelationships of several variables
     b. reduce relationships among variables to a number of key dimensions
     c. discover basic patterns of relationships among variables
     d. all of the above
     e. only b and c are correct
         ANS: D
         PGS: 455-457

26. Which of the following is NOT an assumption underlying regression analysis?
     a. simple random sampling
     b. discrete variables
     c. at least interval data
     d. absence of nonsampling error
     e. all of the above are assumptions
         ANS: B
         PG: 451

27. You believe that the number of hours people spend in the labor force is a function of age. In fact, you argue that between the ages of 14 and 21 labor force participation, measured in hours, steadily increases. Between the ages of 22 and 60 it remains fairly constant. From ages 61 on it steadily declines. To analyze data you should use
     a. curvilinear regression
     b. partial regression
     c. multiple regression
     d. path analysis
     e. analysis of variance
         ANS: A
         PGS: 450-451

28.   Professor Henley calculated a squared multiple correlation coefficient. It was .36. This means that
      a.   36% of the variance in the final score was explained
      b.   60% of the variance in the final score was explained
      c.   6% of the variance in the final score was explained
      d.   13% of the variance in the final score was explained
      e.   Henley erred in the calculation
      ANS: A
      PG: 450

29.   Basically, path analysis attempts to
      a.   study a relationship between two variables with a third variable held constant
      b.   examine a nonlinear relationship between two variables
      c.   describe relationships among variables by developing causal models
      d.   determine the irreducible factors underlying a series of variables
      e.   represent relationships as distances between points
      ANS: C
      PG: 452

30.   Professor Triker is interested in examining the occupational mobility of women in the United States. Triker believes that people's first job affects their second job and that job in turn affects their third job, and so on. To analyze the data Triker should use
      a.   factor analysis
      b.   time-series analysis
      c.   two-way analysis of variance
      d.   smallest-space analysis
      e.   curvilinear regression analysis
      ANS: B
      PG: 454

31.   Professor Stanton thought that verbal ability was a function of age. Stanton collected data on people aged 5 to 20. The analysis yielded the following equation: $V = 20 + 3A$ where V = verbal ability and A = age. Stanton was asked to predict the verbal ability of a 30 year old. Stanton should respond
      a.   110
      b.   90
      c.   extrapolation is untrustworthy
      d.   interpolation is untrustworthy
      e.   53
      ANS: C
      PG: 451

32.   Given the following model, which of the following conclusions is INCORRECT?

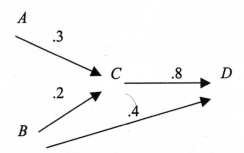

a.   Variable *C* has the strongest direct effect on variable *D*.
b.   Variable *A* has no effect on variable *D*.
c.   Variable *B* has a direct effect on variable *D*.
d.   Variable *C* is an intervening variable.
e.   Variable *D* is last in time.
        ANS: B
        PGS: 452-454

33.   Given the following computer printout from a factor analysis, which of the following
        statements is(are) TRUE?

	1	2	3
1.	.89	.05	.22
2.	.78	.04	.13
3.	.15	.64	.11
4.	.76	.23	.05
5.	.03	.72	.03
6.	.01	.53	.19
7.	.01	.02	.03

a.   There are seven factors.
b.   There are seven variables.
c.   Factor #7 could be eliminated from the analysis.
d.   Variable #2 is most important for factor #2.
e.   Variable #3 tells us nothing
        ANS: B
        PG: 456

34. In a 2x3 table how many cells do we need to fill in before the remainder of the table is determined by the marginal frequencies?
    a. 2
    b. 3
    c. 4
    d. 5
    e. 6
        ANS: A
        PG: 466

35. The formula Y = f(X) tells us that
    a. X is the dependent variable
    b. Y is the dependent variable
    c. f is the dependent variable
    d. Need to know what Y, f, and X represent to determine the dependent variable
    e. None of the above
        ANS: B
        PGS: 447-448

TRUE-FALSE QUESTIONS

1. The regression line that best predicts values of *X* from *Y* is identical to the one that predicts values of *Y* from *X*.
    ANS: F
    PGS: 448-450

2. Generally speaking, the larger the chi square value the more likely it is that the value could be attributed to sampling error alone.
    ANS: F
    PG: 466

3. A disadvantage of factor analysis is that it does not permit hypotheses to be disconfirmed.
    ANS: T
    PG: 457

4. The proportionate reduction in error is related to the strength of the relationship between two variables.
    ANS: T
    PG: 444

5.   Inferential statistics are used primarily for describing samples.
     ANS: F
     PG: 458

6.   Descriptive statistics include both the summarization of univariate distributions and the summarizations of associations between two or more variables.
     ANS: T
     PG: 442

7.   Chi square is based upon a comparison of observed frequencies with the frequencies that would be expected if there was no relationship between the variables.
     ANS: T
     PG: 464

8.   A gamma value of .7 indicates a stronger relationship than a gamma value of .7.
     ANS: F
     PG: 446

9.   If given r you can always compute r squared; however, if given r squared you cannot always compute r.
     ANS: T
     PG: 449

10. Both lambda and Pearson's product moment correlation are based on guessing the mean.
     ANS: F
     PG: 447

11. Pearson's product moment correlation indicates how much of the variance in the dependent variable has been explained.
     ANS: T
     PG: 449

12. The general format for the regression line is $y^{\square} = a + b(X)$. The only observed quantity in this expression is X.
     ANS: T
     PG: 449

13. You should allow the computer to generate the path model.
     ANS: F
     PG: 454

14. A path diagram allows you to determine the effect of one variable upon another both directly and indirectly through an intervening variable.
ANS: T
PGS: 452-454

15. In factor analysis the researcher must specify the number of factors and which variables to load on the factor to allow the computer to generate factor loadings.
ANS: F
PG: 456

16. The output of a factor analysis are artificial dimensions called factors.
ANS: T
PG: 456

17. The beauty of factor analysis is the generation of substantively meaningful factors.
ANS: F
PG: 456

ESSAYS

1. Explain the assumptions underlying the use of tests of significance. Why is there a controversy over the use of these tests?

2. Given the following table:
   a. Calculate and interpret an appropriate measure of association.
   b. Calculate and interpret chi square at the .05 level of significance.

RACE OF OFFENDER BY TYPE OF COUNSEL

	RACE		
COUNSEL	White	Nonwhite	Total
Private	50	25	75
Court appointed	30	50	80
None	5	10	15
Total	85	85	170

3. Illustrate the logic of path analysis by constructing and interpreting a path diagram that traces the relationships among three or more variables.

CHAPTER 17: READING AND WRITING SOCIAL RESEARCH

OUTLINE

I. Reading Social Research
   A. Journals versus books
      1. Reading a journal article
      2. Reading a book
   B. Evaluation of research reports
      1. Theoretical orientation
      2. Research design
      3. Measurement
      4. Sampling
      5. Experiments
      6. Survey research
      7. Field research
      8. Analyzing existing statistics
      9. Evaluation research
      10. Data analysis
      11. Reporting

II. Using the Internet Wisely
   A. Some useful web sites
   B. Searching the web
   C. Evaluating the quality of internet matierals
   D. Citing internet materials

III. Writing Social Research
   A. Some basic considerations
      1. Audience
      2. Form and length of report
      3. Aim of the report
   B. Organization of the report
      1. Purpose and overview
      2. Review of the literature
      3. Avoiding plagiarism
      4. Study design and execution
      5. Analysis and interpretation
      6. Summary and conclusions
   C. Guidelines for Reporting analyses

BEHAVIORAL OBJECTIVES

1. Provide advice for reading journal articles.

2. Provide advice for reading research monographs.

3. Identify questions to ask when assessing theoretical orientations in research reports.

4. Identify questions to ask when assessing research designs in research reports.

5. Identify questions to ask when assessing measurement in research reports.

6. Identify questions to ask when assessing sampling in research reports.

7. Identify questions to ask when assessing experiments in research reports.

8. Identify questions to ask when assessing survey research in research reports.

9. Identify questions to ask when assessing field research in research reports.

10. Identify questions to ask when assessing the analysis of existing statistics in research reports.

11. Identify questions to ask when assessing evaluation research in research reports.

12. Identify questions to ask when assessing data analysis in research reports.

13. Identify questions to ask when assessing the quality of reporting in research reports.

14. Identify some relevant web sites for learning about research methods.

15. Explain how search engines can be used to search web sites.

16. Provide advice for assessing data found on web sites.

17. Provide advice for web citations.

18. Identify the functions of scientific reporting.

19. Explain how the intended audience affects writing a research report.

20. Differentiate the following types of research reports: research notes, working papers, professional papers, articles, and books.

21. Compare the aims of research reports.

22. Explain the importance of stating the purpose and providing an overview in research reports.

23. Explain the role of reviewing the literature in research reports.

24. Provide advice for avoiding plagiarism.

25. Explain the role of describing the study design and execution in research reports.

26. Explain the role of describing the analysis and interpretation in research reports.

27. Explain the role of the summary and conclusions in research reports.

28. Provide guidelines for reporting analyses in research reports.

INFOTRAC EXERCISES

1. Ask students to select an article that interests them and to analyze that report by commenting on its: 1) theoretical underpinnings, 2) methodology, 3) research design, 4) data collection technique, and 5) analyses.

2. Ask students to select 3 articles that interest them and to examine their abstracts. Do the abstracts follow the guidelines suggested by Babbie? If so, how? If not, what is lacking?

INTERNET EXERCISES

1. An interesting site on search engines is:
http://searchenginewatch.com/resources/tutorials.html
Students can use the tutorials on this site to learn more about search engines and how to use them.

2. An interesting site that provides local and global search engines sorted by country is:
http://www.twics.com/~takakuwa/search/search.html
Ask students to select two or three countries and to examine their findings for these countries using the same keywords and multiple search engines.

MULTIPLE CHOICE QUESTIONS

1. Jenny decided to read an article published in *Law and Society Review*. Babbie would urge her to **begin** reading the article by:
   a. Reading the summary and conclusions
   b. Skimming the article noting the section headings
   c. Reading the abstract
   d. Skimming the article completely
   e. Just sitting down and carefully reading the article
   ANS: C
   PG: 473

2. While evaluating a research report, Dr. Childs focused on the research design issue. Which of the following questions would be the **least useful** for evaluating the design?
   a. What was the unit of analysis?
   b. Is the study cross-sectional or longitudinal?
   c. Is the researcher's purpose the statistical description of a population?
   d. Was the purpose of the study exploration?
   e. All of the above would be helpful questions for evaluating the design
   ANS: C
   PGS: 474-475

3. If a reader asks "Who originally collected the data being reanalyzed?" or "When were the data collected?" that reader is most clearly examining the _____ aspect of the research.
   a. Data analysis
   b. Survey research
   c. Theoretical
   d. Field research
   e. Analysis of existing statistics
   ANS: E
   PG:477

4. Which of the following guidelines is(are) **FALSE** for reporting on analyses?
   a. The presentation of data analyses should provide a maximum of detail without being cluttered
   b. If you're using quantitative data, present them so the reader can recompute them
   c. If you're using quantitative data, the reader needs to be able to recompute percentages in the same direction that you used in your presentation
   d. If you're using quantitative data, the reader does not need to be able to recompute percentages in the opposite direction from that used in your presentation
   e. All of the above are **TRUE**
   ANS: D
   PG: 490

5. A _____ locates where specified terms appear on web sites.
    a. Search engine
    b. World wide web
    c. Google
    d. Web page
    e. Http
        ANS: A
        PG: 479

6. Which of the following is **NOT** a suggestion used for evaluating a web site?
    a. Who is the author of the web site?
    b. Does the site advocate a particular viewpoint?
    c. Does the data on the site appear consistent with data from other sites?
    d. Are the data up-to-date?
    e. All of the above are suggested questions for evaluating a web site.
        ANS: E
        PG: 484

7. Abstracts
    a. Should give you a good idea as to whether you'll want to read the rest of the article
    b. Should give you a framework for reading the rest of the article
    c. May raise questions in your mind regarding methods or conclusions
    d. May create an agenda to pursue in reading the article
    e. Should do all of the above
        ANS: E
        PG: 473

8. Which of the following guidelines for reporting on the analysis of qualitative data is **FALSE**?
    a. Provide enough detail so that your reader has a sense of having made the observations with you
    b. Provide only those data that support your interpretations
    c. Provide enough information so that the reader might reach a conclusion that differs from yours
    d. Provide enough detail so that the reader could replicate your study
    e. All of the above are **TRUE**
        ANS: B
        PG: 490

9. Sam wants to prepare a short report on his research for an academic journal. He simply wants to tell the audience about his findings. The most appropriate form for his report is
   a. A working paper
   b. An article
   c. A book
   d. A research note
   e. Any one of the above would be an appropriate form for Sam's work
   ANS: D
   PG: 486

10. Lisa wants to present her tentative findings to a research audience. Her most appropriate form would be a:
    a. Working paper
    b. Article
    c. Book
    d. Research note
    e. Any one of the above would be an appropriate form for Lisa's work.
    ANS: A
    PG: 486

11. Which of the following is **NOT** plagiarism
    a. Using another writer's exact words without using quotation marks
    b. Taking a passage of eight or more words without a citation
    c. Editing another's words and presenting those as your own
    d. Paraphrasing another's words and presenting those as your own
    e. All of the above are plagiarism
    ANS: E
    PG: 488

12. Which of the following statements is **FALSE** about the purpose of a literature review? Literature reviews should:
    a. Point out general agreements and minimize the disagreements among previous researchers
    b. Show where your research fits into the general body of scientific knowledge
    c. Lay the groundwork for your study
    d. Show why your research may have value in the larger scheme of things
    e. All of the above are true of literature reviews
    ANS: A
    PG: 487

13. A typical report begins with a(n)
   a. Literature review
   b. Purpose and overview statement
   c. Analysis and description statement
   d. Summary statement
   e. Conclusions statement
      ANS: B
      PG: 489

14. A good abstract **DOES NOT** include a statement about
   a. The purpose of the research
   b. The findings of each table and graph
   c. The major findings
   d. The methods used
   e. All of the above are included in a good abstract
      ANS: B
      PG: 473

15. Which of the following statements is **FALSE** concerning data on the web?
   a. Information on the web is available to a large proportion of the population
   b. Information that is placed on the web is typically screened for accuracy
   c. Out-of-date data may be reported on the web
   d. University research centers are usually committed to peer review
   e. All of the above statements are **TRUE**
      ANS: B
      PG: 484

TRUE - FALSE QUESTIONS

1. URL and web address are synonyms.
   ANS: T
   PG: 485

2. Some web sites advocate particular political, religious, social, or other points of view.
   ANS: T
   PG: 484

3. A good research report should read like a good novel.
   ANS: F
   PG: 473

4. Research reports are written for one purpose only.
    ANS: F
    PG: 485

5. The aim of a report may be exploration, description or explanation but never action.
    ANS: F
    PG: 487

6. Plagiarism may be intentional or accidental.
    ANS: T
    PG: 488

7. A good summary reviews every specific finding.
    ANS: F
    PG: 490

8. The presentation of data analyses should provide a maximum of detail without being cluttered.
    ANS: T
    PG: 490

9. The term research monograph refers only to a published book.
    ANS: F
    PG: 474

10. It is a good idea to string a reader along, dragging out the suspense over whether X causes Y.
    ANS: F
    PG: 473

ESSAYS:

1. What are six guidelines for evaluating a research report? (NOTE: You can give students an article and ask them to apply the guidelines to that article).

2. What are search engines? Why and how do we use them in our research?

3. Why do researchers take their audience into account in writing a report?

Appendix A

General Social Survey

The General Social Survey (GSS) is a survey done by the National Opinion Research Center on the attitudes, behaviors, and background characteristics of the American population. These surveys have occurred almost annually since 1972 and typically involve samples of about 1500 Americans 18 years old or older. Samples are full probability samples, and the samples reflect multistage area probability samples to the block level. The primary sampling units employed are Standard Metropolitan Statistical Areas or nonmetropolitan counties, stratified by region, age, and race before selection. The units of selection at the second stage are block groups and enumeration districts, which were stratified according to race and income before selection. The third stage of selection involves blocks, which were selected with probabilities proportional to size.

The data file you will be using contains random samples of 500 cases for each of the years of 1975, 1980, 1985, 1990, 1994 (there was no survey in 1995), and 2000, resulting in a total sample of 3000 cases. You may wish to limit your analyses to only one year, do separate analyses for various years, or combine various years in one analysis. Unless you specifically select certain years, your analyses will include data from all years. Be very clear on which subgroups you will use in your analysis. If you use the full sample of 3000 cases across all years to study attitudes toward abortion, for example, changes that occurred in attitudes over the years will not be evident and may even mask relationships you wish to examine between, say, gender and attitudes toward abortion. That is, if women were more likely support abortion in the early years and men in the later years, a table relating gender to abortion support for the entire sample would show few gender differences. Also, some items were not asked in each of the years in the data set. If you see a relatively high number of Asystem missing@ responses for an item on your output, that item probably was not asked in each of the years in the data set. Simply do a crosstab of YEAR by your variables to see which years contain data for your variables of interest.

Be sure you distinguish clearly between independent and dependent variables in your analyses. Many of the typically independent variables, such as gender, age, and race, are located toward the beginning of the data file. Some variables, such as how much people watch TV or their level of education, could be either independent or dependent, depending on your research question. Select an appropriate number of what you consider independent and dependent variables, or as many of each type as indicated by your instructor.

YEAR	1.	Year of sample. 1975, 1980, 1985, 1990, 1994, 2000
ID	2.	Case ID ID number
REGION	3.	Region of interview. 1. New England 2. Middle Atlantic 3. East North Central 4. West North Central 5. South Atlantic 6. East South Central 7. West South Central 8. Mountain 9. Pacific
SIZE	4.	Size of place of interview in 1000s (i.e., add three zeroes). 0. Less than 1,000 Other values reflect actual size of community (add three zeroes)
SIZE3	5.	SIZE, size of place of interview, recoded into thirds. 1. Small 2. Moderate 3. Large
RACE	6.	What race do you consider yourself? 1. White 2. Black 3. Other
SEX	7.	Sex. (Coded by interviewer.) 1. Male 2. Female
AGE	8.	Age. (Determined by asking date of birth, actual ages recorded.)Values reflect actual age.
AGE3	9.	AGE variable recoded into thirds. 1. 18-33 2. 34-51 3. 52-89

MARITAL   10. Are you currently married, widowed, divorced, separated, or have you never been married? ("Separated" and "divorced" recoded to value 3.)
1. Married
2. Widowed
3. Divorced/Separated
4. Never married

DEGREE   11. Highest degree.
0. Less than high school
1. High school
2. Associate/junior college
3. Bachelor's
4. Graduate

REALINC   12. Family income in constant dollars ($1 thru $999,997).

INCOME3   13. REALINC, family income in constant dollars, recoded into thirds.
1. Low
2. Moderate
3. High

FINRELA   14. Compared with American families in general, would you say your family income is far below average, below average, average, above average, or far above average? (Recoded into three categories.)
1. Below average
2. Average
3. Above average

FINALTER   15. During the last few years, has your financial situation been getting better, worse, or has it stayed the same?
1. Better
2. Worse
3. Same

SATFIN   16. We are interested in how people are getting along financially these days. So far as you and your family are concerned, would you say that you are pretty well satisfied with your present financial situation, more or less satisfied, or not satisfied at all?
1. Pretty well satisfied
2. More or less satisfied
3. Not satisfied at all

PRESTIGE   17. Hodge/Siegel/Rossi prestige scale score for respondent's occupation. (Actual score recorded.)

PRESTIG3   18. PRESTIGE, respondent's occupational prestige, recoded into thirds.
1. Low
2. Moderate
3. High

PAPRES   19. Hodge/Siegel/Rossi prestige scale score for father's occupation when respondent was growing up. (Actual score recorded.)

PAPRES3   20. PAPRES, father's occupational prestige, recoded into thirds.
1. Low
2. Moderate
3. High

RELIG   21. What is your religious preference? Is it Protestant, Catholic, Jewish, some other religion, or no religion?
1. Protestant
2. Catholic
3. Jewish
4. None
5. Other

ATTEND   22. How often do you attend religious services? (Recoded into four categories.)
1. Less than once a year
2. Once a year through several times a year
3. About once a month through almost weekly
4. Every week or more

BORN 23. Were you born in this country?
1. Yes
2. No

CHILDS 24. How many children have you ever had? Please count all that were born alive at any time (including any you had from a previous marriage).
0-7. Actual number (e.g., 3 means 3 children)
8. Eight or more

CHILDS3 25. CHILDS, number of children, recoded into thirds.
1. Zero
2. One or two
3. Three through eight

SIBS 26. How many brothers and sisters did you have? Please count those born alive, but no longer living, as well as those alive now. Also include stepbrothers and stepsisters, and children adopted by your parents.
Values reflect actual number of siblings.

SIBS3 27. SIBS, number of siblings, recoded into thirds.
1. 0-2
2. 3-4
3. 5 or more

PARTYID 28. Generally speaking, do you usually think of yourself as a Republican, Democrat, Independent, or what? (Recoded into four categories.)
1. Democrat
2. Independent
3. Republican
4. Other party

POLVIEWS 29. I'm going to show you a seven-point scale on which the political views that people might hold are arranged from extremely liberal-point 1-to extremely conservative-point 7. Where would you place yourself on this scale? (Recoded into three categories.)
1. Liberal
2. Moderate
3. Conservative

ZODIAC   30. Astrological sign of respondent.
                    1. Aries   7. Libra
                    2. Taurus   8. Scorpio
                    3. Gemini   9. Sagittarius
                    4. Cancer   10. Capricorn
                    5. Leo   11. Aquarius
                    6. Virgo   12. Pisces

TVHOURS   31. On the average day, about how many hours do you personally watch television? (Actual number of hours recorded.)
Actual number of hours

TVHOURS3   32. TVHOURS, number of hours watching television per day, recoded into thirds.
1.   0 through 1 hours
2.   2 through 3 hours
3.   4 through 24 hours

NEWS   33. How often do you read the newspaper-every day, a few times a week, once a week, less than once a week, or never? (Recoded into four categories.)
1.   Every day
2.   A few times a week
3.   Once a week
4.   Less than once a week

OWNGUN   34. Do you happen to have in your home any guns or revolvers?
1.   Yes
2.   No

MAWORK   35. Did your mother ever work for pay for as long as a year, after she was married?
1.   Yes
2.   No

HEALTH   36. Would you say your health, in general, is excellent, good, fair, or poor?
1.   Excellent
2.   Good
3.   Fair
4.   Poor

SATHEALT   37. How much satisfaction do you get from your health and physical condition? (Recoded into four categories.)
      1.   Very great deal
      2.   Great deal
      3.   Quite a bit
      4.   Fair amount or less

Please tell me whether or not *you* think it should be possible for a pregnant woman to obtain a *legal* abortion if. . .(applies to items 38B44)

ABANY   38. The woman wants it for any reason?
      1.   Yes
      2.   No

ABDEFECT   39. There is a strong chance of serious defect in the baby?
      1.   Yes
      2.   No

ABHLTH   40. The woman's own health is seriously endangered by the pregnancy?
      1.   Yes
      2.   No

ABNOMORE   41. She is married and does not want any more children.
      1.   Yes
      2.   No

ABPOOR   42. The family has a very low income and cannot afford any more children?
      1.   Yes
      2.   No

ABRAPE   43. She became pregnant as a result of rape?
      1.   Yes
      2.   No

ABSINGLE   44. She is not married and does not want to marry the man?
      1.   Yes
      2.   No

CHLDIDEL 45. What do you think is the ideal number of children for a family to have? (Recoded into five categories.)
1. Zero or one
2. Two
3. Three
4. Four or more
5. As many as you want

AGED 46. As you know, many older people share a home with their grown children. Do you think this is generally a good idea or a bad idea?
1. A good idea
2. Bad idea
3. Depends (volunteered)

Now I'd like your opinions on a number of different things. Some people agree with a statement, others disagree. As I read each one, tell me whether you more or less agree with it, or more or less disagree. (Applies to items 47-49.)

ANOMIA5 47. In spite of what some people say, the lot (situation/condition) of the average man is getting worse, not better.
1. Agree
2. Disagree

ANOMIA6 48. It's hardly fair to bring a child into the world with the way things look for the future.
1. Agree
2. Disagree

ANOMIA7 49. Most public officials (people in public office) are not really interested in the problems of the average man.
1. Agree
2. Disagree

I am going to name some institutions in this country. As far as the *people running* these institutions are concerned, would you say you have a great deal of confidence, only some confidence, or hardly any confidence at all in them? (Applies to items 50-54.)

CONEDUC   50. Education?
                   1. A great deal
                   2. Only some
                   3. Hardly any

CONCLERG   51. Organized religion?
                   1. A great deal
                   2. Only some
                   3. Hardly any

CONLEGIS   52. Congress?
                   1. A great deal
                   2. Only some
                   3. Hardly any

CONPRESS   53. Press?
                   1. A great deal
                   2. Only some
                   3. Hardly any

CONTV   54. TV?
                   1. A great deal
                   2. Only some
                   3. Hardly any

COURTS   55. In general, do you think the courts in this area deal too harshly or not harshly
                   enough with criminals?
                   1. Too harshly
                   2. Not harshly enough
                   3. About right (volunteered)

GRASS   56. Do you think the use of marijuana should be made legal or not?
                   1. Should be made legal
                   2. Should not be made legal

CAPPUN   57. Do you favor or oppose the death penalty for persons convicted of murder?
                   1. Favor
                   2. Oppose

DIVLAW 58. Should divorce in this country be easier or more difficult to obtain than it is now?
1. Easier
2. More difficult
3. Stay as is (volunteered)

HITOK 59. Are there any situations that you can imagine in which you would approve of a man punching an adult male stranger?
1. Yes
2. No

POLHITOK 60. Are there any situations you can imagine in which you would approve of a policeman striking an adult male citizen?
1. Yes
2. No

GUN 61. Have you ever been threatened with a gun, or shot at?
1. Yes
2. No

GUNLAW 62. Would you favor or oppose a law which would require a person to obtain a police permit before he or she could buy a gun?
1. Favor
2. Oppose

HUNT 63. Do you (or does your [husband/wife]) go hunting?
1. Yes, respondent does
2. Yes, spouse does
3. Yes, both do
4. No, neither respondent nor spouse hunts

HAPPY 64. Taken all together, how would you say things are these days-- would you say that you are very happy, pretty happy, or not too happy?
1. Very happy
2. Pretty happy
3. Not too happy

HAPMAR   65. Taking things all together, how would you describe your marriage? Would you say that your marriage is very happy, pretty happy, or not too happy?
1. Very happy
2. Pretty happy
3. Not too happy

SATCITY   66. How much satisfaction do you get from the city or place you live in? (Responses recoded into four categories.)
1. A very great deal
2. A great deal
3. Quite a bit
4. A fair amount or less

SATFAM   67. How much satisfaction do you get from your family life? (Responses recoded into four categories.)
1. A very great deal
2. A great deal
3. Quite a bit
4. A fair amount or less

SATFRND   68. How much satisfaction do you get from your friendships? (Responses recoded into four categories.)
1. A very great deal
2. A great deal
3. Quite a bit
4. A fair amount or less

SATJOB   69. On the whole, how satisfied are you with the work that you do-would you say that you are very satisfied, moderately satisfied, a little dissatisfied, or very dissatisfied? (Responses recoded into three categories.)
1. Very satisfied
2. Moderately satisfied
3. Dissatisfied

SEXEDUC   70. Would you be for or against sex education in the public schools?
1. For
2. Against

PRAYER 71. The United States Supreme Court has ruled that no state or local government may *require* the reading of the Lord's Prayer or Bible verses in public schools. What are your views on this-do you approve or disapprove of the court ruling?
1. Approve
2. Disapprove

BUSING 72. In general, do you favor or oppose the busing of (Negro/Black/ African-American) and white school children from one school district to another?
1. Favor
2. Oppose

TRUST 73. Generally speaking, would you say that most people can be trusted or that you can't be too careful in life?
1. Most people can be trusted
2. Can't be too careful
3. Depends (volunteered)

HELPFUL 74. Would you say that most of the time people try to be helpful, or that they are mostly just looking out for themselves?
1. Try to be helpful
2. Just look out for themselves
3. Depends (volunteered)

GETAHEAD 75. Some people say that people get ahead by their own hard work; others say that lucky breaks or help from other people are more important. Which do you think is most important?
1. Hard work
2. Hard work and luck equally important
3. Luck

POSTLIFE 76. Do you believe there is a life after death?
1. Yes
2. No

PREMARSX   77. There's been a lot of discussion about the way morals and attitudes about sex are changing in this country. If a man and a woman have sex relations before marriage, do you think it is always wrong, almost always wrong, wrong only sometimes, or not wrong at all?
1. Always wrong
2. Almost always wrong
3. Wrong only sometimes
4. Not wrong at all

HOMOSEX   78. What about sexual relations between two adults of the same sex-do you think it is always wrong, almost always wrong, wrong only sometimes, or not wrong at all?
1. Always wrong
2. Almost always wrong
3. Wrong only sometimes
4. Not wrong at all

FEAR   79. Is there any area right around here-that is, within a mile-where you would be afraid to walk alone at night?
1. Yes
2. No

FEHOME   80. Do you agree or disagree with this statement? Women should take care of running their homes and leave running the country up to men.
1. Agree
2. Disagree

We are faced with many problems in this country, none of which can be solved easily or inexpensively. I'm going to name some of these problems, and for each one I'd like you to tell me whether you think we're spending too much money on it, too little money, or about the right amount. Are we spending too much, too little, or about the right amount on. . .(Applies to items 81-89.)

NATCRIME   81. Halting the rising crime rate?
1. Too little
2. About right
3. Too much

NATARMS   82.   The military, armaments, and defense?
1.   Too little
2.   About right
3.   Too much

NATCITY   83.   Solving the problems of the big cities?
1.   Too little
2.   About right
3.   Too much

NATDRUG   84.   Dealing with drug addiction?
1.   Too little
2.   About right
3.   Too much

NATEDUC   85.   Improving the nation's education system?
1.   Too little
2.   About right
3.   Too much

NATENVIR   86.   Improving and protecting the environment?
1.   Too little
2.   About right
3.   Too much

NATFARE   87.   Welfare?
1.   Too little
2.   About right
3.   Too much

NATHEAL   88.   Improving and protecting the nation=s health?
1.   Too little
2.   About right
3.   Too much

NATRACE   89.   Improving the condition of Blacks?
1.   Too little
2.   About right
3.   Too much

The next questions are about pornography--books, movies, magazines, and photographs that show or describe sex activities. I'm going to read some opinions about the effects of looking at or reading such sexual materials. As I read each one, please tell me if you think sexual materials do or do not have that effect. (Applies to items 90-92.)

PORNINF   90. Sexual materials provide information about sex?
                      1. Yes
                      2. No

PORNMORL   91. Sexual materials lead to a breakdown of morals.
                      1. Yes
                      2. No

PORNRAPE   92. Sexual materials lead people to commit rape?
                      1. Yes
                      2. No

PORNLAW   93. Which one of these statements comes closest to your feelings about pornography laws?
                      1. There should be laws against the distribution of pornography whatever the age
                      2. There should be laws against the distribution of pornography to persons under 18
                      3. There should be no laws forbidding the distribution of pornography

RACLIVE   94. Are there any (Negroes/Blacks) living in this neighborhood now?
                      1. Yes
                      2. No

RACMAR   95. Do you think there should be laws against marriage between (Negroes/Blacks/African-Americans) and whites?
                      1. Yes
                      2. No

RACPRES   96. If your party nominated a (Negro/Black/African-American) for President, would you vote for him if he were qualified for the job?
                      1. Yes
                      2. No

APPENDIX B

InfoTrac® College Edition
User Guide
for the Instructor

Contents:

INTRODUCTION

InfoTrac College Edition is a fully searchable online university library containing complete articles and their images. Its database gives you access to hundreds of scholarly and popular publications–all reliable sources, including journals, magazines, encyclopedias, and newsletters. Updated daily, the *InfoTrac College Edition* database also includes articles dating back as much as four years. And every article within the database can be easily printed for reading and reference purposes or quickly arranged into a bibliography.

24 Hours a Day

InfoTrac College Edition means anytime, anywhere Internet access to thousands of articles, from school or home. Student subscribers receive a personalized "account ID number" that gives them unlimited access to *InfoTrac College Edition* for four full months at any hour of the day, anywhere they happen to be. The 24-hour, four-month subscription will launch your students on a quest for knowledge for term papers, class assignments, and lab projects, and you can be rest assured that your students' Internet research will be complete and based exclusively on reliable published sources; what's more, it's not just abstracts!

Use it as Part of Your Course

InfoTrac College Edition also does something for you, the instructor. It gives you the flexibility to require outside readings–an online reader–without sinking your students' textbook budgets. *InfoTrac College Edition* can be integrated into your course syllabi. With your free subscription, you can use it to prepare lectures and assignments, or to build a reader from the database for your discipline.

QUICK TIPS FOR THE CLASSROOM

InfoTrac College Edition is an excellent tool to introduce students to researching subjects. You can use it to prepare lectures and outside assignments or to build a reader from the database for your discipline. Students will appreciate the ease of online research, especially when writing papers, preparing class presentations, or researching a key topic. Below are some suggestions on how to incorporate *ICE* in your classroom.

Writing Assignments
- Provide a topic to your students to research in *ICE*. Have them choose one article that interests them and have them write a thesis on that specific article and construct an outline.
- Point students to *ICE* as an excellent reference and information source when preparing their term papers.

Study Questions
- Prepare a list of study questions on a lecture topic and have the students research and answer them using *ICE*.
- Have students explore answers to the end-of-chapter study questions of the book using *ICE*.

Reading Assignments
- Select specific articles and assign them to your students for further reading.
- Use as a vehicle for critical thinking.

Classroom Activities
- Divide the classroom into groups and provide them with a topic to research and discuss for the next class. Have each group present their discoveries and summary of that topic.
- Set up classroom debates by providing a subject and assigning students to research a pro or con stance to discuss in class.

GETTING STARTED

Go to *http://www.infotrac-college.com*

Click "Enter InfoTrac College Edition."

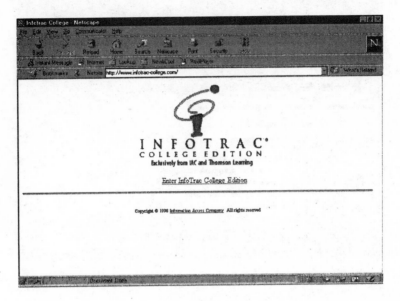

Enter your passcode. **Keep your passcode card safe.** (We cannot replace it.) You will need it every time you log in to ICE.

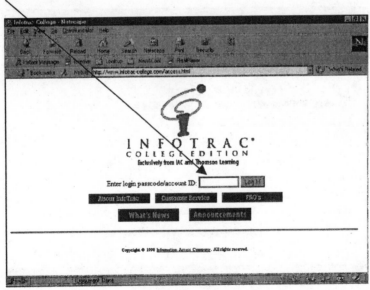

Registration

If you are using InfoTrac College Edition for the first time, you will need to complete the registration form. Any items in **bold** type must be completed before your account can be activated.

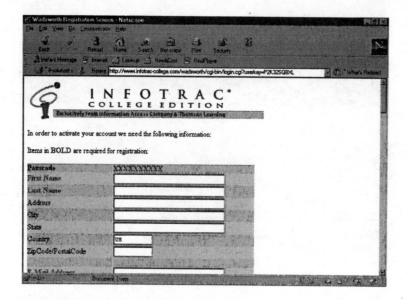

If required items are missing or invalid on the registration form, an error message from Customer Service describing the problem will appear. Simply click the "Back" button on your browser's toolbar to return to the registration form.

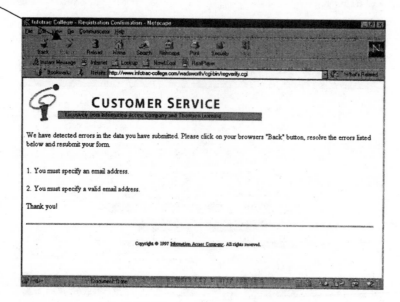

After the registration form is successfully completed, you will be asked to confirm that all information is accurate. Click on the "Submit" button to send your completed registration form.

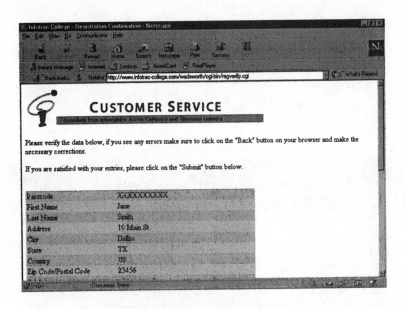

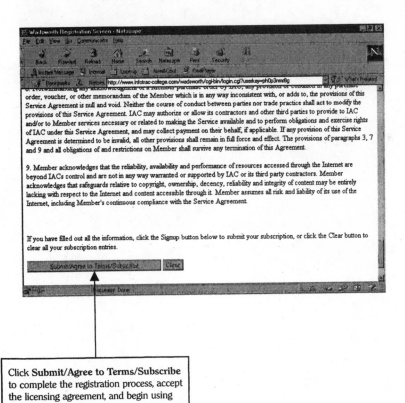

Click **Submit/Agree to Terms/Subscribe** to complete the registration process, accept the licensing agreement, and begin using InfoTrac College Edition.

USING INFOTRAC COLLEGE EDITION

The Header Bar

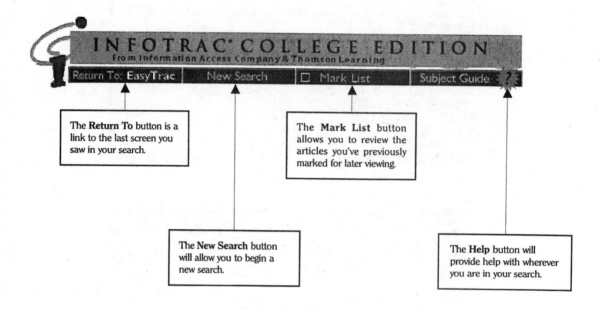

The **Return To** button is a link to the last screen you saw in your search.

The **Mark List** button allows you to review the articles you've previously marked for later viewing.

The **New Search** button will allow you to begin a new search.

The **Help** button will provide help with wherever you are in your search.

EasyTrac Searching

After signing in, the EasyTrac search screen will appear. EasyTrac is designed for basic research needs. You can research articles via Subject Guide or Key Words. Type in the topic you would like to research.

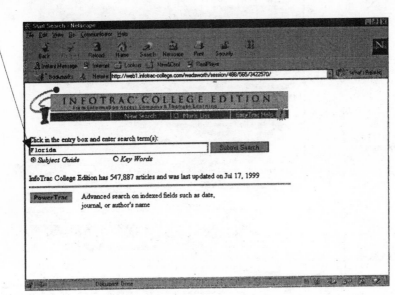

There are two ways to research your topic, by Subject Guide or Key Words.

Subject Guide allows you to do a broad search on a topic. The Subject Guide screen lists all headings containing your specific topic along with the number of articles/citations found with each heading. Clicking on the "View" link will take you to the specific articles/citations for that heading.

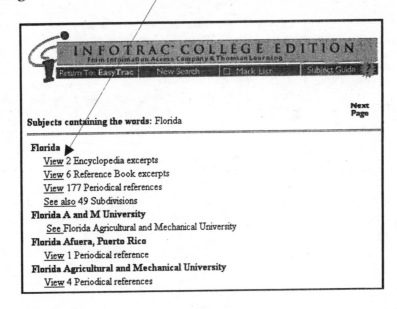

Key Word search is more effective when looking for a specific topic, title, author name, or product. The Key Word search will give you a list of articles containing the key word topic. Click on "View" to link to the article.

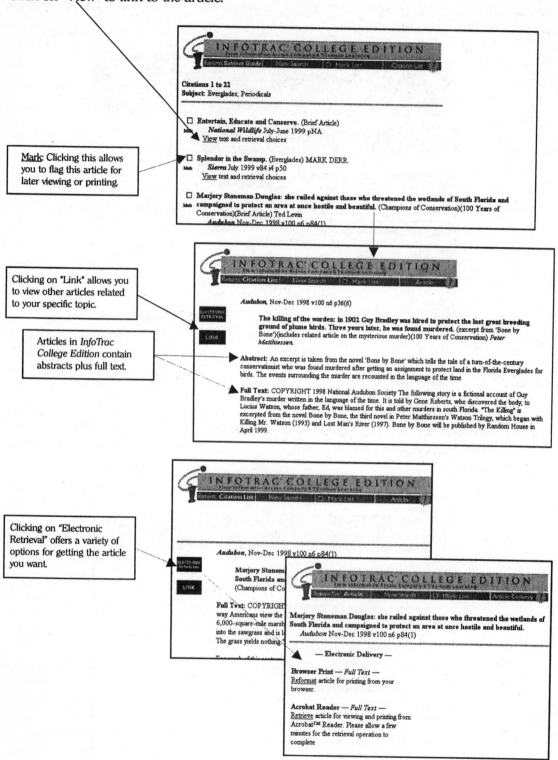

Mark: Clicking this allows you to flag this article for later viewing or printing.

Clicking on "Link" allows you to view other articles related to your specific topic.

Articles in *InfoTrac College Edition* contain abstracts plus full text.

Clicking on "Electronic Retrieval" offers a variety of options for getting the article you want.

PowerTrac Searching

To begin a more advanced search on a topic, click on "PowerTrac."

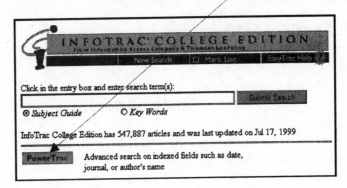

The PowerTrac search provides a variety of ways to search the database for articles. The "Choose Search Index" drop down box displays the indices available in this database.

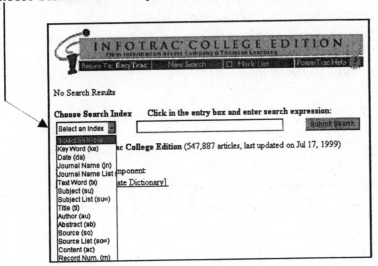

For example, by clicking on "Journal Name" and typing the name of a specific journal, this will search the database for all articles pertaining to that journal. Simply click on "View" to see the complete list of articles.

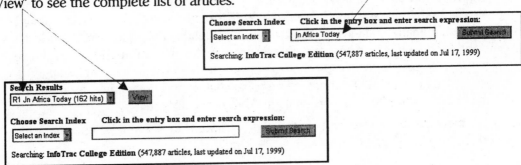

What is an Index? Each article is indexed by certain variables. These indices include the article's author name, where and when it was published, etc. You can search the following indices by using their **Index Abbreviations** (listed in parenthesis below).

Indexes for Searching in PowerTrac:

Abstract (ab): Includes words from article abstracts as well as from any author's abstracts.

Author (au): Authors are indexed in surname/given name order; for example, "nelan bruce w." It's best to search in surname-first order. Enter a surname and, optionally, a given name.

Content (ac): Lets you locate all records with full text and eliminate those without. To search this index, enter the word "fulltext."

Date (da): The date the article was published.

Journal Name (jn): The name of the magazine or periodical.

Journal Name List (jn=): Provides a list of magazines or periodicals in which the search topic appears.

Key Word (ke): Words in article titles and authors, as well as subjects, people, companies, products, vocations, events, etc., featured in articles.

Record num. (rn): A full record always includes a unique record number. If you note a record number, you can easily find the record again with the record number index.

Source (so): Lets you search for records by the source from which they're taken (e.g., encyclopedia or newsletter).

Source List (so=): Lets you browse an alphabetical list of subjects that contain the word or words you type.

Subject (su): Lets you search for references by the topic under which they are indexed.

Subject List (su=): Provides a list of references by topic.

Text Word (tx): Composed of words from the body of articles and reports.

Title (ti): The title index is composed of all words in article, report or book titles.

Using Wildcards in PowerTrac Searches

At times, you might want to find more than just exact matches to a search term. For instance, you might want to find both the singular and plural forms of a word or variant spellings. Wildcards let you broaden your searches to match a pattern.

InfoTrac provides three wildcards:

- An asterisk (*) stands for any number of characters, including none. For example, **pigment*** matches "pigment," "pigments," "pigmentation," etc. The asterisk wildcard can also be used inside a word. For example, **colo*r** matches both "color" and "colour."
- A question mark (?) stands for exactly one character. Multiple question marks in a row stand for the same number of characters as there are question marks. For example, **psych????y** matches either "psychology" or "psychiatry" but not "psychotherapy."
- An exclamation point (!) stands for one or no characters. For example, **analog!!** matches "analog," "analogs" or "analogue" but not "analogous."

If you see a message about a search being invalid, you'll need to add at least one character before one of the wildcards.

TROUBLESHOOTING & FREQUENTLY ASKED QUESTIONS

If you are experiencing any technical difficulties, you can send a form to Technical Support from the ICE Customer Service page, or you can send an e-mail to *wp-support@infotrac-college.com*.

Q: *What are the system requirements to run InfoTrac College Edition?*

A: Netscape Navigator v3.0 or later, Internet Explorer v3.0 or later.

Q: *If I have a problem, what information do I need to provide in my message to InfoTrac customer service? When will I receive a response? How do I submit information?*

A: Click on the Customer Service button on the welcome screen. You will be prompted for all necessary information.

Q: *How do I access the on-line help file?*

A: Each Screen has context sensitive help. Just click on the help button.

Q: *What if I lose or forget my passcode/account ID?*

A: Please keep your passcode/account ID card safe. We **cannot** replace lost passcodes/account IDs.

Q: *Will I be reminded or notified before my subscription expires?*

A: Yes.

Q: *Is that a 0 (zero) or an O (oh) in my passcode/account ID?*

A: Passcodes/account IDs contain no vowels. It's a 0 (zero).

Q: *How often is the database updated?*

A: InfoTrac SearchBank databases are updated every business day. Daily publications such as newspapers are indexed on a daily basis. Weekly publications as well as those with time-sensitive content are indexed and abstracted within the same day or within 1-3 days of receipt.

APPENDIX C

WebTutor ™ Integration Tips
for the Instructor

Contents:

Tips for Integrating Thomson's
WebTutor™on Blackboard into your Course

Feature	Description - Benefit
THOMSON PROVIDED CONTENT	
Chapter Summary Materials	Students will be able to view summary material tied directly to their course textbook. These can include, but are not limited to Chapter Outlines, Summaries, internet exercises, interactive games and PowerPoint presentations.
Multimedia Content	Our WebTutor advantage products offer the added advantage of video clips, simulations and/or simulations.
Quizzes	Allow students to practice what they have learned in the textbook. Quiz results are automatically entered into the BB gradebook. Students can take quizzes multiple times, or if the instructor prefers, they can allow only one attempt, set a time limit, or specify a password for students to take a quiz. These quizzes include content not found in the instructor test bank and can be edited by the instructor.
Flashcards	Flashcards allow students to review key terms from the textbook. Because students learn in many ways, flashcards (w/audio) allow students to hear the pronunciation of the term and in some cases, the definition. Flashcards are especially beneficial to the ESL or Learning Disabled student.
Web Links	Web links help keep the course current for the instructor and provide numerous opportunities for students to do additional research or project-based activities right on the web. Each WebTutor product comes pre-loaded with web links designed to enhance the course.
Discussion Topics	Threaded Discussion or Bulletin Board systems allow students and instructors to engage in a lively, on going discussion, anytime or anywhere. All Thomson WebTutor products come pre-loaded with suggested discussion topics. Of course, instructors and students can add their own.
PowerPoint Presentations	Many WebTutor products include PowerPoint presentations keyed to the textbook.
InfoTrac College edition	Students have access to InfoTrac College edition offering 24/7 access to millions of articles from scholarly journals and popular periodicals. Students can search by keyword or subject. A must-have resource for any course that involves research.
Bb formatted Test banks	Instructors can request a Blackboard-formatted version of the ExamView testbank files for creation of their own quizzes and tests.
COMMUNICATION TOOLS	
Integrated Calendar	An integrated calendar provides the ability to view information at the institutional, course, and personal level.
Web Mail	Blackboard has third party software embedded in the product to seamlessly link to students existing email accounts.
Virtual Classroom	The Virtual Classroom allows for real-time, communication with the class and combines chat, whiteboard technology and a web browser into a synchronous learning tool. There are many possible uses for chat including virtual office hours, group study sessions or projects, and guest speakers. All chat sessions are logged for the instructor to view - even if they are not an active participant.
Threaded Discussion or Bulletin Board	Threaded Discussion or Bulletin Board systems allow students and instructors to engage in a lively, on going discussion, anytime or anywhere. This tool has many applications including discussion of course topics, debates, or general discussions about course issues. Instructors can create private discussion forums, or allow students to post anonymously. Instructors may assign a student moderator.

Group Pages	Group pages allow the instructor to create collaborative learning environment on-line for specific group of students. This is useful for group projects and presentations.
Announcements	An announcement feature allows instructors to post time sensitive information to their class.
STUDENT MANAGEMENT TOOLS	
Course Statistics	Instructors can generate reports on the class or an individual student showing when and how students are accessing their course. Instructors can use this tool to monitor students progress and identify problem areas in a timely manner.
Online Gradebook	Allows instructors to view all students registered in the class and the results of their graded online quizzes and assignments.
Item Analysis	Allows instructor to get detailed item analysis of any quiz or survey item.
Item Tracking	Allows instructor to gather tracking details by student or class on any content item within the course. Report shows number of hits, days and times visited, etc.
T.A or Grader Access	Allows instructor to add a level of access to Teaching assistants or graders for assistance with grading.
Recycle Course	Allows instructors to recycle their courses from term to term without losing their customization. Student rosters, Bulletin Boards, online gradebook, Virtual Classroom archives are reset in preparation for the next term.
CUSTOMIZATION OPTIONS	
Look and feel	Instructors have complete control over the look and feel of their course - they can change button names and colors, add text and images and their school logo if they choose.
Instructor Profile	Instructions can add a profile with contact information for themselves or other key resources such as teaching assistants.
Quizzes	All quizzes are fully editable. Instructors can also create their own quizzes, or pools of questions for additional study or exams. Using the pools feature, instructors can generate randomized quizzes.
Content	Instructors can edit, delete or hide any content provided in the WebTutor product. They can also add their own content as well as re-sequencing the way the current content is presented.
Add additional Blackboard tools	Blackboard provides additional functionality for instructors wanting to take their course to the next level. Here are just a few: a student/instructor dropbox and an Electronic Blackboard for notetaking.
HOSTING OPTIONS	
Locally Hosted - RECOMMENDED	For schools that have Blackboard 5.5 or higher, Thomson will provide the school with an access key so that they can download the content cartridge to their local server. Blackboard provides additional technical support to supplement resources available on campus.
Centrally hosted	For schools that do not have Blackboard 5.5, we provide a hosted option (through Blackboard). All centrally hosted courses include technical support directly from Blackboard.

**For additional information, including Frequently Asked Questions, tours, and downloadable Instructor and Student guides, visit us at
http://webtutor.thomsonlearning.com**

Tips for Integrating Thomson's
WebTutor™on WebCT into your Course

Feature	Description - Benefit
THOMSON PROVIDED CONTENT	
Summary Materials	Students will be able to view summary material tied directly to their course textbook. These can include, but are not limited to Chapter Outlines, Summaries, internet exercises, interactive games and PowerPoint presentations.
Multimedia Content	Our WebTutor Advantage products offer the added advantage of video clips, animations and/or simulations.
Quizzes	Allows students to practice what they have learned in the textbook. Quiz results are automatically entered into the WebCT gradebook. Students can take quizzes multiple times, or if the instructor prefers, they can limit the number of times, set a time limit, or specify a specific time when the quiz is available. These quizzes include content not found in the Instructors Testbank and can be edited by the instructor.
Flashcards	Flashcards allow students to review key terms from the textbook. Because students learn in many ways, flashcards (w/audio) allow students to hear the pronunciation of the term and in some cases, the definition. Flashcards are especially beneficial to the ESL or Learning Disabled student.
Web Links	Web links help keep the course current for the instructor and provide numerous opportunities for students to do additional research or project-based activities right on the web. Each WebTutor product comes pre-loaded with web links designed to enhance the course.
Discussion Topics	Threaded Discussion or Bulletin Board systems allow students and instructors to engage in a lively, on going discussion, anytime or anywhere. All Thomson WebTutor products come pre-loaded with suggested discussion topics. Of course, instructors and students can add their own.
PowerPoint Presentations	Many WebTutor products include PowerPoint presentations keyed to the textbook.
InfoTrac College edition	Students have access to InfoTrac College edition offering 24/7 access to millions of full-text articles from scholarly journals and popular periodicals. Students can search by keyword or subject. A must-have resource for any course that involves research.
COMMUNICATION TOOLS	
Integrated Calendar	An integrated calendar can serve as a syllabus tool for instructors and allows them to enter information and key dates for the course. A pop-up window will always notify students when NEW information is placed on the calendar. Instructors can also create a link that will take students directly to a content page (chapter summary, quiz, etc). Students (and instructors) can also use the compile feature to print all assignments for a selected date range. Private entries are also allowed.
e-mail	An integrated e-mail system automatically builds a directory for the course as students create accounts. Students are not required to have an external email account to use WebTutor.
Chat	Chat allows for real-time, synchronous communication with the class. There are many possible uses for chat including virtual office hours, group study sessions or projects, and guest speakers. All chat sessions are logged for the instructor to view - even if they are not an active participant.

Threaded Discussion or Bulletin Board	Threaded Discussion or Bulletin Board systems allow students and instructors to engage in a lively, on going discussion, anytime or anywhere. This tool has many applications including discussion of course topics, debates, or general discussions about course issues. Instructors can create private discussion forums, or allow students to post anonymously.
Whiteboard	A real-time tool that allows you to upload images or presentations for students to view. Instructors or students can draw to the whiteboard.
STUDENT MANAGEMENT TOOLS	
Progress Tracking	Instructors will receive reports on each student that allow them to identify students first and last login, a distribution of hits, percentage of content visited and a complete history of all pages visited. Instructors can use this tool to monitor students progress and identify problem areas in a timely manner.
Participation in Discussion	Instructors will receive information about students participation in the discussion area including the number of items read, the number of original postings and the number of follow up postings. In an online environment, this is a great tool for instructors to measure a student's participation in class.
Student Management - Gradebook	Allows instructors to view all students registered in the class and the results of their graded online quizzes and assignments.
Item Analysis	Allows instructor to get detailed item analysis of any quiz or survey item.
Page Tracking	Allows instructors to see which students have accessed pages of content (from a path) - both the number of times and the time spent. Using this information, instructors can identify where students are spending their time and which areas of the course either need work, or additional reinforcement in class.
Grader Management	Allows the instructor to add graders to the course who have access to quiz information for assistance with grading.
Course RESET	Allows instructors to reset portions of their course for easy transition from term to term without losing their customization. Instructors can reset the student database, e-mail, Bulletin Boards, grader database, chat logs, the calendar tool, and the page-tracking tool.
CUSTOMIZATION OPTIONS	
Look and feel	Instructors have complete control over the look and feel of their course - they can change screen colors, add text and images, counters and their school logo if they choose.
Syllabus Tool	Provides a template for instructors to create their course syllabus. Alternatively, can upload an existing syllabus from a Word, or HTML file.
Quizzes	All quizzes are fully editable. Instructors can also create their own quizzes, or banks of questions for additional study or exams. Randomized quizzes can be created by using the Question Set feature. Additionally quizzes can be set up to prompt students for a password or require that a student is accessing the quiz from a certain IP address.
Content	Instructors can edit, delete or hide any content provided in the WebTutor product. They can also add their own content as well as re-sequencing the way the current content is presented.
Selective Release of Content	Instructors can choose to release content based on certain criteria such as date or time, to a selected group of students, or based on the result of quiz scores.
Add additional WebCT tools	WebCT provides additional functionality for instructors wanting to take their course to the next level. Here are just a few: an assignment dropbox, student presentation areas or homepages, image libraries, audio and video files, and more.

HOSTING OPTIONS	
Locally Hosted **RECOMMENDED**	For schools that have WebCT, Thomson will provide the school with a content cartridge that they can install on their local server. Instructors and students also receive technical support from WebCT as well as the resources they have available on campus.
Centrally hosted	For schools that do not have WebCT 3.x or higher, we provide a hosted option (through WebCT). All centrally hosted courses include unlimited technical support directly from WebCT for both instructors and students.

For additional information, including Frequently Asked Questions, tours, and downloadable Instructor and Student guides, visit us at http://webtutor.thomsonlearning.com